BASIL DAVIDSON

Modern Africa

LONGMAN

London and New York

Longman Group UK Limited
Longman House, Burnt Mill, Harlow, Essex CM20 2JE England

Associated Companies and throughout the world

Published in the United States of America
by Longman Inc., New York

© Longman Group Ltd 1983   Set in 11/12 Plantin Roman

First published 1983   Produced by Longman Group (FE) Ltd
Fifth impression 1986   Printed in Hong Kong

British Library Cataloguing in Publication Data

Davidson, Basil
   Modern Africa.
   I. Africa—History—1884-1960
   2. Africa—History—1960
   I. Title
      960'.3   DT29

ISBN 0-582-65525-0

Library of Congress Cataloging in Publication Data

Davidson, Basil, 1914—
   Modern Africa.

   Includes bibliographical references and index.
   I. Africa—History—1884-1960. 2 Africa—
History—1960— . I. Title.
DT29.D384 1983   960'.3   82-14941
ISBN 0-582-65525-0 (pbk.)

Acknowledgements

The publishers thank the following for permission to use photographs in the text: Africana Museum for p. 41 top right; Associated Press for p. 154 top left; Ghana Information Services for p. 40 top right; Kenya Railways, Nairobi for p. 41 bottom right; Popperfoto for p. 88 bottom left and p. 155 bottom left; Robinson Sport Foto for p. 155 bottom right; John Topham Picture Library for p. 88 top left and p. 88 top right; UNESCO, Paris for p. 155 top left; United Nations, New York for p. 154 bottom left, 154 bottom right and 155 top right; United Press International Inc. for p. 40 bottom left, 40 bottom right and 88 bottom right; WHO for p. 154 top right. The publishers regret that they are unable to trace the copyright holders of the photos on p. 40 top left, p. 41 top left and p. 41 bottom left, and apologise for any infringement of copyright caused.
The cover photos were kindly supplied as follows: top left – building the Uganda railway (Kenya Railways Corporation); below right – Senegalese troops on the march in the Cameroons (1914–16) (Popperfoto); top right – signalling the start of a political meeting in Lesotho; centre left – anti-government protest by Kenyan students; centre right – Independence Day, Nigeria; below left – white students support black protest in South Africa (all Camera Press Ltd).

Contents

Part Three   The nationalists win through

v

Preface

This book has been written for students preparing for a variety of intermediate and senior level examinations in which a knowledge of the history of modern Africa is required.

Designed for use with other detailed national histories, it presents these histories within the framework of an all-African overview of events, trends, movements, ideas, dates, and personalities between about 1914 and 1980.

While the book therefore concentrates on the wide range of subjects and themes required for full examination syllabus coverage, it is hoped at the same time that teachers, college students and other readers will find here a useful and stimulating record and synthesis.

Basil Davidson

List of maps

PART ONE

Under foreign flags: 1914–1930

Part One studies changes and developments in the years 1914–1930. Among questions examined in its chapters are:

Chapter 1 The early years of our century
What was the colonial partition?
How did the First World War (1914–1918) affect Africans?

Chapter 2 Colonial Africa: to 1930
How did the colonial systems work?
Who paid for them, and how?
What did the colonial systems do to African land, labour, and trade?

Chapter 3 African responses: to 1930
What was colonial 'pacification'?
Who were the early leaders of anti-colonial protest?
What were the Ethiopianist and other religious movements?
What was the migrant labour system, and how did it work?
Who were the 'educated few', and why were they important?

Chapter 4 Key ideas for progress
Who began the Pan-African movement, and why?
How did the ideas of modern nationalism begin and spread in Africa?
What were the National Congress of British West Africa, and the African National Congress of South Africa?
What was the policy of 'assimilation'?
How did nationalism take shape in North Africa? Who were the early leaders of Islamic nationalism?
What were the *Salafiyyah*, the *Wafd*, the *Destour*, the *Etoile Nord–Africaine*?

CHAPTER 1

The early years of our century

Africa's history was already long and famous before our century began. The early kingdoms of the Nile valley took shape five thousand years ago, and still in the distant past many other kingdoms, in West Africa and elsewhere, came into existence. In every region, Africans had many centuries of their own development.

The twentieth century has continued this old development of civilisations in Africa. But new ideas and ways of life have also been at work. These include new forms of government; religion and trade; the use of coins for money; reading and writing; and various ways of production by machine. At the time of the colonial partition, and partly because of it, all these gained new influence.

Partition of Africa

Partition means 'dividing up' or 'sharing out'; and colonial means 'foreign rule' or 'foreign settlement' or both. The colonial partition was the sharing out of Africa among strong empire-building powers such as Britain, France and Germany; and several weaker ones such as Portugal, Italy, Belgium and Spain.

For a long time, during the century before this one, these powers quarrelled over the shares of Africa that each wanted to get. But in 1884–85, at a conference in Berlin (then capital of a united Germany) they agreed to invade and take Africa without fighting each other. They marked out 'spheres of interest'. Each invaded the continent within its own 'sphere'.

Many African peoples tried to defeat these invasions. But the Europeans were too strong; and the partition was almost complete by the beginning of our century. Most of the colonial frontiers – the frontiers, today, of independent African states – were fixed on the map by the end of 1901. Only Ethiopia, and in a lesser way Liberia, remained free.

That is how the colonial systems or empires came into existence: seven of them until 1918, when Germany's system was ended, and then six. These systems differed greatly in detail, as we shall see. Sometimes, wherever kings or chiefs were willing and able to work

3

with colonial government, the systems operated by what was called 'indirect rule'. Otherwise, the colonial governments ruled 'directly' through their own white officials and African servants.

But all the systems, in essential ways, operated with the same assumptions and for the same purpose. Each of them was racist and exploitative. They used colonial power to treat Africans as inferior to Europeans, justifying this by a whole range of myths about a supposed 'white superiority'. The purpose of using colonial power in this way was to make Africans serve the interests of European colony-owners.

These systems brought some gains as well as many losses, for their history was a contradictory process. We study it in three main periods. First, from the First World War of 1914–18 to the great economic depression which began in 1929–30. Secondly, through the 1930s to the end of the Second World War of 1939–45. Thirdly, through the struggles of modern nationalism to the end of the colonial empires. After that, in the fourth part of this book, we study the years of Africa's regained independence.

Before 1914

The colonial powers partitioned Africa by agreement with each other. But they still had to invade and occupy the colonies thus marked by lines on the map. They did this by crushing African resistance wherever it appeared. At first, European troops were used, as well as troops from other colonies such as India and the West Indies. After 1900, African troops under European officers did most of this work.

Military occupation was far advanced by 1914. Even so, colonial rule by military force was often weak or incomplete; large areas remained outside its control. Yet the colonial systems were now 'in place'; and the time was ripe to make them produce wealth for their owners. At this point, however, there came a mighty interruption.

The First World War 1914–18

The colonial powers managed to keep the peace between each other in Africa. But their rivalry in Europe proved too strong for them. In 1914 a huge and terrible conflict broke out between Britain, France and Russia on one side, and Germany with Austria-Hungary on the other. This war spread through Europe and killed millions.

Each power drew upon its colonies for men and money. For the first time on any scale, Africa was pulled into the quarrels of the

4

outside world. The consequences were many and deep. They were military, social and economic, and political.

On the military side, African men were taken into the European colonial armies either as soldiers or as porters and servants. Sometimes this was done by enlarging colonial regiments already in existence, such as the British West African Frontier Force, the French *Tirailleurs*, the German *Schütztruppen*, the Belgian *Force Publique*. Men joined for the wages that were paid, or in obedience to quotas imposed on their chiefs.

Yet these small colonial forces were not enough. Huge French losses on the 'Western Front' in France (so called to distinguish it from the 'Eastern Front' in Russia) soon led the French government to demand more African troops, and conscription (forcing men to join an army) then began. Much the same was done by the British on a smaller scale, especially in East Africa, to obtain porters and other service personnel needed in Britain's war against the Germans in Tanganyika.

Armies of men vanished into the jaws of this monstrous war. From first to last, the French raised about 211,000 troops from their West and Equatorial colonies, some 270,000 from their North African colonies, and about 40,000 from Madagascar. How many of these died has never been exactly found out. But it is generally accepted that about 200,000 Africans lost their lives in French war service.

For the British forces, Nigeria provided some 17,000 fighting men and 58,000 service personnel; many were sent to East Africa, where about 1,000 were killed. The Gold Coast (Ghana) raised some 10,000 men with losses on the same scale; Sierra Leone and The Gambia also played their part. The greatest African losses were in the British campaign against the Germans in Tanganyika. Upwards of one million East Africans were forced to become porters for the British. Of these, perhaps as many as 100,000 were killed by military action, hunger and disease. The Germans, Portuguese and Belgian colonial authorities all relied on a 'call-up' of African troops and porters, at times in large numbers and often by force. As with much else in the colonial period, overall figures of African losses through one or other form of war service have remained a matter for dispute; but it seems unlikely that total African losses were less than 300,000 men. The real figure may have been higher still.

Broader consequences of the war

Colonial governments were obliged to give money, as a contribution to war expenses, to their respective home governments in Europe. This scarcely applied to the German colonies, which were quickly taken over by Britain, France and Belgium (and by South Africa in the case of Namibia), or, like Tanganyika, were cut off from Germany. But most of the British and French territories had to provide money from taxation. Even as small a territory as The Gambia provided £10,000 out of its total budget for 1914 of £122,225.

The war was a profoundly disturbing influence as well as an expensive one. Many rural communities were shaken or undermined. Countless families were deprived of active men taken for war service. Others tried to evade recruitment by hiding themselves or moving to another territory. There was frequent armed resistance to war service in several of the territories of French West Africa; and clashes with the colonial authorities were many. Natural disasters such as the spread of epidemics combined with food shortages to spread hunger and death. All this was bad for rural life, and was indeed a prelude to the great rural poverty of later years.

There were long-term consequences of a different kind. Especially in British West Africa, such African traders who had managed to remain active in the export market were squeezed out of business. British firms took advantage of war conditions to strengthen their hold on export-import trade. They took over, for example, the share of that trade formerly held by German firms. The war years were in fact the period in which a handful of major British trading companies secured control of all big-scale business; and much the same was true of French companies in the French territories. In this important respect, the war years completed the dispossession of Africans that the colonial conquests had begun.

As a political result, the colonial 'share out' was revised. Germany, in losing the war, lost its colonies: one in East Africa (Tanganyika, with Ruanda/Urundi); one in South-West Africa (Namibia); two in West Africa (Kamerun – or Cameroun as it was afterwards called – and Togo). Each of these was attacked by the powers allied against Germany, and chiefly by the British. German resistance lasted longer in Kamerun, and was ended only in February 1916. But in Tanganyika a skilful German commander, General Paul von Lettow Vorbeck, fought a guerrilla war against the British and their allies until the war in Europe ended. By so doing, he forced the British into a major military effort, during which, as we saw, tens of thousands of Africans lost their lives.

These four German colonies were divided among the victorious powers as 'mandated territories' of a newly-born League of Nations.

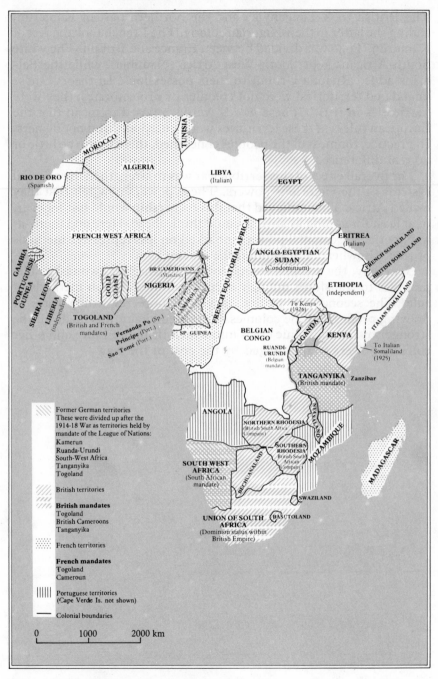

Fig. 1   Colonial boundaries in Africa in 1919

The British took Tanganyika and the northern part of Kamerun, adding the latter to their Nigerian colony. The French took the rest of Kamerun. Togo was divided between France and Britain. The white South Africans kept South-West Africa (Namibia), while the Belgians added Ruanda/Urundi to their possessions. In theory, these 'mandated territories' were not colonies or protectorates; they were 'territories in trust'. These words were supposed to mean that the European rulers of these territories were 'guardians' and not owners. In practice, for most of the peoples concerned, there was to be little or no real difference.

The overall effect of this terrible war was to strengthen the colonial systems of the victorious powers. These powers now felt that they owned Africa. They believed that this ownership would last for ever, or at least for as long as anyone could think ahead. Here and there, as in Nigeria, the colonial power embarked on less repressive methods of rule; elsewhere, it was often the reverse.

Generally, the colonial rulers now set themselves two tasks. The first was to transform military occupation into civilian methods of rule. The second was to find new and more rewarding ways of drawing profit from the colonies. This second aim was made all the stronger by the economic crisis into which Britain, France and other colonial powers were plunged by the cost of the war.

CHAPTER 2
Colonial Africa: to 1930

Many hundreds of states and communities of earlier times lost their independence to the various European colonial powers. Most lost it completely. A few, as in Northern Nigeria, managed to keep some local power to govern themselves. But their power was small, and always under colonial control even when this was called 'indirect'.

Another great change had come to them. All were gathered into some fifty colonies marked out by frontiers that were new. Few of these frontiers took any account of African interest or convenience. Many cut through the territory of former states or united communities, leaving one part in one colonial system and another part in another colonial system.

The Somali people, for example, were divided into four colonial systems: those of Britain (Somaliland), Italy (Somalia), France (Djibouti) and Ethiopia (Ogaden). Some Makonde of East Africa were in (German, then British) Tanganyika; others were in (Portuguese) Mozambique. A majority of the numerous Mandinka of West Africa were included in the French system, but others were in neighbouring (British) Sierra Leone and The Gambia. Many Hausa were in (British) Nigeria, while others were in (French) Niger.

So the immediate results under colonial rule were loss of power on one hand, and new kinds of disunity on the other.

From military to civilian rule

After the First World War of 1914–18, the victorious colonial powers continued to crush resistance and put down protest. This was misleadingly called 'pacification', or 'making peace'; and it was largely completed during the 1920s.

As this system of repression succeeded, the colonial powers moved from military to civilian forms of rule. They kept their colonial armies, now manned by African soldiers under European command. But they handed the tasks of government to non-military officials, while, at the same time, building police forces (again composed of Africans with European officers) so as to make sure the officials were obeyed. In short, they organised colonial civil services.

These civilian governments were various kinds of dictatorship, sometimes mild and at other times harsh. All power was placed in the hands of top governors who received orders from their national governments in Europe, but who, on the spot, could usually decide as they wished. Under the top governors were sub-governors; and under these were regional and provincial officers (sometimes called 'residents' in the British system); and under these again were local or district officers. These political officials were flanked by other services: for public works, health, education, and so on.

The officials were never many. By the 1930s, for example, the vast colonial area of French West Africa was divided into 118 *cercles* (districts), each governed by a French *commandant* (district officer). About 40 million Nigerians, in 1938, were governed by some 380 British political officials with another 1,163 in service departments (such as public works, education, health).

All these officials were Europeans. The racist nature of colonial rule made sure that no Africans could reach positions of responsibility in the colonial services. Only as late as 1942 was there a first departure from this rule, when two African assistant district officers were appointed in Gold Coast (Ghana).

A big consequence flowed from this situation. Being few and all European, the officials had to work, in practice, through a multitude of African interpreters, policemen, servants, or local chiefs appointed by colonial government. This meant that most people were governed in the details of everyday life by puppets or clerks who might abuse their positions, take bribes, act as bullies or otherwise serve their personal interests. That did not happen everywhere, but it happened often. In this important way, the colonial systems were not only systems of repression; they were also systems of corruption.

One reason why the officials were never many was that they and their services had to be paid for. Each colony was run by the rule that the cost of colonial government must not be allowed to cut seriously into colonial profits, or prove a burden to European taxpayers in Europe. Very few Africans had asked for colonial rule, but all Africans had to pay for it.

They had to pay for it by taxes in money; and this was widely resented. 'Taxation troubles' were many; often they were violent. There were various methods of raising taxation-money. One way was to make each family-head, or worker, pay an annual amount. Another was to make each hut-owner pay a tax. A third was to tax imports and exports. Colonial officials found it difficult to get this necessary money, but they persisted. For example: in the second half of the 1920s (1924–29) Kenya's Africans paid a total of £553,000 in personal taxes, a large percentage of all the money that they earned. By 1930 about two-fifths of all the money for government in Nigeria was being paid by direct and personal taxation of Africans, mostly farmers; the rest came from import-export taxes (customs and excise).

Some of this taxation money was used to pay the salaries and other costs of European officials and their families. Some of it was used for the benefit of the colonised populations. The richer colonial powers, such as Britain and France, built clinics, brought in doctors, and began to combat malaria and epidemic diseases. All the colonial powers built primary schools and trained teachers, although some left this primarily to Christian missionaries, mostly European. These were among the gains of colonial rule. But these gains could never be large because they had to be paid for by taxation money. And that money was never enough to spread their gains very far (see also p. 14 in this chapter and Chapter 5, p. 50).

Many officials were honest and hard-working, and with goodwill towards the peoples they governed. But all had to work within the rules of the colonial systems. The most important of these rules applied to land, labour, and trade.

Economic consequences

Land and labour

Though they all operated in the same ways basically, there were two kinds of colony: those with many European settlers, and those with few or none. We shall call them 'settler colonies' and 'non-settler colonies'. For Africans, it was generally much better to be in the second kind of colony than in the first. This was because the interests of European settlers were placed before the interests of Africans.

With a few exceptions, notably in Ivory Coast, West Africa remained free of European settlers apart from businessmen and others who were long-term residents rather than settlers. The reasons for this lay partly in the climate, believed to be bad for Europeans, but even more because local Africans, as in Nigeria and Ghana, successfully resisted the arrival of settlers. Elsewhere on the continent there were few colonies without settlers. By the 1920s these Europeans formed important minorities, still small in numbers but large in influence, in British East Africa, Central and Southern Africa; in South Africa, white settlers already had full control of government. Settlers became numerous in the Portuguese colonies of Mozambique and Angola; in the Belgian Congo (Zaire); in some parts of Italian Africa (notably Eritrea); and in French North Africa and Madagascar.

We may note here that different kinds of settler communities also appeared on the scene. Small numbers of Lebanese came to West Africa, and Greeks and others to other colonies. Much larger numbers of people from the Indian sub-continent also came to East Africa. Of these, about 32,000 were Indians brought to Kenya and Uganda as 'indentured labourers', or contract workers, so as to help in building the railway from Mombasa, on the coast, to the shores of Lake Nyanza (then called Lake Victoria by the Europeans). About 6,000 of these 'indentured labourers' stayed in East Africa after work on the railway was finished.

Most of these Asian newcomers, apart from the railway workers, were welcomed by the colonial authorities as useful middle-men in local trade and enterprise.

Meanwhile, a much larger immigration of Indians had begun in the British South African territory of Natal where the growing and harvesting of sugar required cheap labour in large quantity. In 1872 the number of Indian 'indentured labourers' in Natal was about 5,000; by 1886 the total had risen to 30,000 and to 60,000 by 1899. Thereafter the number of Indians continued to rise, although the practice of 'indentured labour' was gradually discontinued. In 1974 the total number of Indians in South Africa, mostly in Natal, was about 700,000 (or 2.8 per cent of the country's whole population). All were subject to the pains and penalties of the *apartheid* system; and most had to work for white employers for very low wages and in bad living conditions. In short, they suffered in the land of their birth just as the Africans suffered.

Wherever settlers came from Europe, increasing quantities of the best land were taken from African farmers and sold to the settlers at give-away prices. The worst cases occurred in South Africa and Algeria. Already by 1914, a large part of the fertile land of northern Algeria had been taken by European settlers; and the total of such land continued to grow in size until the 1950s. In South Africa a government law of 1913 went even further. This law turned over about nine-tenths of all land to European ownership, so that South Africa's big African majority was allowed to own land only in one-tenth of their country. (See the map on p. 149).

This taking of land occurred in all the settler colonies. As early as 1920, for example, a big part of the fertile, high plateau country of Angola was in European ownership. Over two million hectares of the still more fertile highlands of Kenya were likewise sold or given to European settlers by the British colonial government.

12

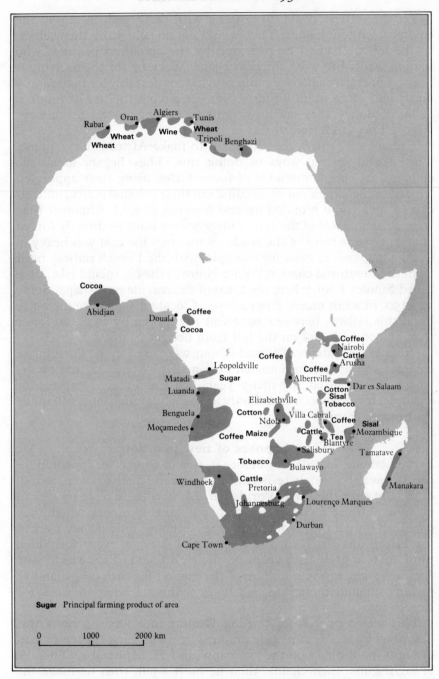

Fig. 2 Areas of principal European farming settlement in Colonial Africa

Yet the settlers could do nothing with their land, in any of the colonies, without labour. They would not do field-work themselves; so the labour had to be provided by the colonised peoples, who seldom wanted to work for Europeans. Working for themselves, as farmers or craftsmen, they could provide comfortably for their family needs and often more besides. Not yet having the use of modern forms of money, they saw no advantage in going to work for money-wages. They preferred to stay at home.

The colonial rulers therefore had to make Africans leave home. They found several ways of doing this. They began, in all the colonies, by simple methods of force. Often using their appointed 'chiefs' or 'headmen', or by sending out their colonial police, officials caused men to be rounded up and brought to work wherever they were needed. Most of the early railways were built by directly forced labour; so were most of the roads. Sometimes the cost was heavy in lives. That was the case, for example, with the French railway built from the equatorial coast at Pointe Noire to the big inland lake, then called Stanley Pool, where the town of Brazzaville took shape. Some 127,250 'fit adult males' from a host of local villages were forced to build this railway between 1921 and 1932; even by 1928, no fewer than 10,000 had died on the job from hunger or disease.

Other large systems of forced labour were used in the Portuguese colonies and in Italian Somalia; but smaller systems existed everywhere. They lasted for many years. In the French empire, for example, forced labour ended only in 1946, but much later still in the Portuguese empire.

The purposes of new taxation

Forced labour, like slavery before it, was of course very wasteful of life. It was also strongly resisted. More peaceful methods were found, especially after the First World War. Mostly, these were by way of taxation. African men were made to pay taxes in money which they could get only if they worked for wages: that is, only if they worked for Europeans. In Kenya, for example, Africans were forbidden until 1926 to grow cash crops on their own land. This was to stop Africans from winning a share of the market for cash crops, and so earning enough money to pay taxes without having to work for Europeans.

This whole process of turning farmers into wage-workers was described by an African trade unionist in 1929. 'First the white man brought the Bible,' said the Zimbabwean J.H. Mphemba. 'Then he brought guns, then chains, then he built a jail, then he made the native pay tax.'

Taxes paid for colonial government. They also forced Africans into the labour pool. Either village men went to work for wages, or else the police came for them. Largely by this method, the Southern Rhodesian (Zimbabwean) mining industry was manned, through the 1920s, by upwards of 40,000 African workers each year.

These men suffered much. Their wages were very low, their conditions of work very bad. Between 1900 and 1933 more than 30,000 African workers lost their lives in Southern Rhodesian mines: some 3,000 by accidents, and 27,000 by diseases caught at work.

Similar methods of getting labour for colonial needs spread all over the continent. They removed great numbers of men from rural life. They often ruined rural stability and peace. There were officials who protested; but they spoke in vain against the huge labour demand from foreign mining companies and settler plantations.

Export crops and food

A different situation came about in all those non-settler colonies, chiefly in British West Africa and parts of French West Africa, where African farmers could produce crops for the export market. Here, men could mostly stay at home in their villages, or work for neighbours. These farmers were rapidly successful in growing crops for export, notably cocoa, groundnuts, palm kernels, cotton, and afterwards coffee. Unhampered by settler interference, they showed skill and enterprise. They moved with the times. They took every chance to grow and sell more.

That was a gain brought by the colonial systems: it joined these farmers to expanding markets in the rest of the world. But it was a gain with several big handicaps. One of these handicaps had to do with the prices for which these farmers could sell their export crops. The prices were fixed by foreign companies which controlled the export trade. Such companies made their profit from the difference between the low prices they paid to local African suppliers and the much higher prices for which they sold these crops in Europe or America. Supported by colonial governments, the companies made this price-difference as big as they could.

Several consequences followed. First, the profits made by foreign companies from this price-difference did not stay in the colonies. They were sent back to Europe. So the skill and enterprise of successful farmers was turned into a way of transferring wealth from colonies to countries overseas. The more that Africans produced, the bigger was this transfer. That was one of the chief reasons why gains brought by colonial systems were repeatedly cancelled out, or turned into losses, by the way those same systems worked in practice.

Secondly, even the most successful farmers often got into debt because their costs of production were not covered by the prices they were paid. Their debt was made worse by the general lack of any proper facilities for borrowing money from banks. Even the Gold Coast's cocoa farmers, though producing most of the world's cocoa in those times, were often in debt through no fault of their own.

Another consequence was long-term. The more that farmers turned to export crops, the less food could they grow for local use. Because of this, local food shortages began to be felt as early as the 1930s. For the same reason, such food shortages would afterwards become much worse. Continuing on the same lines, even though independent, many African states today have to import expensive foreign food because their farmers do not grow enough food at home. Here was another way in which the colonial systems set a pattern of export that was bad for the majority of people (see also Chapter 19).

The contradictions of 'progress'

Certainly, when our century began, the methods and organisation of African production and business greatly needed modernising. Those ways had served well in the days before modern machinery and methods of finance. Nobody anywhere produced better cloth, for instance, than the weavers of West Africa; but they produced it on hand-looms. African miners produced all the gold used for money in Europe long ago; but they did it by hand-methods in shallow mines or by panning the rivers. African traders used many things for money, such as brass manillas, salt bars, and above all, cowrie shells; but they seldom used coins or banknotes.

The greater strength of the colonial powers came from the fact that their own countries had already carried out this work of modernisation. All of them had passed through an industrial revolution – in other words, their hand-production had given way to machine-production. So what did their coming to Africa do for the modernising of Africa?

The answer again is contradictory. It did something, but not much; and each gain tended, in practice, to be cancelled out by a larger loss. The colonial period brought in, for example, the use of coins and notes. These went quickly into common use. Even as early as the ten years of 1901–1911, British West Africa (but chiefly Nigeria) imported silver coins (made in England) to the value of nearly £3.5 millions; and in 1911 the use of rods and manillas, as forms of money, was officially ended.

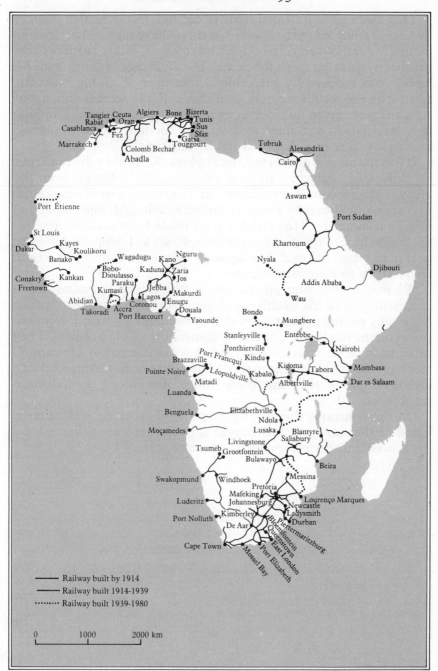

Fig. 3 Railways in Africa, with dates of construction

That was a gain: it helped trade to expand. But in settler colonies this use of coins led to the labour system we have seen earlier, leading in turn to rural poverty. In non-settler colonies, where farmers could prosper by growing crops for export, the advantage of using coins for money was reduced by the colonial take-over of all big business, again with the results we have seen above. Banks were founded, but Africans were given no share in owning or running them. Shipping lines expanded, but they were always foreign. Great wholesale businesses were launched, but not by Africans.

It was the same with machine technology. Railways were built, but by European engineers; in most of the settler colonies, even the engine drivers were always European. Deep mines were dug for the first time, but always by foreign companies using African labour and foreign technicians. Huge profits were made from these mines, but the lion's share of the profits went always back to Europe or America; in this way too, colonial development meant the transfer of wealth from Africa to countries overseas.

We may briefly sum up. Generally, the colonial systems aimed successfully at taking wealth out of Africa: by means of cheap mining labour; by paying prices to export crop farmers that were lower than prices on the world market; and by controlling all big business. They brought in modern technology, but they transferred to Africans no technical skills of any importance. They did not modernise Africa's means of production and trade. They introduced no industrial revolution.

On the contrary, they set up patterns of working and earning, based on the aim of wealth-transfer abroad, that were going to leave great problems for independent Africa to solve.

CHAPTER 3

African responses: to 1930

How did the people of those days respond to colonial rule and its demands? Of course the answers of Africans varied from colony to colony, and from one colonial system to another. Their first need was to study and understand their new rulers. Their next need was to make the best of things.

Most chiefs – whether they were real ones appointed by their peoples, or false ones appointed by the colonial authorities – found that they could defend their positions by serving the new rulers. Some chiefs, as in parts of Nigeria or Uganda or Kenya, even found that they could improve their positions. Many traders, though kept out of big business, found that they could still make a living in small business, even sometimes a better living. Many farmers went into export crops with good results. Generally, people welcomed the chance of modernisation wherever this appeared. There was now an opportunity, though still a small one, of sending children to primary school, and even, in rare cases, to secondary school.

One big response, in short, was adjusting to the system: what historians have called 'accommodation'. Having resisted the colonial invaders in vain, Africans naturally looked for ways of getting a place inside the new systems, or even of turning these systems to African advantage. Some of these ways of accommodation, as we shall see, were to lead on to the later rise of modern nationalism and its way of escape from foreign rule. Broadly, ways of adjusting were sought by all who had the chance to do that.

But the great majority of people, above all in the settler colonies, had no such chance. They were too poor or powerless to join the social groups, or the 'better-off classes', for whom accommodation could offer something useful. The new ways of working and earning kept them fixed in their poverty and ignorance; the gains of colonial rule passed them by. For them, the choice was a hard one: to give in, or to revolt.

'Pacification' in practice

Many responded by revolt. They continued their resistance of former years, but now with new reasons for their action. They protested against forced labour, against their loss of land to settlers, against colonial taxation and much else. Such protests were sometimes peaceful; at other times they resorted to violence in reply to the violence of the colonial systems.

To all these protests, whether violent or not, the colonial powers replied with some form of 'pacification'. No year in this period passed without campaigns of 'pacification' in one region or other, and often in several. These campaigns were designed to repress, or to frighten.

If there was a violent protest to repress, many troops or armed police were used. If there was only a threat or fear of violent protest, a show of force was put on. Troops were marched about. An official circular of the Belgian Congo government laid it down, in 1924, that 'military promenades are one of the best ways of preventing any idea of revolt, of making the natives carry out their legal duties, and of keeping up habits of work among them.' The wording of that circular is interesting. It shows that the colonial powers, in this case the Belgian Congo government, were always thinking that Africans might revolt. It uses the word 'natives', meaning Africans, as a term of colonialist contempt. And it speaks of the need to keep up 'habits of work', as though Africans never worked when left to themselves.

What the 'legal duties of natives' and their 'habits of work' could really mean, in those colonial years, may be seen from another example, that of Italian Somalia. In 1930 an Italian official wrote home to his government, in Italy, that these 'duties' had become too heavy. This worried official reported that methods of forced labour in Somalia were 'a good deal worse than slavery'. If a man were a slave, he said, his master would care well for him; otherwise, if the man died from overwork, his master would have to buy another slave. But forced workers cost nothing. 'So when a Somali native dies after being given to an employer, or becomes unfit for work,' wrote this official, 'the employer simply asks the government to give him another.'

Those years saw countless protests and revolts against such treatment. Often they were small, 'lost in the backlands', barely noticed even in the colonial records. But sometimes they were big protests and long wars. These were revolts, led by outstanding men, against more than bad treatment. Beyond that, they were revolts aimed also at winning back independence.

Early attempts at national liberation: two examples

In 1899, seeing his country invaded by foreign powers, a young but learned Muslim of Somalia sent out a call for war against them. Raising 5,000 men, at first with only 200 rifles, the Sayyid Muhamad Abdille Hasan began by attacking British colonial forces. He also tackled the Italian invaders (in Somalia) and the Ethiopian invaders (in Ogaden). He began to build a united new Somali nation, even though several Somali clans refused to follow him.

Only in 1920 were the Sayyid and his 'Dervish Army' (so called after the revolt of the Mahdia in the eastern Sudan) finally defeated. With the First World War at an end, the British sent fresh troops against him, and aircraft to bomb his fortress-capital at Tale. But the Sayyid had launched a new and powerful idea of Somali unity. Nowadays he is remembered as the founder of the modern Somali nation.

In that same year of the Sayyid's defeat in Somalia, another Muslim leader took the same road in northern Morocco. Abd al-Krim al-Khattabi (the Writer or the Learned) launched a revolt against Spanish colonial rule. He won a great battle at Anual, defeating some 60,000 Spanish troops with only 3,000 of his own, and set about founding a free republic in the north Moroccan mountains of the Rif.

Abd al-Krim's plan was to unite the Berber-speaking clans of that Moroccan region, put an end to the social inequalities of their way of life, introduce modern education and other services, and prepare for Moroccan independence in the modern world. He went far to realise his plan before he and his republic were overwhelmed, in 1926, by a combined Spanish and French army of some 800,000 men. Yet he too was not forgotten. A judgment on him by the French army's intelligence service, in 1925, spoke for what the world has remembered of this extraordinary man:

> Abd al-Krim is not a warrior trying to be a king. He is not a *Mahdi* come to renew Islam. He is a nationalist seeking to liberate the territory. He is a patriot aiming to throw off a foreign yoke.

With men such as the Sayyid Muhamad and Abd al-Krim, we can see that protest and revolt went beyond a response to bad colonial treatment; these men went beyond an effort to win back the old independence of the past. They looked forward to a new kind of independence, moving with the times. So the political effects of the colonial systems were already, even in those early years, beginning to have their counter-effects. The banners of national liberation were beginning to wave in the winds of political development.

The notion that people should free themselves by going forward to new ideas rather than going back to old ideas made progress as the 1920s passed by. Other important personalities show this. So it was that Harry Thuku, a clerk in the colonial administration of Kenya, led new forms of protest and political organisation in those same years. He and others formed a group, in 1921, which they called the Young Kikuyu Association; and it is in this Association that historians have found some of the origins of Kenya nationalism.

Other thoughtful men followed the road of peaceful political organisation in those years, and in many colonies. Their plan was to build unity by political work, and to use this unity for the common good. We shall come back to this subject.

Independent churches and religious protest movements

To combat the colonial invasions, people had asked for the help and guidance of ancestral spirits, and of priests who spoke for those spirits. Some of these priests had become the leaders of anti-colonial rebellions, as in the great rising of the Shona and Ndebele against British invasion of their country, Southern Rhodesia (Zimbabwe), in the 1890s.

But now, after some twenty years of colonial rule, people looked more often for new kinds of spiritual guidance. Many in Africa south of the Sahara turned to the Christian teachings of European missionaries. Then they often found that these missionaries were also part of the colonial systems to which the missionaries preached submission and obedience. This led Christian Africans to form new churches of their own, or else – as in South Africa – to join independent church communities already in existence.

The movement for independent churches was another form of anti-colonial protest. It had begun long before in South Africa, colonised by settlers in an earlier time. Its leaders were inspired by the Bible message that 'Ethiopia will stretch out its hands to God': meaning by Ethiopia not just the country of that name but all the lands of black people. Many Ethiopianist churches were founded in the far south of the continent. They drew multitudes of believers, for they preached the truth that God was not part of the colonial systems, but was for the salvation of everyone. From South Africa the same movement spread elsewhere: to Central, East and West Africa.

After 1920, the various trends of the independent church movement became still more important, and suffered more persecution. They gave people fresh hope and confidence outside the ideas of

22

obedience to colonial rule; and the colonial authorities therefore feared them. Notable among the new churches founded in these years was the Church of Jesus Christ on This Earth, launched in 1921 by Simon Kimbangu in the Belgian Congo (Zaire). In joining this church, people of the Belgian Congo expressed spiritual resistance to colonial rule, and were sorely persecuted by the Belgian authorities.

Another independent movement, a little older, was the Church of the Children of Israel founded in South Africa by Enoch Mgijima. Like the followers of Kimbangu, those of Mgijima had to face colonial persecution. In 1921 their congregation refused to move from land which the racist government of South Africa had marked out for Europeans only. South African troops killed 163 and wounded 129 of these peaceful African Christians.

Religious protest took many shapes. Their aim was not to form political organisations, or to move towards the ideas of nationalism. Protesters wanted, in a religious way, to get rid of 'the evil of the times'. But since this evil was often identified with colonial rule, their aim was also anti-colonial. An important case was the movement known usually as Watchtower, originally launched in central Africa in the 1890s but active later in a number of colonies. Often its members refused to pay colonial taxes, or broke other colonial laws. So the colonial authorities set out to suppress them, and found this difficult.

Watchtower had several offshoots. One of them was the Watchman's Society founded by Kenon Kamwana of Nyasaland (Malawi) in 1937. It was directly anti-colonial. 'We are the children of God,' Kamwana told his followers, 'and must therefore pay no attention to the laws of the *boma* [colonial government] . . . People must not be afraid to break government laws.'

All these independent Christian responses were an aspect of African protest against the colonial systems, and above all against the colonial belief that God wanted white people to rule over black people.

Such responses were not only Christian by inspiration. There were continued examples of spiritual resistance to colonial rule by Africans who remained true to their own religions. Also, large movements of Muslim protest occurred south of the Sahara as well as north of it. They tried to give people fresh self-confidence in the face of colonial conquest and repression. In Senegal, for instance, a movement called the *Muridiyya* took shape through the teaching of Ahmadou Bamba (1850–1927). Bamba himself did not directly challenge colonial rule, but the effect of his teaching was to cause his followers to challenge it. The French exiled Bamba to Gabon and then to Mauritania, and allowed him to return to Senegal only under house-arrest. Another movement of Muslim spiritual protest was the *Hamalliyya* in French Soudan (later Mali) led by Sheikh Hamallah (1883–1943).

New social groups, or classes-in-the-making

It would be wrong to think of this period only in terms of protest or revolt. There was much of both, for the colonial systems were instruments of conquest and repression. But they were more than that, they were also instruments of social reorganisation. This was in line with colonial needs, and Africans had to adjust to it as best they could. Produced by industrialised countries, the colonial systems changed many ways of working and living. They brought into existence new social groupings, as well as the beginnings of the social classes into which industrialised peoples were divided.

This social reorganisation went much further after 1930, and again after 1940. But it was already at work before 1930. We have seen part of it in the 'forcing out' of African labour for colonial mines and plantations.

This 'forcing out' of labour created a new social grouping of men who worked for money-wages and who, increasingly, had no other means of livelihood. Consider one example. Africans had mined tin on the Jos Plateau (of central Nigeria) for more than 2,000 years. Using handicraft methods, they were independent producers who combined their mining with farm work. Then foreign companies, using machinery, took over the Jos mines after our century began. In 1910 there were 50 such companies in Nigeria employing 15,000 miners; and, by 1928, Nigerian tin-miners totalled nearly 40,000. But these men had ceased to be independent producers. They had become wage-workers.

The same happened wherever foreign companies dug deep mines: for gold in South Africa, for copper in Northern Rhodesia (Zambia), for coal and other minerals elsewhere. Huge numbers of wage-workers were employed. Nearly always they were workers brought from another place, or another colony, employed on contracts for a year or more at a time. In short, they were *migrant workers*.

As a new social group, which had never existed before on any such scale, migrant workers did not form a new, integrated class of workers, or what industrialised countries call a working-class. As migrants, they had one foot in the wage-work of the mines or plantations, but another foot in their villages at home. Here was what we have seen earlier: Africans were brought into the modern

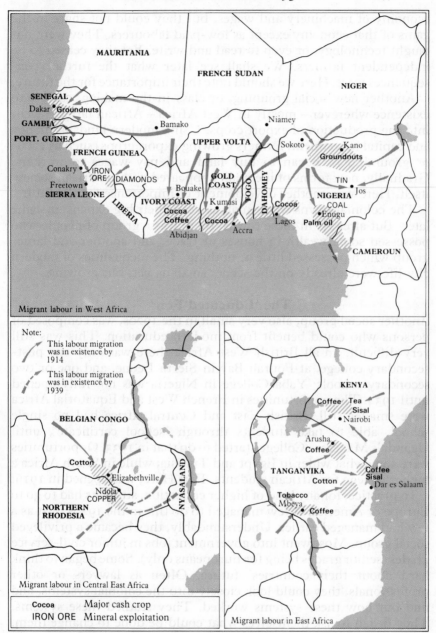

Fig. 4 Patterns of labour migration in Colonial Africa. Only the main migrant-labour flows are shown. (For Southern Africa, see page 144.)

25

economy of machinery and wages, but they could not share in the gains of that economy except as low-paid labourers. They were not taught technology, or even to read and write. Yet they ceased to be independent farmers. We shall see later what the further consequences were. Here we should note their importance for the future.

Another new social grouping, or class-in-the-making, came into existence wherever – mostly in West Africa – African farmers went into the production of export crops. Using modern kinds of money and capital investment, farmers growing export crops (such as cocoa or groundnuts), began to buy land and pay wages to workers. Gradually, new forms of inequality appeared within African society itself. Here was another development of importance for the future.

The colonial towns were small as yet. Their big expansion came later. But already, in these towns, there was a group of people who possessed some wealth in houses or trade, and another and larger group which possessed little or nothing. The inequalities of modern city life were already on the scene: small as yet, but growing.

The 'Educated Few'

Another social group, also very small in the 1920s, was composed of persons who could benefit from modern education. This was still very difficult. In all British West Africa there was only one post-secondary college, at Fourah Bay in Sierra Leone, and one or two secondary schools; Yaba College in Nigeria was not fully opened until 1934. The opportunities in French West and Equatorial Africa were smaller still. British East and Central Africa had no single school, able to take students through 'school certificate', until Uganda's Makerere College started to do that in 1933. Opportunities were somewhat wider in Egypt and Tunisia; while in South Africa a higher college for African students, Fort Hare, was opened in 1916.

In practice, for any kind of higher education, students had to go to Europe or America. A few managed to do this in the 1920s, just as a few had managed earlier. Understandably, they became a privileged social group. Most went into government jobs in junior civil-service grades (senior grades being for Europeans only). Some began to think hard about their countries' future. Often as lawyers or other professionals, they could look closely into the colonial systems, and find out how these systems worked. They studied these systems. They began to ask themselves what could be done to change them.

It was largely through this group, the 'educated few' or the 'intellectual élite', that the ideas of nationalism, and the struggle for political advance, now began to be known and accepted.

26

CHAPTER 4

Key ideas for progress

In those days, thinking about the future, educated persons saw two big obstacles to any progress. One of these was raised, and always built higher, by the racism of the colonial systems. The Africans, this racism insisted, are inferior. They have made no history. They have created no civilisation. They cannot rule themselves: we superior Europeans must do it for them.

These were foolish untruths, because Africans had made history, and built civilisations, and ruled themselves, through countless years before any colonial ruler came upon the scene. Yet these untruths, however surprising this may seem today, were widely believed in those early decades of our century. That was partly because the colonial rulers were far advanced in machines and modern technology, and they consequently claimed that they had 'invented everything'. Partly it was because children in colonial schools were taught this same racist lesson. Africa's own development was never mentioned or discussed.

Here was one obstacle to progress: a steady and continual downgrading of African brains and skills, of Africa's real achievements. There was a second obstacle. This was raised by the division of Africa's peoples into some fifty colonies. In nearly every one of the colonies, many ancient communities or states suddenly found themselves inside the same colonial frontier, and part of the same colony. But although thus thrown together, they were still divided – by their own history, but also by the divisive methods of colonial government.

On the one hand, few of these many states and communities had ever felt the need to combine together in the past. On the other hand, the colonial systems tried hard to prevent them from combining now. Unless they did combine together now, who was going to listen to any big demand for change? Yet how were they to find common ground?

We shall return to this subject later in the context of modern tribalism and nationalism (see Chapter 7). Meanwhile, in the 1920s, two powerful ideas began to circulate, the one aimed against the first obstacle, the other against the second obstacle. The first idea was Pan-Africanism. The second idea, linked to the first, was national union or nationalism.

The Pan-African movement: origins, early aims

'Pan' is a Greek word meaning 'all'; so Pan-African means 'all-African'. But the first form of the Pan-African movement was not directly concerned with Africa. It was concerned with the black communities, of African ancestry, who lived in North America and the Caribbean (West Indies). These black peoples had come from many African peoples and cultures. But they had lost their languages and cultures during the time of slavery. Liberated from American slavery, they were united by remaining the victims of American and colonial racism. They were united, we can say, by their colour and by their sufferings.

Some of these black people, during the last century, came to believe that they could become free and equal only if they left America. But where, then, should they go except to the homeland of their ancestors? A 'Back to Africa' movement developed; and this was how Liberia came to be founded by black people from the USA. The same idea developed further: into the idea that all black peoples should unite in defence of their common interests, and against racism.

So the first form of this movement was, really, a 'Pan-black' or Pan-Negro movement which took shape outside Africa. Yet the Pan-African movement, even in this early form, also stood for the defence of Africans in Africa. One of the actions of the first Pan-African congress, held in London in 1900, was to protest to Britain's Queen Victoria against racist rule in South Africa and Rhodesia.

That first congress was attended by 32 delegates. Of these, eleven were from the USA and ten from the West Indies, but only four directly from Africa. Yet its proceedings raised high the truths of African equality and achievement; and its importance was well marked by educated persons in Africa, notably in West and South Africa. The Nigerian *Lagos Standard*, a newspaper that was owned as well as edited by Africans, hailed the congress of 1900 as 'an event in the history of race movements which, for its importance and probable results, is perhaps without parallel'.

Leading spokesmen for the liberating ideas of Pan-Africanism were soon on the African scene. Among them was the West Indian and later Liberian diplomat, Edward Wilmot Blyden (1832–1912). During the 1920s, powerful help for the same ideas was given by two outstanding men across the Atlantic. One of these was the Jamaican Marcus Moziah Garvey (1887–1940), who in 1914 founded an organisation in New York, called the Universal Negro Improvement

Association, and whose influence was felt widely across Africa. Another was the black American William Burghardt DuBois (1868–1963), a great student of African history who eventually became a citizen of Ghana.

This movement could do nothing to change the colonial systems, for it had no power. Yet it played a useful part in telling the world about Africa's problems under colonial rule. It spoke up for colonised Africans at a time when few of these could make their voices heard through colonial walls of silence. A second congress was held in Paris, in 1919, where the victorious powers of the First World War were holding their peace conference. A third congress took place in London and Brussels in 1921; a fourth in London and Lisbon in 1923; and a fifth in New York in 1927.

But by this time, the middle of the 1920s, the ideas of the Pan-African movement were developing towards a new form. This was that Africans must find their own way towards unity and freedom. Black Americans could help, but their problems were different; they could not lead Africa. Any sound plan for African progress, declared a leading Gold Coast thinker, Kobina Sekyi (1892–1956) in a book written during 1925, 'must be controlled and directed from African Africa and thoroughly African African.'

In this new form, the 'Pan-black' or 'Pan-Negro' idea grew into a much more directly Pan-*African* idea. This would reach its full development only with the sixth Pan-African congress, held in Manchester (England) in 1945, when leading African nationalists combined in new demands for African independence. And that was the congress which then led on to the Organisation of African Unity (see Chapter 20). Meanwhile this revised form of Pan-Africanism was accompanied, during the 1920s, by the second idea we have noted above: the idea of *national union*.

National union

This idea was also not quite new in the 1920s. It had taken shape some years earlier among the educated few of British West Africa, especially in the towns of Cape Coast (in the Gold Coast/Ghana), Lagos (in Nigeria), Freetown (in Sierra Leone), and Bathurst (Banjul in The Gambia). These men had more freedom than Africans in other colonies. Though barred from senior government jobs, they were able to discuss politics without fear of the colonial police. They could publish newspapers of their own.

These men studied Europe, and saw that the basis for the

independence of European peoples was that they were organised into nations: into states, that is, whose peoples had a single national loyalty and accepted a single national culture. (In fact, many European states had various loyalties and cultures. But each had one that was dominant, and this was the basis of their nationhood.)

Now the idea that the various peoples in a colony could become free only if they combined together as a nation, like the Europeans, had already been heard in earlier years. Influential in promoting this kind of idea, for example, was the Aborigines' Rights Protection Society, founded in Gold Coast in 1897. In 1911 another Gold Coast thinker, S.R.B. Attoh Ahuma, published an important book called *The Gold Coast Nation and National Consciousness*. He called for Africans to be proud of their heritage and history. He argued that they must found modern nations.

Attoh Ahuma, like other early thinkers of this kind, was caught in a contradiction. He stood for African progress. But he shared the contempt of educated persons for the people of the rural areas. This early idea of national union, in other words, expressed no confidence in the ability of Africans to grow from their own historical roots and cultures. It taught that Africans must follow the lessons of European history, and copy European ways of organisation. But this, in fact, was just what the colonial rulers were also teaching.

'Let us help each other to find a way out of Darkest Africa,' wrote Attoh Ahuma in his book of 1911. 'We must emerge from the savage backwoods, and come into the open where nations are made.' That was the opinion of nearly all the educated persons of those days; and it was understandable. To become educated to a high level, they had to live in Europe and learn in European languages. Home again, they tended to live like Europeans, losing touch with their own peoples. They became what Kobina Sekyi, in a play of 1915, called 'social hybrids': persons 'born into one race, and brought up to live like members of another race.' Such was the 'been-to' fate in those times.

Yet these 'social hybrids' of the 1920s, mostly in British West Africa, played an important part. They found the common ground on which different peoples, gathered within a single colony, could make progress towards independence: the common ground, that is, of national union. They said that Africans must become nations. But they also said more, and this, too, was to be important. They said that Africans must become nations by adopting the British system of government, and not by adapting the systems formed in Africa's own history. As the Nigerian historian E.A. Ayandele has written, 'it was they who conceived the "modern" Nigeria which embraced the myriads of states and kingdoms of the pre-colonial era.'

Founders of modern nationalism: West Africa

A new move towards the development of nationalism came in 1920.
Forty-five members of what the Gambian historian J. Ayodele
Langley has called 'the lawyer-merchant class' in British West Africa
– the spokesman of the educated few – gathered at the Accra Native
Club (in the Gold Coast) during March. There they founded the
National Congress of British West Africa (NCBWA), with sections
in each of the four colonies (Nigeria, Gold Coast, Sierra Leone, The
Gambia).

The aims of this congress combined the idea of national union with
that of pan-Africanism. As to the first, its leaders believed that they
must press the British to allow them to join colonial parliaments, then
known as legislatures. These were mostly advisory bodies in each
colony, and had no power. But the men of the NCBWA believed that
these legislatures could develop into democratic parliaments, and, in
time, into national parliaments.

At the same time, the NCBWA leaders argued that educated
Africans must combine their efforts across colonial frontiers. They
pressed the pan-African idea. Their president, the Gold Coast lawyer
J.A. Casely Hayford, told the third NCBWA conference:

> As there is an international feeling among all white men, among all
> brown men, among all yellow men, so must there be an inter-
> national feeling among all black folk.

Even at its first conference, in 1920, the NCBWA demanded progress
towards 'a united West Africa' of the four colonies.

Active in these discussions, besides Casely Hayford and other
Gold Coasters, were well-known Nigerians such as the Reverend
Patriarch Patrick Campbell, the medical doctor Richard Savage, the
newspaper editor Thomas Horatio Jackson, and Prince Bassey
Ephraim of Calabar. Dr Herbert Bankole-Bright was in this respect
the leading Sierra Leonian, while E.F. Small was prominent among
Gambians.

Not all the lawyer-merchant class agreed. The Nigerian lawyer Sir
Kitoyi Ayasa rejected the congress policy on the grounds that 'we
have a Yoruba nation and a Hausa nation, but so far we have no
Nigerian nation.' He thought the NCBWA was going much too fast.
So did the British, who rejected all the congress demands. The
NCBWA went on having occasional meetings till 1933, but gradually
the 'four-colony union' idea was forgotten. In sum, the NCBWA
failed to make any progress. But it pointed the way, clearly, to the
future of nationalism.

The chief weakness of the NCBWA was that its members were all privileged 'hybrids' who were against calling on the mass of people for any support. They wanted small steps, small reforms, which would ensure that they would become the leaders of the nations they talked about. They wanted to be junior partners with the British in the hope that one day they could become equal partners. The time had yet to arrive when nationalism would have mass support, and demand full independence. Then, as we shall see, the British would have to listen.

Little or nothing was heard of these ideas of national union, during the 1920s, in British East and Central Africa. There, the educated few barely existed as yet; while the European settler communities, slowly growing stronger, took it for granted that they, and not the African majorities, were going to dominate the future of those countries.

The African voice in South Africa

Here the key date was 1910. In that year the British imperial government in London withdrew Britain's political power from South Africa, and gave all this power to the two white minorities, those who spoke English and those who spoke Afrikaans (a local language descended from the Dutch language of the earliest white settlers). This was done by an Act of Union. The four countries of earlier South Africa (Cape Colony, Natal, Orange Free State, Transvaal Republic) were combined into one country, the Union of South Africa.

The whites of the four former states disagreed in many ways, but they were firmly united against the blacks: against, that is, the African majority and the two minorities of Coloureds (persons of mixed origin) and Asians. The Afrikaner (Boer) whites were severely racist by doctrine, habit and tradition. The English-speaking whites were the same, or else, if they were new immigrants, soon became so. Handed all local power in 1910, these two white communities competed with each other for the spoils and benefits. But they at once agreed with each other in passing laws, for the whole Union, which reduced or eliminated rights and opportunities for black people.

Their chief idea was to drive Africans into labour-service for white farms, white industries, and white families. One of the harshest of these new racist laws was the Land Act of 1913. It denied Africans any right to own land in nine-tenths of the whole country, even though the Africans, at that time, outnumbered the whites by four to one. With other laws of the same kind, this Land Act was a big

32

reinforcement of the South African racist system which, becoming ever worse, would later develop into *apartheid* (see Chapter 16).

African farmers and chiefs protested in vain, for the whites had all the power and used it without mercy. Protests by educated Africans were also made. These were the work of a small number of men who had managed to secure some modern education through missionary colleges, or overseas. They included John Tengu Jabavu, John Dube, Pixley Seme, Solomon Plaatje and others. Meeting in 1912 at Bloemfontein, in the Orange Free State province of the newly-formed Union, they launched the South African Native National Congress. Still free to organise in public, they wanted this congress to speak for a united African voice, against the united white voice, in all the four countries of the Union. So this congress was another early combination of the ideas of unity and nationalism.

The white rulers paid no attention. They went on building up their racist system. Here, too, the educated men had yet to call for mass support; like those of the NCBWA, most were moderate and cautious. In 1923 they changed the name of their organisation to the African National Congress of South Africa (ANC). The ANC was able to hold out against growing persecution; in spite of its weakness, it proved to be another 'parent of the future'.

The policy of 'assimilation'

Africans had to face a somewhat different kind of racism in the French colonial empire. At least in British West Africa, the British always said that they had a 'mission' to lead Africans to independence, though by immensely slow steps. The French also said that they had a mission: not, however, to lead Africans to independence, but to lead them towards becoming citizens of France. On this French view, Africans could never have independent states of their own; they could only become part of 'greater France'. They could not rebuild their civilisations in the modern world; they could only join French civilisation.

This was called the policy of 'assimilation', or 'being absorbed'. It meant that African people, to become free, had to become black French people. In practice, assimilation was impossible for nearly all Africans in the French empire. Throughout French West Africa in 1926, for example, there were more than 13 million Africans. But fewer than 50,000 of these were French citizens, and most of that small percentage were in the single colony of Senegal. All the rest were 'natives' (*indigènes*) subject to forced labour and other racist laws; as late as 1945, the number of assimilated West Africans was still below 100,000. The assimilated number was even smaller in other French colonies in Africa.

Yet these small groups of black French citizens were important. They were the ones who could get some modern education, and develop new ideas about the future. Because of the French policy of assimilation, they began to demand a bigger chance for Africans to become French citizens; only much later did they start to think about demanding national independence. They made no progress in the 1920s or even later. They had much less freedom than educated persons in British West Africa. Their position was more like that of Africans in the British settler colonies of East and Central Africa.

The history of African newspapers underlines this. Thanks to missionary schools, British West Africa had gifted editors and journalists who were able to use their skills. Even by 1900, Sierra Leone had known as many as 34 African newspapers at one time or other; the Gold Coast had had 19, Nigeria seven. The best of these papers continued to appear. They were a big part of city life; they contained a lot about politics, and were often critical of colonial rule. But in French Africa, as in British East and Central Africa, there were few or no independent African newspapers. Editors and journalists in those colonies risked stiff punishment, and sometimes suffered it, whenever they wrote critical articles.

In the other African empires, the ideas of nationalism, or of any kind of progress for Africans, made even smaller gains; mostly, there were no gains. The Belgians ran their vast Congo colony as a stiff dictatorship. The Portuguese, Italians and Spanish did the same. All of them talked of having a mission to help Africans. But their words were even emptier than those of the British and French.

The Portuguese colonialists, for example, repeatedly claimed to be doing a great deal to 'civilise Africans'. But as late as 1970 the number of blacks in their colonies who were treated as 'civilised', because they had the status of assimilated persons, was less than one in every three hundred in Guiné (now Guinea-Bissau); while the numbers of 'civilised blacks' were not much greater in Angola or Mozambique. All the rest were treated as the objects of unlimited colonial exploitation. Even the few assimilated Africans were arrested, beaten, or exiled if they launched any serious anti-colonial protest.

North Africa: Islam and nationalism

Colonial rule came to North Africa at different dates, and not as any direct result of the 'share-out' conference in Berlin of 1884–85. The French invaded Algeria as early as 1830, and took control of Tunisia in 1881. The British were in full command of Egypt by 1890, and, as a result of their defeat of the Mahdia, they were ruling the Sudan soon after. In 1912 the French assumed control of Morocco, while in 1911 the Italians launched a long and bitter invasion of Libya.

These invaded peoples kept strong links with Islam in the Middle East. It was from there too that they took their new ideas about self-defence by national union. Those ideas were the creation of several important Islamic thinkers such as Jamal al-Din (1838–97), who was born in Iran but known as al-Afghani. He was a founder of the idea of Pan-Islam, of the cultural and political unity of Muslims everywhere. Another was an Egyptian follower of al-Afghani's, Muhamed Abduh (1849–1905). A third was a Syrian, Muhamed Rashid Rida (1865–1935), who became one of the founders of Arab nationalism in the Middle East.

Their teachings spread into Libya and the three countries of the Maghrib (Tunisia, Algeria and Morocco), and were welcomed by patriotic Muslims. But with colonial rule both new and strong, these patriots found it hard to know what best to do. Two schools of thought developed.

One school believed that the best course was to reform Muslim society by strong reliance on the traditional teachings of Islam, notably those of the predecessors or founders of Islam, and especially of the Prophet Muhamad and his companions. Using early Muslim principles, together with later concepts of banking, law codification and education, the thinkers of this group generally believed that specifically Islamic ideas and methods would enable their peoples to meet the challenge of the modern world. This traditionalist reform movement was often called the *Salafiyyah* (after *salafun*, 'predecessors').

A second school of thought, which eventually became much stronger than the first, was no less loyal to Islam; but its thinkers believed that their effort could succeed only by adopting secular (non-religious) ideas and methods of organisation. They urged that the oppression of imperialist nations could be thrown off only by forming anti-imperialist nations, and, therefore, anti-imperialist movements and parties of nationalism in their countries.

These two groups were both opposed to colonial rule. But their difference of opinion about how best to oppose it continued for many years. It made national union more difficult.

As time went by, the secular trend won wider support. Modern forms of politics began to emerge. As early as 1906, three political

35

parties were formed in Egypt. But the first strongly nationalist party appeared there in 1918. This was the *Wafd*. A party of Egypt's lawyer-merchant class, more numerous than elsewhere, the *Wafd* called for negotiations with Britain to end the country's colonial situation.

For their part, the British wanted to keep military and economic control over Egypt. But they had no interest in governing the country; they were ready for Egyptians to do that. So they partly agreed with the *Wafd*. In 1922 they recognised Egyptian independence, but stayed in power behind the scenes. The *Wafd* continued to lead Egyptian politics, but there was no weakening of British control until the 1950s (see Chapter 10).

Other North Africans watched these political moves. What could they do to follow them? Little or nothing in Libya, because colonial war continued there right down to 1932. This war had begun with Italian invasion in 1911. At first the Italians fought the Turkish forces of the old Ottoman empire, but these Turks withdrew from Libya in 1912. Then the Italians found themselves faced with a new and more powerful Libyan armed resistance, organised by such patriots as Ahmad Sharif and Umar al-Mukhtar, and by the *Sanussiya* – originally a movement of Muslim religious inspiration, founded long before by Sidi Muhammad al-Sanussi. Under the leadership of Sharif and Mukhtar the resistance of the *Sanussiya* and of other Libyans was overcome by the Italians only in 1932, and after years of ruthless warfare.

Things went differently in Tunisia, next door. Shortly before 1914, educated persons in Tunisia formed the Young Tunisian Party, and later pressed for a share with the French in governing Tunisia. In 1920 they and others formed another party, the *Hizb al-Hurr al-Dasturi*, or *Destour* as the French called it. Its aim was to persuade the French to allow Tunisia to return to its constitution (*Dastur*) of 1860, under which the educated few could have some political power in a parliament. To this the French paid no attention. Also, the French ignored demands for better wages and conditions put forward by Tunisian workers organised in new trade unions.

Algeria's situation was still more difficult. Most of Algeria was governed as part of the 'home country' of France, but strictly in the interests of the white settlers in Algeria. These settlers persecuted the Algerians by a powerful racism like that of the whites in South Africa. They believed that Algeria could never be anything except a region of France, and governed by French people.

Trying to improve their situation, Algerian leaders were divided on what best to do. In this period of the 1920s, most agreed with

36

Sheikh Ben Badis. Although an Algerian patriot, Ben Badis believed that Algerians must accept French rule at least for a time of 'guardianship'. 'The Algerian nation,' he said in 1925, 'is weak and insufficiently evolved. It feels a vital need to come within the protecting wing of a strong and civilised nation.' That nation was France. This was really just what leading nationalists in West Africa were also saying then. Let us try to make progress, they were saying, but for the time being under British colonial leadership.

Not all Algerian spokesmen agreed with Ben Badis. The Amir Khaled al-Kader, descendant of a great Algerian leader of the 1830s, spoke for the independence of Algeria. But he was ahead of his time; he had to end his life in exile.

A more important trend took shape, across the Mediterranean, among Algerian migrant workers in France. Even by 1926, because there was no work for them at home, these numbered about 18,000. They were badly paid, lived poorly, and needed to combine in self-defence. In 1926 a young Algerian nationalist, Messali Hadj (1898–1974), began to lead this self-defence movement. He formed the *Étoile Nord Africaine* (North African Star) in France, and the *Étoile* soon had thousands of Algerian members. For North Africa, this was the first big anti-colonial party whose leaders and most members did not belong to the lawyer-merchant class. They were workers with revolutionary ideas. Soon their demands went beyond better conditions; soon they were demanding Algerian independence. They began to take their ideas and demands back to Algeria, and to spread them there. A tremendous struggle lay ahead.

Morocco was allowed to keep its own king and local officials when the French seized control in 1912. But it was not long before the French were taking all the big decisions in governing Morocco, and most of the small decisions too. Their control was shaken, in 1920–26, by Abd al-Krim's war of independence in the Rif mountains (see p. 21). After that, they brought Morocco under tighter French control (as the Spanish also did in their northern zone). There was no effective political resistance at this time by Morocco's educated class. Yet here, too, new struggles lay ahead.

SUMMARY

Resistance and Adjustment

During the 1920s, the colonial systems were fully installed. 'Pacification' was completed. Military government was followed by civilian government.

Many continued to resist colonial government and taxation: sometimes by revolt, often by new movements of religious protest, or else by moving across colonial frontiers. Many others thought it more sensible to adjust to the system and make the best of things. Most chiefs did that; so did persons who served colonial government as appointed 'chiefs', 'headmen', police, interpreters, soldiers. Especially in non-settler colonies, farmers found they could make money by growing crops for export instead of growing food for local use.

All these trends began to make big changes in African ways of earning and living. Old ways of life began to break down. New ways of life began to be looked for. There was now a bigger demand for modern education. People wanted their children to understand this modern world from which the colonial systems had come. But schools, as yet, were few. For most children there was no chance of going to school.

New ideas about politics, about Africa's future, began to circulate: especially, the ideas of pan-Africanism and of national union, or nationalism. But as yet, with exceptions here and there, only the educated few of the lawyer-merchant class had these ideas. As yet, there was little or no talk of trying to win mass support for nationalism.

PART TWO

Colonialism under strain:
1930–1945

Herbert Macaulay (1864–1946) Sometimes called 'the father of Nigerian nationalism', Macaulay founded the Nigerian National Democratic Party. Later, with Nnamdi Azikiwe and others, he led campaigns for Nigerian political advance.

Casely Hayford (1866–1930) The prominent Ghanaian lawyer, writer and nationalist leader. He was active till 1914 in the Gold Coast Aborigines' Rights Protection Society, and founded the National Congress of British West Africa in 1920.

Harry Thuku (1895–1970) Early leader of Kenyan political resistance to colonialism. He founded the Young Kikuyu Association in Nairobi during 1921, and was a pioneer of later nationalist ideas.

Abd al-Krim (1882–1963) Moroccan leader of anti-colonial war against Spanish and French colonialism, and founder of the Rif Republic (1920–26). He stood for Muslim and African unity and independence in the Maghrib.

Messali Hadj (1898–1974) Pioneer Algerian nationalist. He founded the Etoile Nord-Africaine in 1926 and, in 1937, the Parti du Peuple Algerien. Imprisoned by France in 1937, and 1941, he remained an active nationalist after 1945.

Clements Kadalie (1896–1951) Born in Nyasaland (Malawi), he pioneered African trade unions in southern Africa and, in 1919, founded the Industrial and Commercial Workers Union in South Africa, with branches elsewhere in Africa.

Wallace Johnson (1895–1965) Sierra Leonian trade union and political leader. He founded the West African Youth League, and was active in organising protest against Italy's invasion of Ethiopia.

Jomo Kenyatta (1891–1978) Pioneer of Kenya nationalism, in the 1920s he was secretary of the Kikuyu Central Association. After 1945 he became president of the Kenya African National Union and was president of Kenya from 1963.

Part Two is about the years 1930–45. Among the questions it answers are:

Chapter 5 Colonial systems and the Great Depression
What was the colonial economy? How did it differ from African economies before the colonial period?
What was the Great Depression? Why did it mark a turning-point? In what ways did the 1930s differ from the 1920s?
Where did colonial governments find their revenue, and how did they spend it?
What was 'imperial protection'?
When did Italy invade Ethiopia? With what results?

Chapter 6 The Second World War 1939–45
What happened in the Second World War? How did it affect Africa?
What was the Atlantic Charter?
When and where was the United Nations founded?
Did the UN help African progress?
What was the influence of Asian nationalism?
When was Israel founded? The Arab League?

Chapter 7 Towards modern politics
What is meant by the term 'modern tribalism' in the colonial period?
How and why did 'modern tribalism' develop?
What were tribal unions? Why were they formed?
Did tribal unions lead on to modern parties? If so, how and why?
When did new political parties of 'mass politics' begin to appear?
What was the importance of the Nigerian Youth League? The West African Youth League? The Gold Coast (Ghana) 'cocoa hold-up'? The importance of New-Destour and the *Istiqlal*? The Kikuyu Central Association?
What were African reactions to Italy's invasion of Ethiopia?
What was WASU? The *Union Inter-Coloniale*? The League Against Imperialism?
What was the NCNC? The *Ashiqqa*?

Chapter 8 Colonialism in crisis
Why was colonialism in crisis by 1945?
What was 'the flight to the towns'?
What were the effects of migrant labour by 1945?
How and why did mass political movements evolve?
What part was played by African trade unions?

CHAPTER 5

Colonial systems and the Great Depression

If you had been living in the 1920s, you would easily have thought that Africans could never again be free to run their own countries. Only Ethiopia and Liberia had their own governments: everywhere else, the colonial systems were strong and growing stronger. All resistance had failed; only the various ways of accommodation (of 'adjusting') seemed to remain. But even accommodation was far from easy; in the settler colonies, it was still more difficult.

Yet the fifteen years from 1930 to 1945 developed in fact towards a very different outcome. For this was the period when the seeds of a new independence, planted by the hands of early nationalists, began to grow into the harvest of political renewal that came later.

Two major developments encouraged this political renewal. One was the Great Depression, when everywhere in Africa the ways of working and earning, as the Sierra Leonean economist Cox-George has said of his own country, 'suffered a complete slump, touching every sector'. The second development, evolving partly from the first, was the rise of a new political resistance. Sharpened by the economic crisis, this new political resistance began to look for mass support, and, gradually, was going to find it.

The colonial economy: a dependent economy

Only a few parts of Africa, before colonial times, had depended on the outside world. Away from the coast in the vast interior, states and communities depended on themselves and on their neighbours. Slumps or booms in Europe, Asia, or America made little or no difference to them. Their exports were small, as were their imports. At a simple level of life, they could easily provide for their own needs. Troubles in the outside world could barely touch them.

Now all this was changed. Great numbers of men had been pressured into working in mines opened by foreign companies. In this way, Africa became a vital source of minerals for the world overseas. Even as early as the five-year period from 1925 to 1929, African colonies together with white-ruled South Africa produced 56 per cent of all the gold used in the world; 16.4 per cent of the

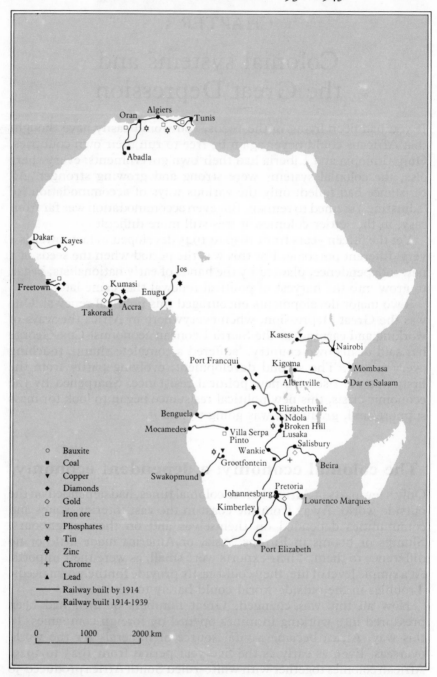

Bauxite
Coal
Copper
Diamonds
Gold
Iron ore
Phosphates
Tin
Zinc
Chrome
Lead
Railway built by 1914
Railway built 1914-1939

0   1000   2000 km

Fig. 5 Mineral exploitation in colonial Africa, up to 1939. The chief railway systems linking the mining areas with the coast are also shown manganese; 12 per cent of the platinum; and much other mineral wealth.

It was the same with farming. Great numbers of men had been pressured, as migrant workers, into producing crops for settlers or on foreign-owned plantations: again for export. Other large numbers, mostly in the non-settler colonies, had also become involved in cash crop production. By 1929, for example, locally-produced cotton provided 80 per cent of all Uganda's exports. Cocoa provided 79 per cent of all Gold Coast exports. Groundnuts represented 98 per cent of The Gambia's exports. Cloves were 61 per cent of Zanzibar's exports. What colonial development really meant in these 'mono-crop colonies' – and there were others like them – was that they were being turned into producers for the overseas market.

So in one way or other, Africa's workers and traders and their families were dependent, now, on the outside world. As long as that world prospered, they could make a living. But if the outside world failed to buy African exports, or bought less of them, or paid lower prices for them, then Africa's livelihood must at once suffer.

This dependence went on getting bigger during the 1920s; and it was deepened, all the time, by the colonial transfer of wealth from Africa to the outside world. For most profits were not used to strengthen the African economies which produced them; they were used to strengthen western European and north American econ-omies. In the years between 1886 and 1934, for example, foreign companies invested some £200 million in producing African dia-monds. In return for this investment, these companies paid out dividends (profits to shareholders) of £80 million in those 48 years. But these dividends (except when paid to white shareholders in South Africa) all went overseas. This was African wealth, but it did not help to develop Africa.

Dependence and wealth-transfer, going hand-in-hand, continued. It has been calculated that about half of all the profits of mineral exports from the Gold Coast (Ghana), between the early 1920s and the end of the colonial period, were sent out of the country, mostly to Britain. Here was one reason why the people of the Gold Coast, for example, had only one government higher-secondary school (Achi-mota College, founded in 1924); the money which could have paid for other schools was sent abroad instead.

The same situation occurred in other mineral-rich colonies. The copper mines of Northern Rhodesia (Zambia), recovering from the Great Depression in about 1935, became immensely profitable. In 1937, their profits were well over £4 million. But of these profits, Northern Rhodesia kept only about £540,000, by way of taxation, while a much larger total (in one way or another) went to Britain and the British South Africa Company which 'owned' the land where the mines were. The rest of the profits went to overseas shareholders. In those years, Northern Rhodesia's African population had no single secondary school because, the colonial authorities said, the country was too poor to be able to afford more.

As in southern Africa, the more profits that were made by the mining companies, the lower were the wages that they paid to African mine-workers. In 1929, for example, the starting wage paid to an African working underground in the Northern Rhodesian copper mines was 30 shillings for every 30 days of work; but in 1940, when the mines had become far more profitable, that starting wage was only 22s 6d. Surface workers had been paid 17s 6d in 1929; in 1940 their wage was down to 12s 6d. These bad wages were another means of enlarging the flow of wealth overseas.

Thus the economic dependence of the colonies on the outside world formed one main aspect of the colonial systems, and wealth-transfer from Africa to countries overseas formed another. We shall discuss the methods of wealth-transfer overseas in detail in Part Four (see p. 189).

For most of the colonial systems, the 1920s were a time of economic expansion. Exports grew, profits rose. Then, quite suddenly at the end of the 1920s, the 'developed' countries of western Europe and North America hit serious trouble. The colonies were dragged helplessly into the same trouble.

1929: economic collapse

It began far away. The scene of the first big drama was the New York Stock Exchange, where Americans bought and sold shares in companies. Signs of economic crisis in western Europe led to fear that the price of shares was about to collapse. This led to panic selling, and collapse soon followed. 'Golden America' plunged itself into years of hardship. More than 3,000 American banks failed by the end of 1931. Soon after, more than 12 million American workers were out of jobs, while Western Europe followed the same downhill path.

World trade slumped, because many exports could not be sold and many imports could not be bought. The consequences for Africa were very bad. In 1929 the total value of the export-import trade of the four British West African colonies was £56 million; by 1931 it had collapsed almost by half to £29 million. The same disaster hit Britain's East and Central African colonies: in 1929 the value of their export trade stood at £40 million; in 1931 it was down to £21 million. The fourteen French West and Equatorial colonies (including the two 'mandated territories' of Cameroun and Togo) met the same hard fate. Their total export-import trade fell from £30 million in 1929 to less than £18 million in 1931; while the trade of the Belgian Congo fell by more than half in those two years. Other colonies suffered in like measure.

As trade collapsed, so did prices. The Belgian Congo was again typical. By 1932 the money paid to cotton-producers had fallen by about two-thirds. For some crops it was worse still: the money paid to Belgian Congo rubber producers fell by 90 per cent between 1929 and 1932.

The collapse did not end soon. Again taking the fairly typical Belgian Congo figures, palm-oil fell by 1934 to less than one-fifth of its 1929 value, and cocoa to little more than one-quarter of its 1929 value. To this general collapse of prices – and therefore of the money to pay producers and workers – there was only one exception. The price of gold scarcely fell at all, because, it was believed, gold would never lose its value. Those who suffered least, in consequence, were the big South African mining companies. But even this did not help South Africa's mine-workers. Because of white South Africa's racist laws and attitudes, their wages were pushed even lower than before.

Though at its worst in the early 1930s, the Great Depression continued for several more years; in some colonies, it lasted until the early 1940s. It bit deeply into everyday life. It was so severe that historians have called it a turning point in our century; and we can easily see why.

Before the Great Depression, the colonial powers believed that they had found all the solutions to the problems of ruling Africa, and making money out of Africa, for countless years to come. Afterwards, they were increasingly worried about the future. And although the Great Depression did not in itself begin to end colonial rule, it helped to create tensions which led to the Second World War. That war, however unintentionally, really did mark the beginning of an entirely new chapter in Africa's history.

Colonial stand-still

The world economic collapse meant that the 1930s, in contrast with the 1920s, were years of colonial standstill or retreat: in production, in prices, and in trade. There were exceptions where new mines were found: the deep mining of Northern Rhodesian (Zambian) copper, for example, began only at the end of the 1920s and expanded greatly in later years. But such exceptions were few.

As wages and prices fell, and unemployment spread, there came another fall, this time in the taxation money that governments could get from Africans, and from export-import taxes. Having less money coming in, they had less money to spend. What were they to cut?

There were two big items they could not cut very much, and which they tried hard to avoid cutting. The first of these annual budget items was the money that the colonial governments had to pay, in interest, on sums of capital they had borrowed overseas, each from its own home government or private lenders, in order to finance such things as railway rolling-stock, lines of rail, and other imported things. The amount of this annual interest payment varied from colony to colony. But a big effort always had to be made to pay it.

The second item in the annual budget of each colony that each colonial government wanted to cut as little as possible, or not at all, was the money spent on European officials, police, security, and the like. So the chief cuts had to come from other items. Among these were benefits of colonial rule in education, health services, and public works such as the provision of better roads. The extent of these cuts varied from colony to colony, but it can be said with confidence that they were made in all colonies, and they were often severe.

Colonial budgets: government spending in the 1930s

The depression in trade continued through the 1930s, but began to ease, in most territories, after about 1935. By that time, however, the spending pattern of colonial governments was firmly established, even if it became possible, here and there, to restore some of the cuts in social services imposed during the worst years of the depression.

This spending pattern varied from one colony to another, and we cannot go into the details here. Yet its main characteristics can usefully be summarised. The following table shows in an approximate way how a number of colonial governments allocated money to their principal forms of expenditure. The figures are each a percentage of total expenditure for each colony for the 1936/37 financial year.

These percentages are only a rough guide, for each colonial system estimated its expenditure in different ways. Yet it can still be seen that the cost of colonial government was high: whether in salaries paid to European officials and in the organisation of colonial civil services, or in the always high cost of police and security services. Funds available for social services had to be correspondingly low.

Annual budget expenditure on main items: 1936/37*

	Government (civil service, police, etc.)	Social services (education, health, etc.)	Colonial economic development
	%	%	%
N. Rhodesia (Zambia)	40.6	21.9	9.4
Kenya	38.9	22.0	14.5
Nigeria	29.3	17.8	11.5
Gold Coast (Ghana)	31.6	28.0	16.3
French West Africa (1937)	20.0	16.0	24.0
French Equatorial Africa (1937)	20.0	11.0	13.0
Belgian Congo (1935)	24.0	12.0	17.0

* Source: Lord Hailey, *An African Survey*, 1945, pp. 1433, 1453, 1456.

'Colonial economic development' – the third column in the table – had a strictly limited meaning. Mostly, it meant money spent on railways, harbours, and other facilities needed by foreign companies, chiefly mining companies. These facilities had nearly all to be built by the colonial government, often using forced labour, because foreign companies would not invest their own money in building them. If there was now, in the 1930s, the beginnings of a communications revolution in Africa, this was primarily for the benefit of colonial interests. Any gain to Africans was incidental.

For such incidental gains, moreover, the colonised peoples had to pay an often stiff price. This price was partly in forced labour and in taxes to colonial government. But it was also in the payment, by government, of debt-interest to foreign lenders. In the Belgian Congo, for example, only 12 per cent of government revenue was spent on education and other social services during the year we are examining, 1936–37. But in the same year the Belgian Congo government was paying, to foreign lenders, about 40 per cent of all its revenues. This was in respect of debt-interest to foreign lenders for railways and other facilities needed to export the produce of the

Congo's foreign-owned mines and plantations. About 20 per cent of the Nigerian annual budget was spent in the payment of debt-interest in that same year, and more than 16 per cent of the Northern Rhodesian (Zambian) budget.

Colonial economic development, in other words, did not mean the development of the colonised peoples. Largely, it meant the development of the means by which foreign companies could increase their profits.

Methods of taxation

We need to say a little more about taxation in addition to the general principles outlined in Chapter 2. Government money, or revenue, came from three sources. One was the taxing of foreign companies. This was the smallest source: not because the profits were small, but, as we have seen, because most of the profits were sent, untaxed, overseas. The second source was the taxing of exports and imports (customs and excise). The third source, and usually the biggest, was the taxing of people. We have already seen how this began. By the 1930s, the system was long in use in all colonies. Some official figures for 1934 give an idea of how matters now stood:

Taxation revenue: 1934*

		Tax from Africans	Tax from non-Africans	% of annual budget revenue
Nyasaland (Malawi)	£ Sterling	129,562	18,970	43.0
Kenya	£ Sterling	544,480	116,495	32.5
Nigeria	£ Sterling	775,010	32,633	18.5
French Equatorial Africa	French francs	37,298,300	1,185,000	57.0
Belgian Congo	Belgian francs	80,709,434	19,764,683	28.8

* Source: Lord Hailey, *An African Survey*, 1945, p. 547.

Generally, taxes on Africans rose during the Great Depression and after, even though conditions of life were harder than before. So did taxes on non-Africans, chiefly on white settlers; but these taxes remained far lower than any such taxes in Europe. Besides this, the amounts of money spent on education and other social services for the settlers and their children were always more, and often much more, than the amounts spent on helping Africans. Here was another reason why there could be very few educated Africans in any of the settler colonies.

Education in settler colonies

Some more figures illustrate that point. In Kenya during 1935, for example, 1,889 European children were in school, paid for by 29.2 per cent of government education money. There were 7,995 Asian and 'mixed-origin' children at school; they got 23.5 per cent. But a total of 100,720 African school children got only 47.3 per cent of the education budget. Taxes paid by Kenya Africans were bringing in nearly five times' more money to government, as the above table shows, than taxes paid by Europeans. But African schoolchildren still got less than half the education budget.

The position in South Africa was still more unfavourable to black students. In 1935, in the former Boer republics of Transvaal and Orange Free State, white students got 92.2 and 93.4 per cent of all public education money, while little more than six per cent was spent on educating the far bigger black population. In the once-liberal Cape province, the big black majority got only 13.4 per cent of public education money, and the similarly big black majority in Natal province got only 15.14 per cent.

Elsewhere, the position varied with the size of settler communities. In Uganda, with few settlers, African children (in 1936) got 89.3 per cent of public education money. In Tanganyika (mainland Tanzania, without Zanzibar) there were more settlers, but African students (all in primary school) still got 77.3 per cent. In British West Africa, without settlers, all public education money went to Africans; and the position was about the same in the French non-settler colonies. Even so, there was little money for secondary education, and, outside Sierra Leone, none for university education.

In this brief analysis of colonial budgets, we have shown how the benefits of colonial rule could never be large, and how the crisis of the Great Depression in the 1930s made them smaller still. There were good colonial officials who regretted this cutting into social services, but they could not prevent it.

Some other results of the Great Depression need to be looked at.

'Imperial protection'

This had to do with tariffs and quotas: with what became known as 'imperial protection', or the effort by each colonial empire to defend its interests and profits against rival empires.

Tariffs are import taxes. Their aim is to raise the price of imported goods, so that locally-produced goods suffer less from foreign competition. Quotas are government restrictions on the quantity of goods that are allowed to be produced or manufactured. Their aim is to prevent prices being lowered by an over-supply of goods.

Each of the colonial powers had always protected their colonial gains and profits; and the poorest colonial powers – the Portuguese, Spanish, Italians – had naturally done it most of all. They treated their colonies as 'private estates of the motherland'.

Much excellent cotton, for example, was grown in colonial Angola. But none of it could be processed there. All of it had to be sold, as raw cotton, to buyers in Portugal, and at prices fixed in Portugal. There it was turned into shirts and cloth. Then these cotton goods were sold back to Angola, once again at prices fixed in Portugal; and the Portuguese government, at the same time, prevented any foreign competitors from selling cotton goods to its colonies. The Portuguese in Portugal, in other words, were able to buy cheap and sell dear in a 'closed' market, and make high profits in Africa, by means of government protection. Here again we see the two aspects of colonial dependence and wealth-transfer.

The Belgians in the Congo had to operate a more 'open' market, because the Congo, by treaty, was supposed to be a free-trade zone. The French treated all their colonies as parts of a greater France, but were strong enough to open their colonies, in a limited way, to foreign competitors. The British, whose free-trade attitudes came from British strength in earlier times, were generally more open in operating their colonial markets.

Now the Great Depression struck these markets. Reacting to it, the colonial powers all participated in a trade war against each other. Tariffs were raised and multiplied. Prices of imported goods therefore tended to rise, even though most people had less money to spend. This hit the colonial peoples especially hard, for few of them had any savings; at the same time unemployment grew fast.

Yet it is likely that the colonial peoples suffered more from quotas than they did from tariffs. Both tariffs and quotas had the same aim, as we have seen: it was to keep up the selling price of goods, especially of manufactured goods. But while tariffs were trade-war weapons, quotas were the outcome of agreement between rival empires. These empires agreed, for instance, to limit the amount of sugar that was produced so as to protect the level of its selling price. In 1937, to follow the same example, a sugar-restriction agreement was imposed on the British East African colonies. The agreement greatly affected Uganda, which was to be allowed to export, in 1938, only one-third of the quantity of sugar exported two years earlier.

Quotas therefore worked in a contradictory way. They helped producers to keep up their selling prices. But they cut down the number of producers who got any price at all; and they made consumers pay more, just when consumers were getting poorer every month.

Other aspects of 'imperial protection' prevented Africans, on a bigger scale than before, from buying goods in the most favourable world markets: from buying, for example, cheap Japanese shirts instead of less cheap European shirts. In fact the whole system of international trade was in a mess, and none of the colonial powers knew how to sort things out. Their own peoples suffered much from this; colonised peoples suffered even more.

Aid for Development: origins

More important in later years, another colonial policy also took shape. Because of its great importance after 1945, and again after the coming of independence, we should understand its origins and how it began. This policy was called 'aid for development'. Later, aid for development was going to be presented as a means of helping to develop Africa for the benefit of Africans. At the beginning, however, it was presented quite differently – and, in the opinion of later critics, more honestly. It was first presented as a way of developing colonies for the greater benefit of their overseas owners. The basic idea, very new at the time, was that colony-owning countries should not only take money out of their colonies; they should also invest a little of their own taxpayers' money there, so that colonies could produce more profits.

The British led the way, in 1929, with a Colonial Development and Welfare Act, the first of later ones of the same kind. British taxpayers' money was to be lent to Africa (against payment of debt-interest) for 'development and welfare'. But then at once the Great Depression came, and only some £6.5 million was lent during the 1930s. Most went into mining equipment and in helping hard-pressed colonial governments to balance their budgets; very little went into welfare.

This, once again, was 'aid for colonial expansion'. Besides, being in the form of loans, it had to be paid for by taxing Africans. Colonised peoples, in other words, were again providing taxation money in order to enable more wealth to be sent overseas. Between 1930 and 1940, for example, Britain made development grants to Northern Rhodesia (Zambia) which totalled £136,000. But in those same ten years the amount of money received by Britain from Northern Rhodesia, by way of taxes on Northern Rhodesia's booming copper mines, was probably not less than £2,400,000. So which country was being developed: Britain or Northern Rhodesia?

French aid policy was not much different. One ambitious plan may be noted. The French wanted to irrigate more than one million hectares of land in the middle Niger (Mali) region, so that African farmers could grow cotton there. The scheme cost (in francs) more than one million pounds by 1937, but was a failure. The farmers of the middle Niger region did not take to it; they believed that cotton-growing would not benefit them. The plan provided for about 1.5 million cultivators. But by 1940 only some 12,000 had actually settled there.

Such schemes could succeed if African farmers approved of them. This was already proved by the Gezira cotton scheme in the (British-governed) Anglo-Egyptian Sudan, today the Republic of Sudan. It arose in 1913 from a demand by British cotton-manufacturers for a bigger supply of long-staple cotton. Sudanese farmers of the Gezira region found that cotton-growing would suit their interests. So they went into it in a big way. Sudanese exports of raw cotton continued to expand; and the Gezira scheme remains today a central part of the country's economy (see also Chapter 19).

Generally, however, aid for development continued to be aid for colonial exploitation.

New conflicts between the imperial powers

Huge and threatening events were meanwhile on the way. Out of the disaster of the First World War, there had come in Italy an especially aggressive system called fascism. Out of the disaster of the Great Depression, there now came in Germany a still more aggressive system of the same kind, called nazism. Both were severe forms of dictatorship, and severely racist. Both were committed to achieve their aims by force.

All this prepared new European disasters. The collapse of the international capitalist system, early in the 1930s, now became linked to the collapse of peace between the big powers; soon enough, the Second World War began. Before it began, however, there was a prelude which greatly concerned Africa. Fascist Italy invaded Ethiopia.

Italy invades Ethiopia

In the Horn of Africa, the colonial partition had let Italy into a large part of the country of the Somalis. Italy had also seized land along the southern part of the Red Sea, and turned this into its colony of

Eritrea. Having done that, Italy proceeded to claim neighbouring Ethiopia as its protectorate, or semi-colony. When the Ethiopian emperor Menelik rejected this claim, Italy went to war but was crushingly defeated by the Ethiopians at Adua in 1896. After that defeat, Italy recognised 'the absolute and unreserved independence of the Ethiopian empire as a sovereign and independent state.' Peace followed.

However, early in the 1930s, Italy's fascist government under its leader Benito Mussolini began shouting for revenge for the defeat of 1896. Claiming that Italy must also have her 'place in the African sun', Mussolini prepared for war.

The first hostilities were provoked by Italian aggression at a place called Walwal in the Ogaden province of the Ethiopian empire. Mussolini demanded that the Ethiopian emperor Haile Selassie must humble himself and pay compensation. The emperor refused, and, seeing the Italians making ready for war, appealed in January 1935 to the world security organisation, the League of Nations, for help to keep the peace.

But the League's help proved worthless, for the League was divided between pro-fascist and anti-fascist powers, with the former stronger than the latter. Despising League protests, Mussolini's bombing planes attacked Adua and Adigrat on 3 October, 1935, and Italy's invading armies followed, entering Ethiopia through Eritrea. Once more Ethiopia asked in vain for League protection. The League condemned the aggression; and 50 member-states, on 18 November, backed a scheme to apply sanctions against Italy. But the scheme failed to include a ban on oil supplies to Italy, while the British government, which controlled Egypt, also refused to close the Suez Canal to Italian ships carrying reinforcements to Italy's invading armies.

Abandoned by the outside world, the Ethiopians fought on alone. But their only well-organised military force was an imperial guard of some 25,000 men, armed with out-of-date weapons. Against this, the Italians sent in very strong forces and took the capital of Addis Ababa on 5 May, 1936. The Emperor Haile Selassie went abroad to find support, but guerrilla resistance continued. The people fought the invaders, and were sometimes led by local chiefs organised in an Ethiopian Patriotic Association.

By 1937 the Italians could claim to have conquered the country, and in 1938 their claim was accepted by the western powers. Mussolini's government boasted that 'Italy has at last got an empire of her own.' Italian farmers were sent out to settle on Ethiopian land: Italian businessmen began to take over Ethiopian trade.

Yet Italy's triumph was brief. As we shall see in the next chapter, the Second World War restored Ethiopia to independence in 1941, and returned Haile Selassie to his throne. Lasting only about five years, Italy's colonial occupation had several more durable effects. Partly for military use, the Italians built some useful roads; against that, their occupation was disturbing and sometimes brutal.

More widely, this painful invasion of Africa's oldest state, made when colonial invasions were supposed to be a thing of the past, aroused great protests throughout the continent. Such protests could not oust the Italians, but they were among the roots of a stronger movement of anti-colonial nationalism in many colonies (see pp. 71–2).

CHAPTER 6

The Second World War 1939-45

Like the First World War, the Second was a breakdown in Europe which brought terrible destruction. Millions died. Cities were destroyed. There seemed no end to the tale of horror. Those who had claimed to be civilising Africans proved once more that they had failed to civilise themselves.

The course of the war

Nazi Germany began the war in September 1939 when it attacked and invaded Poland, then Belgium, Holland, France and (unsuccessfully) Britain, and later, in June 1941, the USSR. Fascist Italy joined Germany in June 1940, and completed the subjection of France. Imperialist Japan joined the nazi-fascist 'Axis' in December 1941, when its air force disabled the American fleet at Pearl Harbour in the Pacific island of Hawaii. Japan then invaded most of south-east Asia as far as the borders of India, and brought many countries into a new but short-lived Japanese empire.

Until late in 1942, the Axis powers won most of the battles. Then the Allies (Britain, USA and USSR, with some smaller partners) began to score big victories. Fascist Italy collapsed in September 1943. Nazi Germany fought on till May 1945, though at a terrible cost to the German people; then the Allies occupied the whole country, with the British and American and small French armies coming from the west and big Soviet armies from the east, and they smashed the nazi system. Imperialist Japan held out till American atom bombs were dropped on Hiroshima and Nagasaki in August 1945, and then surrendered.

African involvement

No part of Africa was untouched by this hugely destructive conflict, but fighting occurred only in two regions: the Horn, and North Africa.

As in the First World War, Africans had to pay in men, labour, and loss of trade. Large numbers were asked or were compelled to serve in the forces of Britain and France. Of some 80,000 African troops in the

57

French armies inside France, perhaps as many as a quarter were lost during Germany's invasion of May 1940. They were killed in action, were murdered after capture by the racist nazi troops, or died of bad treatment in prisoner-of-war camps.

Fighting on after the collapse of France in 1940, Britain raised still larger African forces. From its East African colonies, as well as from Somaliland, Nyasaland (Malawi), and both Rhodesias (Zimbabwe and Zambia), a total of 280,000 men were recruited, mostly by conscription (that is, force); and a large part of these were organised in fighting brigades. Tanganyika provided 86,000 of these soldiers, of whom 2,358 were killed in action or died on active service; while Kenya provided 75,000, with comparable losses.

Demand for soldiers from British West Africa was smaller, but still large. The four western colonies provided 167,000 fighting men, organised in seven brigades: three Nigerian, two Gold Coast, one Sierra Leonian and one Gambian. Most of these West African brigades were then brought together as 81 (West Africa) Division and 82 (West Africa) Division; all but one of the brigades saw active service on the battlefield.

As part of the British army, these African troops drove the Italians out of Somalia, and then destroyed the last of the Italian fascist armies in East Africa in bitter fighting across Ethiopia and Eritrea. Ethiopia was restored to independence, while short-term British military governments were installed in Somalia and Eritrea, pending post-war decisions about the future of those two countries. A leading part was played by the African brigades, for it was the soldiers of 'the Gold Coast, Nigeria and the [East African] King's African Rifles,' proudly reported the Nigerian *West African Pilot*, quoting the British commander-in-chief, 'who broke the backbone of Italian resistance on the entire Kenya and Somaliland fronts after a series of brilliant attacks' across the Juba river and right up through Somalia and Ethiopia. Having done that, these and other African formations went on to fight the Japanese invaders of Burma. Altogether, Africans in British colonies were organised in four Divisions of the British army, as well as in various transport and other service units; and the battle honours on their regimental standards, when they brought them home in 1945, were many.

Some Africans also served in North Africa. Here the British in Egypt had to defend their positions from powerful Italian forces advancing across the plains of the Western Desert (chiefly, of the Cyrenaica region of Libya); and these Italians were soon joined by German forces. For nearly two years the tide of battle swung back and forth in rapid tank warfare. But the British forces won the upper hand late in 1942. They drove the nazi-fascist armies out of Libya into Tunisia. Other British and American armies meanwhile landed in Algeria; very soon, nazi-fascist resistance in Tunisia was completely broken. This ended the war in Africa.

The African war effort and its effects

Outside the armed forces, again as in the First World War, farming and other labour was conscripted on a big scale, and with much the same destructive results. Village people in the British and Belgian colonies were organised or forced into a massive effort to increase production for export. In French West Africa, blockaded by the British because its French colonial rulers had sided with nazi Germany, village people were likewise forced into higher production for the internal market, since there could be no imports.

This long and forced 'war effort', as the colonial governments called it, was severe in its effects on rural peoples. Coming on top of previous years of forced or migrant labour, the strain of these war years deepened rural poverty, further interfered with farming and family life, and drove ever bigger numbers of rural people to seek relief in towns. From about 1940, the numbers of town-dwellers began to grow from few to many.

Like the First World War, the Second forced Africans in many colonies into a huge labour effort to produce more raw materials for export. This greatly reinforced the colonial pattern of export-dependency and wealth-transfer. Europe's economic control became even stronger than before.

But that same 'war effort' in labour and production had other effects. It upset rural stability. It undermined family life. In the settler colonies, as we shall see, the war brought more power to settler communities, thus preparing sharper conflicts. By 1945 the colonial governments were facing social problems they could not solve. In this important respect, the war weakened the colonial systems.

Many of its political effects also weakened the colonial systems; and here we should notice another important difference from the consequences of the First World War. That war of 1914–18 had come too soon after the shock of the colonial invasions and conquests for Africans to grasp its full meaning for themselves, while the major colonial powers, as we have seen, came strengthened out of that war. Now it was different.

The experience of the Second World War gave a new spur to anti-colonial criticism. It brought a new force to the call for anti-colonial change. War experience helped to develop a better political understanding of the colonial systems. It raised political consciousness. One cause of this was the anti-nazi, and therefore anti-racist, nature of the war on the Allied side. Another cause was the promise of the Atlantic Charter (see p. 62).

A Zimbabwean writer has told the following story about a British officer in 1940 who was trying to convince an African to enlist:

'Away with Hitler! Down with him!' said the British officer.
'What's wrong with Hitler?' asked the African.
'He wants to rule the whole world', said the British officer.
'What's wrong with that?'
'He is a German, you see,' said the British officer, trying to appeal subtly to the African's tribal consciousness.
'What's wrong with his being German?'
'You see,' said the British officer, trying to explain, 'it is not good for one tribe to rule another. Each tribe must rule itself. That's only fair. A German must rule Germans, an Italian, Italians, and a Frenchman, French people.'

Having told this story, that Zimbabwean writer commented:

But the extremely wary British officer did not say, 'A Briton, Britons'.
What he said, however, carried weight with the Africans who rallied in thousands under the British flag. They joined the war to end the threat of Nazi domination.

Having joined the war to end nazi domination, many African servicemen began to see that the war should make an end of colonial domination as well. They fought as equals alongside white soldiers. They won battles in distant lands, and this made nonsense of the colonial-white claim to superiority. Many learned to read and write; not a few received technical training. They deepened their understanding. They welcomed the ideas of freedom. They wrote letters home to say so. They contributed to African newspapers. Here are two examples.

Early in 1945, a Nigerian serviceman wrote from India to the prominent Nigerian nationalist leader Herbert Macaulay:

We all overseas soldiers are coming back home with new ideas. We have been told what we fought for. That is 'freedom'. We want freedom, nothing but freedom.

A little earlier a Gold Coast serviceman sent a satirical poem to the *African Morning Post*, of Accra, which printed it. In a parody of Psalm 23 he wrote:

> The European merchant is my shepherd,
> And I am in want;
> He maketh me to lie down in cocoa farms;
> He leadeth me beside the waters of great need;
> The general managers and profiteers frighten me.
> Thou preparedst a reduction in my salary
> In the presence of my creditors.
> Thou anointest my income with taxes;
> My expense runs over my income
> And I will dwell in a rented house for ever!

These ideas were reinforced by another experience of the war. Colonial whites had always claimed that Europeans would defeat non-Europeans. Now the war showed Europeans as defeated by the Japanese, but then the Japanese in turn defeated, and partly by African soldiers. This taught lessons, even if the colonial powers failed to learn them. The Gambian historian J. Ayodele Langley has written that 'the anti-Japanese war was to unleash a decade of nationalism and revolution in South-East Asia and Africa'.

The war made colonial Africa still more dependent in the economic field. But it weakened the social and political control of the colonial governments. Besides this, it greatly weakened the principal colony-owning powers.

International balance of power

The Atlantic Charter and the United Nations (UN)

The colonial powers were weakened for a variety of reasons. First, the French were utterly defeated in 1940, and France had to endure four harsh years of enemy occupation, with great loss of wealth and prestige. The British won the war, but had to fight for their victory to the last man and the last penny. They came out of the war much poorer than before.

Secondly, the USA and then the USSR became 'super-powers' in the post-war world. Neither had an interest in strengthening the British and French colonial systems. On the contrary, if with very different political ideas, both had an interest in weakening British and French rule. Each wished to expand its own trade and influence.

Thirdly, the colonised peoples of Asia began to demand their independence. By the end of the war it was clear that Britain would have to give independence to Burma, India, and Ceylon (Sri Lanka). Asian nationalism became an encouragement to African nationalism.

But African nationalism had already moved ahead in response to the Atlantic Charter of 1941. This was a solemn declaration by President Roosevelt of the USA and Prime Minister Churchill of Britain. It promised that after the Allies won the war they would 'respect the right of all peoples to choose the form of government under which they will live.'

Did this promise apply to the colonised peoples as well as to Europeans, such as the French, who were then under German control and government? Churchill at once tried hard to say no to this question: he had no intention, he said in November 1942, of liquidating the British empire. But Roosevelt insisted that the promise applied to everyone; and in this he was supported by progressive political parties and persons in Britain. If it was wrong for Germans to govern and control Frenchmen, how could it be right for other Europeans to govern and control Africans or Asians?

On that question, leaders of African opinion had no doubts. Hearing of the Charter by radio and newspaper, they hailed it as a promise of freedom after the war. And they were again encouraged by British wartime propaganda in colonial-controlled broadcasts and newspapers. These often said that the great conflict was a war for freedom. They said it not only in English but also in African languages such as Swahili: *vita vya uhuru.*

In these ways, the war began as one thing and developed into a different thing. It began as a conflict between Europeans. But it developed into more than that: it became, at least to some extent, an anti-colonial and anti-racist war as well. Some good came out of the evil.

Then there was a further development in the same direction. This was the foundation of the United Nations, in place of the discredited League of Nations, at San Francisco in the USA during April-June 1945. In line with the Atlantic Charter, and with the policies of the USA and USSR, the Charter of the UN was anti-colonial. Its principles called for progress towards ending colonial rule.

The UN made little immediate difference. The old League 'mandated territories' (the former German colonies) were re-labelled as UN 'trusteeship territories'. But there was one useful new rule. Each colonial power, against tough opposition by all of them, had to make annual reports on each of its colonies; and this rule put those powers on the defensive. At the same time, colonised peoples could send delegations to the UN to state their grievances. Gradually, the UN also became a force for anti-colonial progress. Later, its General Assembly gave a world-wide platform to the spokesmen of newly-independent nations (see also Chapter 20).

India, Pakistan, Sri Lanka, Burma

Rising Asian nationalism gave new confidence to African nationalism. The emergence of new Asian states soon added to that confidence.

India became independent of the British empire, as the two separate states of India and Pakistan, in August 1947. Ceylon achieved its freedom in the following November, when it changed its name to Sri Lanka. Two months later, in January 1948, the Burmese became independent in the republic of the Union of Burma. A new China emerged in 1949. Other Asian peoples took the same road, although some of them, notably those of the former French colonies of Indo-China (Vietnam, Laos, Cambodia), still had to suffer years of colonial warfare.

All this was part of the background to Africa's post-war struggles for independence.

Israel and the Arab League

In May 1948 another independent state emerged, though in different circumstances. The British recognised the right of Jews to have a national home in Palestine; and this became the independent state of Israel. One chief reason for their doing this was to give security to Jews who had survived the mass killings of nazi-occupied Europe, where some six million Jews were gassed to death, or murdered in some other way, by the nazis.

But the Jewish national state of Israel was created at the direct and painful expense of the Arab people of Palestine. Most Palestine Arabs lost homes and land. Against this injustice, a newly-formed alliance of Arab states, including Egypt, launched a long campaign of protest and opposition. They called for the world to recognise the rights of Palestine Arabs.

Created some years earlier, in 1944, this alliance was the Arab League (see also p. 219). Later, the League was joined by newly-independent Arab-speaking and Muslim countries in Africa, including Libya, Sudan, Tunisia, Morocco, Algeria, and also by non-Arab but Muslim Somalia. So the cause of the Palestinian people also became an African cause. Confrontation between the states of the Arab League and an expanding Israel was to lead to repeated warfare.

CHAPTER 7
Towards modern politics

The years between 1930 and 1945 may be called 'the middle colonial period'. They were sandwiched between the early period of conquest and 'pacification', and the later period of colonial withdrawal. We have looked at their main features. For a majority of Africa's peoples, they were years of loss rather than gain. First, there was the Great Depression, lasting through most of the 1930s. Then came the Second World War with all its hardships.

But these experiences taught useful lessons. What did the European rulers really want in Africa? What were they trying to do? Not many Africans had been able to say. Many more now understood. As the answers to such questions came clear, so did the answers to another set of questions. How best could Africans defend themselves? How could they turn to their own advantage what the colonial rulers were doing, or trying to do?

The answers to this second set of questions led to what we have called accommodation, or 'adjustment'. This took many forms, including various kinds of anti-colonial resistance. Africans tried to defend and advance their interests when armed resistance had failed. One result was the formation of modern tribes.

From colonial tribalism to modern nationalism

Africans had worked out their own ways of community life, of living together and governing themselves, through many past centuries. They had created a very large number of different communities or states. Some of these were famous empires or big states whose kings ruled over several or many communities. Others were states whose kings ruled over a single community. Many communities had no kings or chiefs, but independent village governments led by groups of elders.

Each of these old communities had its own territory, language, beliefs and loyalties. Various kinds of political structures held them together: largely, the strength of kinship, of family-ties, together with beliefs that bound each people to its rulers, or to their ancestral shrines and spirits. Age-grades were another 'cement' that could unite men and women of a community's various families or family-groups.

When the colonies were made, the new rulers understood little or nothing about that long and complex development of African political units. They simply thought that Africans lived in 'tribes', even though nobody knew just what the word 'tribe' was supposed to mean. How could these unknown 'tribes' be controlled as cheaply as possible? As the European rulers saw things, that was the big problem.

The problem arose, as we have seen, partly because tax money was never enough to pay for many colonial officials. It was solved partly by using African interpreters, clerks, and so on. But it was also solved by using Africans who were chiefs, or men ready to serve as appointed 'chiefs', and then giving orders through them. Each 'tribe', the new rulers now said, must have its own chief. If no chief could be found, then it was necessary to invent one.

This system ran into difficulty whenever communities would not accept 'invented chiefs'. Sometimes it ran into continuous trouble, as in Eastern Nigeria where the British made use of so-called 'warrant chiefs'. These were invented chiefs who were supposed to rule over Igbo communities who did not have chiefs. But the colonial policy of finding chiefs remained in force, notably among the numerous communities of British East Africa.

Gradually, in many regions, this invention of chiefs had success; and two results followed. One was the combining together of several neighbouring communities under a single chief, or 'paramount' as he was now called. The other was the treating of these combined communities as though they had always formed a single people. Inventing chiefs, in short, led on to inventing tribes.

A good deal of modern tribalism was born in this way; and we need to understand what happened, and why. Let us take three cases from Tanganyika during the 1930s.

Inventing tribes

When the colony was made, officials found a number of communities living along the north side of Lake Tanganyika. These were related to each other in language and custom, but each governed itself through its own elders. At first, officials tried to combine these communities under invented paramounts, so that they could give orders to one man instead of several; but the communities refused. At last, in 1933, the British set up a council of chiefs or elders for these peoples (and two others, the Kukuwe and Selya, living nearby); and from then onwards they were all said to form a single people: the Nyakyusa tribe.

Much further north, south of Lake Nyanza, there lived another set of related but separate communities. Here, for Usumbwa, Kwimba, Buzinza and others, the British were able to appoint paramount chiefs. Then they set about combining these paramountcies into bigger groupings. All of these were then said to form a single people, forming another new 'tribe': the Sukuma tribe.

Eastward towards the Indian Ocean, on the slopes of Mount Kilimanjaro, the British found a number of related Chagga communities, each with its own chief. These communities had begun growing coffee under German rule (before, that is, 1918); and in 1925 they had formed the Kilimanjaro Native Planters' Association to organise the sale of their coffee. This led their chiefs, in time, to form a council of chiefs to defend their traditional authority; and in 1934 this council began to discuss the need to have a paramount chief. The idea of a united Chagga tribe was born.

The process, as we see, became a two-way one. The European rulers wanted to reduce many communities to a few 'tribes' so as to control them more easily. But Africans saw that this forming of modern tribes could also have advantages for them. As the British historian John Iliffe has pointed out, 'Europeans believed Africans belonged to tribes; Africans built tribes to belong to.' In this way they could combine in defence of common interests. Their spokesmen, speaking now on behalf of many people instead of few, could win more power to be listened to by colonial officials.

This idea of forming modern tribes made progress in the 1940s. In 1942, for example, the communities that were gathered by the British into the Nyakyusa tribe took a step of their own. They formed the Nyakyusa Union 'to preserve the good customs and habits of the tribe' – even though the Nyakyusa tribe had never existed in the past.

Other tribal unions quickly followed. In 1945, to give another example, the communities gathered under paramount chiefs south of Lake Nyanza formed the Sukuma Union: even though the word 'Sukuma', in the past, had meant no more than 'north' in the language of their Nyamwezi neighbours.

From unions to parties

Various pressures encouraged this modern tribalism. As towns expanded in the 1940s, people who had come from the rural areas found themselves jumbled together without friends and neighbours whom they knew. They looked for countrymen who spoke the same language, or came from the same district. They began to form tribal

66

associations for their common interest, sometimes called 'welfare leagues', 'tribal unions', or 'progressive unions'. Nigeria alone had many such, as did other colonies.

These tribal unions and associations were not directly concerned with politics, or not at first. They were concerned with helping their members: with solidarity, education, and the coming-together for dances, drumming, and social occasions. As such, colonial governments tolerated them, and even welcomed them. But sometimes they were led by young men of energy and vision; and these soon got interested in politics.

When Harry Thuku and his friends in Nairobi city founded the Young Kikuyu Association in 1921, this was a tribal union to protest against bad wages and work conditions. But it was not long before Thuku and his friends began thinking about anti-colonial politics. In fact, their association became a foundation for the later ideas of all-Kikuyu union, and then of all-Kenya union. In short, the tribal unions and associations helped towards another central development of these same years: the rise of modern nationalism.

This idea of modern nationalism was, in fact, already bringing new political parties into existence. As these appeared, their leaders looked for support to this or that tribal union. Thus Igbo communities in Eastern Nigeria possessed an Igbo Union, strong in the late 1940s, which developed links with the National Council of Nigeria and Cameroons (see p. 73). And in 1948, partly in competitive response to this, Yoruba communities in Western Nigeria gave support to a new Yoruba union called Egbe Omo Oduduwa (Society of the Descendants of Oduduwa, a great Yoruba spirit-ancestor). The principal founder of Egbe was Chief Obafemi Awolowo, who soon after formed a largely Yoruba political party called the Action Group. Here again, we see that tribal unions and new nationalist parties were often intertwined.

A contradiction at work

Modern nationalism was a big advance on modern tribalism. Within each colony, it combined the force of many peoples in pressing for an end to colonial rule. Further, it pressed for freedom by using the political arguments of the Europeans in Europe: arguments which many Europeans found hard to answer. 'If you want,' said the nationalists to the Europeans, 'we Africans were tribes yesterday. But today we are nations. And you yourselves say that nations must be free.' So the new parties of the nationalists went far beyond the small demands of the tribal unions, and pressed for national parliaments and governments. In this far-seeing way was built the great engine of mass pressure which eventually shifted the colonial governments off the scene.

How was this engine put together, and made to move ahead? Those are the great questions we shall examine next. First though, let us just take note of another major contradiction which was now at work. Later on, this was going to give a lot of trouble.

On one hand, there was the colonial organisation of many old communities into fewer new tribes. Each new tribe or grouping, as well as older states or communities which had existed long before, naturally tried to advance its own interests. Often, it had to do this in rivalry with other groupings. That was how colonial rule worked: it played off one grouping or 'tribe' against another. Colonised peoples often found themselves organised against each other, and therefore discouraged from organising together against colonial rule.

In Ruanda-Urundi, for example, the Belgians deepened the natural differences between the Tutsi and Hutu peoples by taking the Tutsi into a sort of 'colonial partnership' against the Hutu. Most colonial powers raised security troops from certain 'preferred' peoples and sent them to keep order among different peoples elsewhere. Migrant workers in the South African mines were organised by the mine-owners into competing groups, setting Zulu against Basuto, and so on. This method of organising peoples against each other was called 'divide and rule'.

On the other side, more and more Africans began to see that escape from colonial rule called for another forward step. This was that the groupings or 'tribes' of each colony should join to form a nation, because only united action could set them free. Yet a new nation made up of competing tribes, each with its own spokesmen and political organisation, would not have unity. It would have disunity. This contradiction between modern tribe and modern nation was going to be one of the hardest problems left to Africa by the colonial period.

New men, new organisations

The ideas of nationalism took shape, among the educated few, long before the 1930s. The story of the African National Congress of South Africa, of the National Congress of British West Africa, and of North African parties such as the Destour in Tunisia, has shown us this.

These were minority movements, restricted mostly to the 'lawyer-merchant class', timid in their protests, opposed to any call for mass support. Their idea was that the colonial rulers should accept them as collaborators, so that, in the end, they would take the place of the colonial rulers. Mostly, the British ignored them, or, now and then, allotted them some nominal importance in the form of a seat on a colonial advisory council. The French and Portuguese ignored them altogether. The Belgians permitted no 'lawyer-merchant' groups to exist.

But now came the beginnings of another change. All through the 1930s, various developments led to this: the miseries of the Great Depression, Italy's invasion of Ethiopia, and then the experiences of the Second World War. A new trend appeared. Leaders and organisations began to turn away from the 'polite politics' of the educated few, and seek, instead, for 'mass politics' among the uneducated many. Weak as yet, this new trend marked another turning-point in African political development during the colonial period.

This emergence of new men and new organisations with tougher ideas about the future occurred in several colonies, notably Nigeria. Herbert Macaulay, sometimes called 'the father of Nigerian nationalism', had formed the first modern party in Nigeria as early as 1923; this was the Nigerian National Democratic Party (NNDP). But it was very much a Lagos party of the educated few, and the British were able to ignore it.

Early in the 1930s, younger men began to call for action. As so often on such occasions, a purely local issue gave them a start. There was discontent with Nigeria's only advanced secondary school, Yaba Higher College in Lagos. Critics said that it was not giving students an education capable of preparing them for leadership in many fields of life. Worse, it was said, the British authorities were stopping any such development. Partly out of this dispute, there came the demand for a new political organisation. In 1933 the Nigerian Youth Movement (NYM) was founded. It quickly developed the vision of a new and united Nigeria: of a Nigerian nation which would take its future into its own hands.

The NYM was the first nationalist movement in West Africa to call for a wide support, and find it. NYM leaders moved out of local Lagos politics; they campaigned in other regions of the country. They went on to win the support of non-Yoruba leaders such as Nnamdi Azikiwe and Ernest Ikoli. They worked out a programme of nationalism. Five years after its formation, in 1938, the NYM made history with a document called the Nigerian Youth Charter.

For the first time in any British colony (or in any African colony except for Madagascar, Cameroun, and Algeria in the French system), this Charter called for complete self-government, and it did so in clear words. Its key passage stated:

> The goal of our activities is a complete taking-over of the Government into the hands of the indigenous people of our country. We are striving towards a position of equal partnership with other member-states of the British Commonwealth of Nations, and enjoying complete independence in the local management of our affairs.

In 1938, this was a revolutionary demand. The colonial authorities ignored it, but thoughtful British observers began to see that something new was on the scene, and that the British in West Africa might soon have to give way. A new confidence was born among African leaders. A new militancy appeared. Mass action was now in the wings of the political stage, and about to appear on it.

As things turned out, that happened first in the Gold Coast. Here, too, new men and new parties were formed. One of these was the Gold Coast Youth Conference (GCYC), founded in 1930 by the lawyer J.B. Danquah (1895–1965). This was a rather conservative organisation, mostly of the educated few, but was ahead of the men of the 1920s. In 1934 it was partly responsible for sending an important delegation to London, asking for constutional improvements.

Much more radical was the West African Youth League (WAYL), founded in 1935 by the Sierra Leonean I.T.A. Wallace-Johnson (1895–1965), a forceful leader who gave a big push to mass politics and pan-Africanism. He distrusted the old school of 'respectables', and believed that progress called for 'new ideas and new vision; new determination and will.' This was close to the ideas of the Nigerian Youth Movement; and the no less forceful Nigerian, Nnamdi Azikiwe (born in 1904), was in fact active both in the NYM and the WAYL. After making a big impact in the Gold Coast, Wallace-Johnson went to London and then transferred his chief scene of action to Sierra Leone, where, in 1939, the British duly imprisoned him for a time.

But the decisive action in the Gold Coast came in 1937, and from an unexpected source. This was the great 'cocoa hold-up' by cocoa-growing farmers. The reasons for it were simple. Nine European companies bought all the cocoa produced for export in the Gold Coast. They had long agreed between themselves not to compete with one another, but to form a 'cocoa pool'. Through this 'pool' they all bought at the same price. Naturally, they pushed this price as low as they could. Finally they pushed it so low that the cocoa-farmers would take it no longer, and stopped all supplies. The British imperial government was forced to appoint a commission of inquiry; eventually this led to buying arrangements which were less exploitative. Though not a directly political movement, the hold-up brought confidence to those who were pushing for political change. The value of mass action was proved.

Elsewhere, the same trend was at work. In Tunisia, impatient with the polite talk of the old Destour, young intellectuals led by Habib Bourghiba (born in 1903) broke away in 1934 and formed the New-Destour, once again with ideas close to those of the NYM and WAYL. In Algeria the *Étoile Nord-Africaine* went from strength to strength under Messali Hadj. When it was banned by the French in 1937, a new party took its place, the *Parti du Peuple Algérien* (PPA). Morocco followed later, with the emergence at the end of 1943 of the *Istiqlal* (Independence) party of Moroccan nationalism.

In Kenya, too, the trend towards national political union saw the development of the Kikuyu Central Association (KCA), as well as mass action by newly-formed trade unions in Mombasa; all these were banned or repressed at the outbreak of war in 1939, but led the way to Kenya nationalism after 1945.

Defend Ethiopia!

The shock in the middle 1930s of fascist Italy's aggression (see p. 55) spurred the new men and their parties to fresh efforts. 'To a great extent', the Ghanaian historian S.K.B. Asante has told us, 'the Ethiopian question played a part in awakening a new generation of West African nationalists.' It helped to create 'a new awareness of Europe's growing strangle-hold on Africa'; and this 'sowed the seeds of nationalism' more widely than before.

Nationalism was developing in many parts of Africa. But the effect of Ethiopia's suffering was clearest in British West Africa, which had more liberty and more African newspapers. Many protests were organised. Especially active were the Nigerian Azikiwe and the Nigeria-based pan-Africanist, Duse Mohamed Ali (1867–1944). In the Gold Coast, Wallace-Johnson launched an Ethiopia Defence Committee. Expelled in 1937, he went to London and, together with West Indian activists C.L.R. James and George Padmore, organised an International African Service Bureau (IASB) with useful results.

A sense of outrage was widespread. The students of Fourah Bay College called for a day of mourning. Masses of ordinary people attended protest meetings. Even behind the 'walls of silence' of the Portuguese colonies, the news brought anger to people who, there, could not openly speak their minds.

The movement to support Ethiopia encouraged the nationalists; it also gave a new support to the ideas of Pan-Africanism. The NYM Charter, for example, was partly a reaction to the Italian fascist invasion. Chief H.O. Davies of the NYM was among those who now felt, as he said later, that 'we were against not only the Italians, but the whole system of imperialism and colonialism.' Reaching Kwame Nkrumah in London, news of the invasion found the future Ghana leader 'praying that the day might come when I could play my part in bringing about the downfall of such a system.'

At home and overseas: new rallying points

Many currents of African thought and action flowed into the rising tide of nationalism. Events and influences overseas reinforced them; and we have noted some of these. Another derived from the influence of young men and women who had gone overseas for the education they could not get at home. They were not many: even in 1932, there were in France only twenty-one students from tropical Africa, and not many more in Britain. There were none at all in Belgium, and the merest handful in Italy and Portugal.

Few though they were, those in Britain and France made themselves heard. In Britain, this was partly through the West African Students' Union (WASU), formed in London in 1925 by the Nigerian Ladipo Solanke (1884–1958) with the help of the Sierra Leonean Bankole-Bright and the moral support of the Gold Coast leader, Casely Hayford. WASU was under colonial supervision, and could not act directly. But its London hostel proved a useful meeting-place for discussions about the future. Later, Africans in Britain found a more effective means of action through the IASB (see p. 71).

Africans in the French colonies found protest in this period both difficult and dangerous. Some of them, such as the notable Dahomey (Benin) thinker Louis Hunkanrin (1887–1964), suffered much colonial persecution and were obliged to go into hiding or to accept exile. Hunkanrin himself was nonetheless able to attend the Pan-African Congress held during 1921 in London, Brussels and Paris. Others went to Paris and stayed there, finding the political atmosphere less oppressive than at home. Prominent among those who were politically active in Paris during the 1920s were another Dahomeyan called Touvalou Huénou (1887–1925), and the Senegalese Lamine Senghor (1889–1927), who should not be confused with the later Senegalese president of the same name, mentioned below. A third was the Algerian leader Messali Hadj. Other men followed them during the 1930s, notably the Soudanese (Malian) Tiémoko Garan Kouyaté (— –1942), and the Senegalese Léopold Sedar Senghor (1906–   ).

These men, and others like them, found friends and allies among European liberals, socialists, and communists; some turned to journalism and wrote vivid articles in Paris-based African newspapers such as the *Cri des Nègres*. They acquired experience of European political ideas, and, through the communists, learned about the meaning and history of the Russian revolution of 1917. Among pro-African organisations active in the 1920s and 1930s were the leftwing *Union Inter-Coloniale* and the *League Against Imperialism*. These were support organisations which helped African activists, when overseas, to win useful contacts and political experience. A few individuals went to the USA for higher education. Among these were Nnamdi Azikiwe and other young Nigerians, the Ghanaian Kwame Nkrumah, the Malawian Kamuzu Banda. All were to play a leading part in their own nationalist movements after the Second World War.

At home, meanwhile, the anti-colonial aspects of the Second World War added their influence. In Nigeria, 1944 saw the launching of the first of the big nationalist parties of later years, the National Council of Nigeria and the Cameroons (NCNC), with Macaulay as president and Azikiwe as general secretary. The older nationalism had asked only for small advances, but this new one asked for much more. Azikiwe sketched its demands during 1944 in his Lagos-published *Political Blueprint of Nigeria*, writing that:

we who live in this blessed country of Nigeria know that until we are in control of political power, we would continue to be the footstool of imperialist nations . . . We are fed up with being governed as a crown colony . . . We are nauseated by the existence of an untrammeled bureaucracy which is a challenge to our manhood . . .

There were other such moves elsewhere. Once Somalia was liberated in 1941 from Italian colonial rulers, its political spokesmen began to organise; and for a time the British military government in Somalia allowed them to do this. In 1943 they formed the Somali Youth League (SYL). A year earlier, in the Sudan, the National Unionist Party (*Ashiqqa*) had emerged under Ismail al-Azhari; and in 1944 Sudanese students in Cairo founded the Sudan Movement of National Liberation (SMNL). As a communist organisation, the SMNL was made illegal; but it led to the later formation of the Sudan Communist Party, among the first of its kind to be formed in Africa after the launching of the South African Communist Party in 1921.

These are only a few examples; new men and new parties were widely at work. Everywhere there was talk of a fresh start after the

73

war was over. 'After the war, what?' asked a headline in the Tanganyika African newspaper *Kwetu* (*Our Place*), in May 1942, and its editor, Erica Fiah, followed with another question:

Will the African native be allowed a better place and a little more voice and responsibility in the administration of his country, or will he continue to remain a clerk, last on the list, as he has always been?

Three years later, in 1945, a Gold Coast soldier in India wrote home to the nationalist thinker and writer Kobina Sekyi. 'We have made up our minds,' he told Sekyi, 'to help build the country, free from all oppression, and in our oath to the Lord, we shall never miss you [forget you] in all our plans to build our motherland . . .' Though far away in India, he wrote that 'we are discovering the truths of Wallace-Johnson's writings: and I would to God that He gives us more Wallace-Johnsons when we come back home . . .'

And so it was to be. By 1945 the whole scene was set for dramatic changes.

CHAPTER 8

Colonialism in crisis

Peace opened in 1945 on a different world from that of 1939: different in the balance of world power, different in the condition of the colonies. The colonised peoples now had a better chance of making progress.

Big anti-colonial struggles, and then struggles for independence, soon began by peaceful means wherever peaceful means proved possible; otherwise, they began by violence. In the next part of this book we shall follow these always difficult and often heroic struggles for freedom. But first we need to look at the condition of the colonial systems as they emerged from the strains and changes of the Second World War.

As we saw in Chapter 6, while Britain and France were much weakened by the war, the USA at once became a 'super-power'. For the USA had both won the war and become much richer because of the war. Its reserves of money were now enormous; its powers seemed to be without limit. But although the USA was the ally of Britain and France, America's leaders had little wish to help the British and the French to keep their colonies. On the contrary, leading Americans believed that the old pre-war empires should be done away with. Instead, the colonised peoples should have political independence, while, at the same time, they became part of a new international world system under indirect American control or influence.

Not yet strong, but soon to become another 'super-power', there was also the USSR. Though from a political standpoint contrary to that of the USA, the USSR was also against the old pre-war empires. Yet its influence in Africa, exercised through a few African communists or through other African revolutionaries, was still very weak. (Later, through trade agreements, financial aid, and diplomatic relations, Soviet influence became much stronger. But this could scarcely begin to happen till the 1960s.)

All these developments pushed Britain and France on to the defensive. The same happened to the small colonial powers: Belgium, Portugal, Spain; while Italy lost its colonies altogether in the Second World War, just as Germany had lost its colonies in the First.

Although the colonial grip on Africa was, in fact, beginning to

75

loosen, there was still one country where independent minority government was more firmly in control. Racist South Africa, as we shall see later, became stronger as a result of the war.

The colonial systems undermined

Weakened though they were, the colonial powers in 1945 still thought they had enough strength to keep their colonies for a long time ahead, and, outside West Africa, for the rest of the twentieth century or longer still.

In West Africa, the British and French were now ready to give way to some African demands. But their idea was to give way by small steps that would long delay the coming of independence (see also Chapter 9). Outside West Africa and most of the trusteeship territories under UN supervision, none of the colonial powers was ready to give way to any African demand. In the settler colonies, the white minorities now seemed to hold the future in their hands.

The rise of African nationalism was going to change all this. Meanwhile another pressure was also at work in the background. This was the real condition of the colonised peoples when peace came. For reasons we have discussed, it was a condition of poverty and social upheaval; by 1945, in fact, this meant that all the colonial systems were deep in trouble.

Half a century had passed since the chief colonial invasions. About a quarter of a century had gone by since the last big campaigns of 'pacification'; and the colonial systems had since become firmly planted within their colonial frontiers. Many results had followed. Some of these, of course, were contradictory. That has been the nature of all big historical developments.

Let us take, for example, the field of public health. The richer colonial powers – Britain, France, Belgium – campaigned to some extent against tropical fevers and diseases, whether by inoculating people or by other means. Colonial hospitals and clinics helped to reduce the number of children who died at birth or soon after. From about this time, or late in the 1940s, the size of most African populations was found to be growing faster than before.

This new wealth of people could be a big gain for the continent. But it could be a gain only on condition that these bigger populations could be fed, and could find jobs, housing, and other necessities. Above all, more people meant that there had to be more food. And this was where the chief trouble came. For the colonial systems now revealed that they were generally unable to increase the growth of food-production in line with the growth of population.

Why was this? The biggest part of the answer is that the colonial systems all wanted to produce more crops for export. They had succeeded rather well in doing this; but the more they succeeded, the less land and labour were left for producing food. In Algeria, to offer one example among many, the French took more and more fertile land for producing wine to send across the Mediterranean to France. But the land they took was land on which Algerians, before, had grown an abundance of food for themselves. So the Algerians had less food, just at the time when their numbers were growing bigger. It has been calculated that the amount of food in cereals, available to an average Algerian person in 1945, was little more than half the amount available in 1900.

Many peoples who grew crops for export began to suffer from a shortage of home-grown food: in the cocoa-rich Gold Coast, in Nigeria, in many of the settler colonies. Here and there they gained from better public health. But everywhere they lost by having less to eat, or by having to pay higher prices for food in shorter supply. And the loss began to be bigger than the gain. In Nigeria, said a report of 1947 to the British parliament, 'over 20 million people are living on an agricultural subsistence of a very low order, and malnutrition [hunger] and disease are widespread.' In other colonies, notably the Belgian Congo, official reports pointed to the same deepening poverty.

Yet the colonial powers, though they knew these facts, still believed that the colonies must help Europe to feed itself. Big efforts were made, after 1945, to export still more than before. Tanganyika, for example, had suffered a famine in its central region during the Second World War; many had died of hunger. Yet the biggest project now undertaken by the British authorities was an ambitious scheme to clear bush to grow groundnuts, not to grow local food. It proved a disastrous failure, and cost the British a loss of £35,870,000. But it was not the only scheme of that kind. Another, the Yundum egg scheme in The Gambia, failed at a cost of £900,000.

Such projects for producing food or other crops for export to Europe continued to be called 'colonial development and welfare'. But for whom was the development, and for whom the welfare?

Other results of the colonial systems enlarged a crisis that was now widely felt.

Effects of migrant labour

The steady increase of migrant labour in many colonies was one of these results. Especially in central and southern Africa, and to a lesser

77

extent in French West Africa, bad consequences were already obvious in the 1930s. From Nyasaland (Malawi), for example, large numbers of men were working for long periods in Southern Rhodesia (Zimbabwe) and South Africa. A Nyasaland government inquiry sounded a note of alarm as early as 1935:

> The whole fabric of the old order of society is undermined when 30 per cent to 60 per cent of the able-bodied men are absent at one time. It is easy to criticise that old order, but it worked: the community was stable; and there was give and take [within the community]. Emigration destroys the old order, but offers nothing to take its place. The family-community is threatened with complete dissolution.

The warning went unheeded. By 1946 there were more than 200,000 migrant workers employed in mines and plantations in Southern Rhodesia; of these, 62 per cent came from Nyasaland and Northern Rhodesia. One out of every three African workers in Southern Rhodesia was from outside the country; but their families, for the most part, were still at home in their villages in Nyasaland and Northern Rhodesia. An even larger number of migrant workers from several colonies in central and southern Africa were employed in South Africa.

With their men away on work contracts lasting for a year at a time, or longer, villages decayed. Wherever forced labour was still much used, the decay was greater still. In 1945, a Belgian Catholic missionary, Father van Wing, wrote that village people in Ruanda-Urundi during the Second World War 'were treated without mercy. One term of forced labour followed another.' It was the same in the Belgian Congo, but the end of the war did not end that treatment. Back in 1928 a government commission had urged that women, old people, and children in the Belgian Congo should no longer be forced to build and maintain roads. Yet, as late as 1947 we find the same commission still having to urge the very same thing, commenting:

> There can be no doubt that it is the forced labour services on roads which are the most unpopular, either because they mean long journeys to work, or else because they mean painful toil, often even for mothers of young children and for pregnant women.

After 1945, more and more village people left for the towns in the hope of finding a better life. Even children left, often on their own. As another Belgian missionary wrote from the Belgian Congo:

78

At the beginning of October 1952, I was making my usual tour to register children for the regional primary schools. At Makalelu Tseke, a school which serves about 25 villages, I had called for 147 boys who were now old enough to begin their first year, I was much surprised to find that of these 147 boys, 34 had gone to Léopold-ville [now Kinshasa, the country's capital]; and not one of them was old enough to have to pay [and so try to escape] tax.

Already the colonial towns of Africa had begun to grow as village people left to escape an increasing poverty. Now these towns grew much faster. Several as much as doubled in size during the Second World War. Dar es-Salaam, the capital of Tanganyika, was one of them; Léopoldville (Kinshasa), the capital of the Belgian Congo, was another; there were many more.

The towns expand

Was this a gain? Living in town was a kind of modernisation, a way of getting into the 'modern' world. Villages were backward, often boring. Towns, by contrast, could be thought to have bright lights, piped water, better wages, even some buses and cars. Yet these expanding towns had few or none of those things. The colonial rulers did not want this flight from the countryside. They wanted families to stay in villages, and men to be available for migrant labour. They did little or nothing to provide houses and services for the multitudes who came.

So the new arrivals had to live in shacks and huts they built for themselves from flattened-out cans, canvas, or whatever they could find. Seldom was there piped water; often there was no electric light. Worse still, there were too few jobs. A few lucky newcomers might be able to buy a second-hand truck; most could not afford a bicycle. Even those who found jobs got little money. In the settler colonies, for example, the rule in towns was to pay wages to each worker as though he was unmarried. If he was married, it was held, then his family in the rural area could provide for itself.

Getting worried about these bad conditions in the towns, the British government in London appointed a royal commission, in 1953, to find out the facts in British East Africa. Its members took a lot of evidence; and the more evidence they took, the more worried they became. Here is what they found in the city of Nairobi, capital of Kenya, and reported in 1955:

The wages of the majority of African workers are too low to enable them to obtain accommodation [housing] which is adequate to any

Fig. 6 Urban growth in Africa, 1945–80: a sample of 12 important cities

standard. The high cost of housing relative to wages is, in itself, a cause of overcrowding, because housing is shared to lighten the cost. This, with the high cost of food in towns, makes family life impossible for the majority.

Just pause for a moment to think about the last seven words of that quotation. Wages were so low in the capital city of Kenya, after half a century of colonial rule, that family life had become impossible for the majority of Africans living there. Could that royal commission have spoken more clearly about the crisis of the colonial system? Better wages were sometimes paid elsewhere; but also worse wages. Tens of thousands of migrant workers worked every year in the rich gold mines of South Africa. These mines made large profits, but, largely, because of cheap labour. In 1910, when the Union of South Africa was formed, mining wages for Africans were low. Forty years later, those wages were lower still in real terms: in terms, that is, of what they could buy.

Of course there were pockets of fair prosperity. Cocoa-farmers in the Gold Coast and Nigeria now got rather better prices than before. Chagga farmers in northern Tanganyika did well with coffee. Mouride producers of groundnuts in Senegal could make good money. But most rural people had no share in these gains. Here and there, workers in new industries were able to unite in trade unions, and improve their wages. Yet these, too, were a minority of industrial workers.

All this was part of the social crisis of the colonial systems. It formed the challenging but difficult ground on which the new nationalists had to take their stand. Small or bad educational systems were another part of that ground.

Colonial schools: new source of anti-colonial criticism

An Africa without modern schools and teaching could never make progress; everyone agreed about that. The provision of this kind of education ran into three big obstacles. One problem was that money for schools and teaching was always in short supply. In every colony, most children had no chance of going to school because no schools existed for them. By 1945, even in the less backward colonies, the proportion of children who could go to school was smaller than one in every ten. Literacy (reading and writing) was still a rare skill. In the more backward colonies – those of Portugal after 1945 – the proportion of Africans who had been able to learn this skill was smaller than one in every hundred.

A second obstacle was the poverty of parents. Few could afford school fees, books, clothes, or journey-money if getting to school required a bus journey. Even if they sent their children to school, those sons and daughters could seldom stay for more than one year, or perhaps for two. The situation in Northern Rhodesia (Zambia) was typical of most colonies. In this copper-rich colony in 1942, there were said to be fewer than 90,000 school-students (for a total African population, then, of about 2 million people). Yet only 3,000 of these were in the fifth year, and only 35 were in 'early secondary' classes. Of the few children who went to school, most stayed too short a time to be able to learn much of use.

A third obstacle was the nature of colonial education. When young people managed to get to school, and stay at school, what could they learn? Reading, writing, a little arithmetic, and religion were the main subjects taught; in the first year or so, they were usually the only subjects taught. Later years included some history and geography, and perhaps one or two other subjects. But all these subjects were taught from a racist standpoint: tending to show that whatever came from Europe was good or useful, and that whatever came from Africa was either the reverse or not worth studying. In history, for example, British colonial schools taught about British kings and heroes, French colonial schools taught about French kings and heroes, and the smaller empires did the same. The general assumption behind such teaching was that Africans could not solve their own problems, but Europeans must show them how.

By 1945, however, a lot of people began to see that there was something wrong with this lesson. The economic depression of the 1930s and the Second World War had taught a different lesson: that Europeans had not been able to solve even their own problems, let alone the problems of Africa. And from this different lesson there came a new mood of questioning, of criticism. It was the point at which, after 1945, schools which were intended to teach students to accept and even to admire te colonial systems began to turn into schools where students became increasingly critical.

African teachers sometimes took the lead. They began to reject the attitudes and content of colonial textbooks. They tried, instead, to find ways of teaching the values of African life and history. They, and their older students, also began to turn to modern politics; and this was one way in which the Nigerian Youth Movement grew, and Wallace-Johnson's West African Youth League also.

The same trend took shape elsewhere. In Kenya, an independent schools movement had been formed as early as 1929. It wanted to get away from the racist lessons of colonial schools, and promote, instead, a respect for African dignity and history. Strong among the

Kikuyu of central Kenya, where colonial racism was also strong because of the white settlers who lived there, this Kikuyu Independent Schools Association (KISA) helped to win wide support, later on, for the politics of nationalism and for the Kenya African National Union (KANU).

From elitist parties to mass movements

Various events and experiences of the fifteen years from the start of the Depression to the end of the Second World War – from 1930 to 1945 – widened understanding of the modern world. We can say that these years, gradually, produced a change in mental scale.

Many people now lived outside the small world of village or lonely farm. Often they lived in a harder world of towns, low wages, the search for jobs. But it was also a bigger world of new things and new ideas. Earlier people had learned to adjust to a small world. Now they learned to adjust to a bigger world. That meant, among the rest, thinking about politics.

With this change of scale, the narrow nationalism of earlier years had to change as well. Less and less, after 1945, were anti-colonial politics discussed only in the private houses of lawyers, clergymen, doctors or chiefs. More and more, political talk moved out to the verandah. Then this outward development of discussion moved further. Anti-colonial politics stepped off the verandah and went into the street, into many streets, and into the rural areas.

Here was a second change of scale, reflecting the first. It marked an end of the small world of élitist politics and parties – of politics and parties for the educated few – and a beginning of a big world of mass politics and parties for large numbers of people.

Leaders looked now for wide support; more and more, they found it. Some had thought of doing this in the 1930s, and a few, like Azikiwe and Wallace-Johnson, had really done it. Now the search for wide support became a general thing wherever the colonial rulers would allow it. Only the British and French rulers allowed it, but they had most of the colonies. People in their colonies could give a lead for people in other colonies, like those of Belgium and Portugal, where all political action stayed forbidden.

The new mass parties, at this stage, were of several kinds. Very few of them had any tight organisation or list of members; nearly all were movements rather than organised parties. Some of these movements called for the united action of all the people in a colony; these were movements or parties of national union. Others looked for their main support only from a single people in their colony; these were ethnic or regional movements and parties.

Yet others had a strong religious loyalty. Such, for instance, was the Somali Youth League. This was a national party which was also an ethnic party, because nearly all the people of Somalia are Somalis. It was also a party with a strong religious loyalty to Islam, an unifying force in this case because nearly all Somalis are Muslims.

Yet all these parties operated in much the same ways. Talented or privileged men took the lead and appealed for mass support. Often persecuted, such parties had to have a loose form of organisation. Besides this, most people were not yet familiar with modern ways of political action. They needed time to learn. It was largely through this process of learning modern politics that the great engine of mass pressure was set in motion.

Growth of workers' action: trade unions

Wage-workers in colonial towns began to organise themselves into trade unions, so as to improve their wages and conditions of work, before the Second World War: in Tunis, for example, as early as the 1920s; in Kenya's great seaport of Mombasa during the 1930s; and in towns in other colonies. But all the pre-war trade unions or workers' associations met with colonial repression; they could make little headway.

During the Second World War – and here was another of its anti-colonial consequences – the British decided that they would allow trade unions in colonies where trade unions had been previously forbidden; and the new French government, emerging in 1945, decided they would do the same. The smaller colonial systems continued to forbid Africans to form trade unions. So did the racist South Africans. A big strike by African mineworkers in the South African gold-mines, in 1946, was put down by armed police with great violence.

But new trade unions could appear in the British and French colonies. They could also act with success. A greatly impressive railway workers' strike in French West Africa, during 1946, showed both power and discipline. A trade union federation for Tunisia was formed by Ferhat Hached in 1945, but there things went differently. Passing to strike action in 1947, Tunisian trade unionists lost 32 killed and some 200 wounded at the hands of the colonial police or army; Hached himself was later killed by racist political murder.

Different, again, was the situation in Northern Rhodesia (Zambia). Strong strike action there by African workers in mines and railways in 1945 led to the formation, three years after, of a powerful African

84

mineworkers' union, and of other unions. Those are only three examples, among many, of a new workers' ability to act together. The same occurred, for example, in Kenya, Tanganyika (Tanzania), Sierra Leone and elsewhere.

Struggling against colonial wages and conditions of work, the new trade unions could not stand aside from modern nationalism. They became part of it. In Northern Rhodesia, for example, the new African mineworkers' union gave solid support to the politics of national independence. Some of the most forceful leaders of the new unions – Siaka Stevens in Sierra Leone, Sékou Touré in Guinea, Tom Mboya in Kenya, to mention only three – became political leaders. Here was another proof of mass support for the new parties.

SUMMARY

Agencies of modernising change
1930–1945

Two kinds of agency or influence for modernising change were at work in these years. One kind consisted of positive agencies which encouraged people to change their ideas and hopes in response to them. The other kind consisted of negative agencies: people changed in reaction against them.

Among the positive agencies we have discussed were:
1 A new pan-African patriotism inspired by protest against the fascist Italian invasion of Ethiopia.
2 Development of associations, co-operatives, and social groups producing crops for export, and their efforts to improve prices (for example, the Gold Coast cocoa hold-up).
3 The wartime promise of the Atlantic Charter.
4 Encouragement from successes of Asian nationalism.
5 The anti-colonial ideas of ex-servicemen.
6 The weakening, because of the war, of the chief colonial powers; and the post-war influence of the USA and USSR.
7 Changes of scale in the thought and action of uneducated as well as educated persons.
8 New readiness of political leaders to look for mass support.
9 Formation and militancy of new trade unions.

Among the negative agencies were:
1 Hardships of the Great Depression of the 1930s.
2 Other hardships imposed during the Second World War.
3 Flight to the towns: low wages, bad housing, jobs hard to find.
4 Colonial repression of nationalist protest.

PART THREE

The nationalists win through

Kwame Nkrumah (1909–1972) Ghanaian national leader and socialist thinker. He founded the CPP in 1949, won internal self-rule for Gold Coast (Ghana) in 1951, and led his country to independence in 1957. President of Ghana until 1966.

Chief Luthuli (1898–1967) He became president of the African National Congress of South Africa in 1952. As an active champion of freedom from racist rule, he won worldwide acclaim, culminating in the award of the Nobel Prize in 1960.

Patrice Lumumba (1925–1961) Outstanding national leader of Belgian Congo, he became the first prime minister of Zaïre (then Congo-Kinshasa) in 1960, but was murdered by separatist enemies in 1961.

Amilcar Cabral (1924–1973) Founder of PAIGC, a movement of national liberation in Guinea-Bissau and Cape Verde. A great revolutionary thinker of the 20th Century, he received worldwide recognition. Murdered in 1973.

Part Three considers questions arising from the growth and success of African nationalist movements, in freeing their countries from colonial rule, during the years after the Second World War. Among these questions are:

Chapter 9   The conditions of decolonisation
How did British colonial policy begin to change after the Second World War?
In which kind of colonies did peaceful pressures fail to win progress?
In which ways did 'world factors' influence the conditions of decolonisation?
Liberia and Ethiopia were partial exceptions in the process of decolonisation. Why was this? What happened there?

Chapter 10   Raising national flags: north-east Africa
What was agreed by the Anglo-Egyptian Treaties of 1922 and 1936?
What happened in Egypt in 1952, and with what consequences?
How did Sudan become independent?
What happened to the Somalis, and the Eritreans?

Chapter 11   Libya and the Maghrib
What led to the Islamic Republic of Libya?
Which influences led to the independence of Tunisia, of Morocco?
Why was the struggle for independence especially harsh in Algeria?
How did the Algerians win?

Chapter 12   South of the Sahara: French colonies
What was the Brazzaville Declaration? The French Union? The RDA? The 'enabling Act' of 1956?
How did Sékou Touré oppose de Gaulle?
What was the French plan for indirect control?
Who was Um Nyobé? What was the UPC?
What events led up to Madagascan independence?

Chapter 13   British West Africa
What were Britain's 'small steps' in Nigeria?
How did Nigerian regionalism take shape? With what results?
What was the UGCC? The CPP? How did they differ?
What did Ghana's independence mean for the rest of colonial Africa?
How did Sierra Leone and The Gambia win independence?

Chapter 14   East and Central Africa: British settler colonies
What was the most important difference between Britain's colonies in

West Africa and in East and Central Africa?
What was 'closer union'?
How did TANU develop? Why was TANU successful?
What happened in Zanzibar before and after independence?
What stood in the way of Ugandan national unity?
Which were Kenya's chief problems? What was KAU?
What led to the Kenya Emergency? What happened during and after it?
What was the Central African Federation, and why was it dissolved?
What did the Malawi Congress Party achieve for Malawi? UNIP for Zambia?
Why was the Rhodesia Front formed? What did it do?
How did Zimbabwe's war of liberation develop, and end?

Chapter 15   In other empires: Belgian, Portuguese, Spanish
Who was Patrice Lumumba? Why was he important?
What was the legacy of colonial disunity in Ruanda and Burundi?
When were PAIGC, MPLA, FRELIMO formed? Why did they have to launch wars of liberation, and with what results?
What advances were made in Liberia under Tubman? What happened in Ethiopia in 1974?

Chapter 16   The 1980s: unfinished business
What plans did the South African regime develop after 1960?
How did these plans affect Namibia? How did SWAPO develop?
What is *Apartheid*? What were SASO, Black Consciousness, the Soweto rising?

CHAPTER 9
The conditions of decolonisation

Decolonisation, when it came, proved to be a complex and varying process. Each country added its own chapter to the story. Often these chapters were fruitful; sometimes they were also painful. All of them are important in the history of modern Africa, and are reviewed in this Part of the book.

But first it will be useful to stand back from the detail, and to summarise or re-state the main trends and themes in this decisive process by which Africans, advancing out of the constraints imposed by foreign rule, began to shape their independent future.

Why did Britain, and then France, begin to consider withdrawing from some colonies? Why did they continue to refuse to withdraw from other colonies? Why did the lesser colonial powers, notably Portugal, delay or stubbornly refuse? What different methods did Africans have to use in order to win their independence? Why were there built-in limits to the amount of independence that could be won? Lastly, how have world factors influenced the progress that could be made, and what were these world factors?

Some detailed answers to these basic questions are given in the chapters on decolonisation that follow here. Other answers, concerning the problems after independence, are considered in Part Four.

The imperialist powers take stock

We saw in Chapter 8 that the principal colonial powers were weakened by the Second World War. Britain could win against the Axis powers – nazi Germany, fascist Italy, imperialist Japan – only at very great cost in national wealth. France had been entirely defeated; she limped from the war in ruin. Belgium had also been defeated. Italy was on the losing side, finally, and forfeited all her colonies. And although the USA was a most powerful force amongst the victorious Allies and came out of the war with increased wealth, it had no interest in helping to maintain the empires of its business rivals.

Yet none of these external events could alone have led to decolonisation without the pressures set in motion by the colonised peoples themselves. For although the colonial systems were deep in their own social and economic crisis, the resulting pressure was added to by a rising tide of African nationalism; this now made ever stronger demands for progressive change. So the colonial powers could hope to go on dominating Africa in the old way only with a big increase in European officials, police, armies and investment. Not only would this be very expensive, but it also carried no guarantee of continued success.

So it became wise to think about how to dominate Africa in a new way. Looking at this difficult problem after 1945, the British were the first to begin to see that they might do well to retreat before the oncoming tide of nationalism: at least in West Africa, as well as in some other colonies where there were few or no British settlers. If they gave way in the political field, cautiously, slowly, they could hope to safeguard their interests in the economic field.

These economic interests were also undergoing an important change. More and more, after 1945, they became the new interests of major companies or corporations which began to operate in many different countries and in different colonial systems. This had happened to some extent in earlier years, but then the companies had been much smaller and more limited in their influence. Now the biggest corporations, the oil corporations among them, had grown into veritable giants, and their operations were practically worldwide. This new mode and scale of operation represented a further development of the world capitalist system. Recognising this change, people began to call them 'multi-national' companies, because they operated in many national territories, or else 'transnational' companies, because they operated across many frontiers.

These big corporations – notably the largest, which were American – naturally wanted to operate in every country, or in every colony, where they could make good profits. But the old colonial empires, each guarding or at least trying to guard its own monopoly in its own colonies, got in the way of the new 'multi-nationals'. So the interests of the new corporations were not identical with the interests of the old colonial monopolies. On the contrary, the interests of the 'multi-nationals' lay in weakening or even destroying the old monopolies. This added a new pressure, even if indirectly and behind the scenes, towards getting rid of the political controls which safeguarded the old monopolies, and, to that extent, towards strengthening the position of African nationalists who were demanding political independence.

In West Africa, at least by 1950, the British and after them the French began to make ready to withdraw their colonial government and its political controls, intending to do this in such a way as to safeguard their long-term economic interests. It was obvious, of course, that this could succeed only if newly-independent countries remained within the Western or capitalist system to which Britain and France belonged. This, in turn, meant making political concessions of a kind that could avoid or prevent any far-reaching or revolutionary changes. It meant trying to ensure that there were built-in limits to the amount of independence that Africans could win and use. From the British and French standpoint, in short, the great need was to modernise the relationship between themselves and their colonies, and to bring that relationship into line with the requirements of 'multi-national' capitalism.

This was to be part of the meaning of neo-colonialism, or new colonialism, after independence came (see also Chapter 18). It was obviously an intelligent policy from the European or American standpoint, but it did not take shape all at once. The policy of creating neo-colonialism was developed gradually, and sometimes in a contradictory way, as often happens in history. Whatever one may think of its consequences for Africa, this policy has to be seen as an attempt by the principal powers to deal with their colonial crisis while, at the same time, protecting the substance of their interests – a substance, of course, that was economic rather than political. As time went on, the policy became clearer and was more consciously pursued.

Little by little, as the ideas of neo-colonialism developed, the chief powers were helped by finding African leaders who felt that they had no real alternative but to go along with these ideas. They were men who sincerely believed that Africa could progress to full independence only by successive stages in agreement with the colonial rulers, although, as well, there were others who merely looked to their own careers. They rejected a struggle for any far-reaching or revolutionary change in the relationship between their countries and Europe or America on the grounds that any such struggle was wrong, or was in any case bound to fail. There were some revolutionary thinkers, very few in number and at that time with very little influence, who thought differently. They believed that political independence on the lines of neo-colonialism would lead to a new surrender to the interests of big outside powers. It may be worth recalling what one of them wrote in 1964. The leader of the liberation movement in Portuguese Guiné (now Guinea-Bissau) and Cape Verde, Amilcar Cabral (1924–73), questioned whether the fundamental aim of the imperialist countries was not to prevent:

the enlargement of the socialist camp, liberate the reactionary forces in our countries stifled by colonialism, and enable these forces to ally themselves with the international bourgeoisie [middle class].

Only a handful of nationalists saw matters in this way, and even they did not question the nationalist strategy of pushing for political independence as a first step to further development later on. In any case it took some years for the new policy of the principal colonial powers to develop to a point where it was widely understood. Gradually, as this development went on, the old kind of direct colonial dependence was replaced by a new kind of dependence, indirect and chiefly economic.

Could this new kind of dependence be avoided, or at least reduced? If there were strong African leaders who were nonetheless willing to become junior partners in the new multi-national economic system, were they not right and sensible? Could they, realistically, have acted in some other way? Was there, in those years, any good alternative? These are questions for discussion. We shall return to these questions in Part Four.

The duty of the nationalists

Meanwhile, during the 1950s or later, the nationalists had a prime and urgent duty to their peoples. They had to take the first steps towards liberation. These steps were to get rid of the direct and political controls of the colonial systems, throw off the racism and oppression associated with those systems, and free their countries from foreign rule. After that, and with this useful amount of freedom, a further struggle against indirect control, a struggle for a large measure of economic independence, could then begin, or, at least, could become possible.

The British, in these circumstances, began to move towards political concessions in West Africa. With somewhat different results, they were followed by the French; later, by the Belgians; later again, by the Spanish.

Only the Portuguese refused. Portugal's rulers were convinced that they would lose everything in Africa if they gave up their direct control. This was partly because Portugal was itself too weak and economically backward to try for a neo-colonial relationship, and partly because Portugal was ruled by a fascist-type dictatorship which believed that Portugal's colonies were the 'glory' of Portuguese civilisation. Desperately, Portugal hung on to the last possible moment (see Chapter 15).

Peaceful pressures or counter-violence?
Africa's nationalists had therefore to face a wide variety of situations. In British West Africa (see Chapter 13), they were usually able to make progress by peaceful pressures. The same was largely true in many of the French colonies (see Chapter 12), and sometimes elsewhere as well.

Yet peaceful pressures never worked in colonies of large European settlement. There the nationalists could make progress only by opposing the violence of the colonial systems with the use of their own counter-violence.

These differing conditions of decolonisation, as we shall find in Part Four, greatly affected the individual countries after independence was finally won. In a number of ex-colonies it proved possible, and sometimes easy, for the former colonial power to impose neo-colonial limits on independence, and, at least in the early years, to decide or direct the policies of the newly-independent governments. Some of these governments, as for example in the Central African Republic, were little more than instruments of continued foreign rule.

But wherever colonised peoples were obliged to use their own counter-violence against the violence of the colonial systems, the later imposition of neo-colonial limits became much more difficult to achieve. These peoples could win their wars of independence only by destroying the colonial systems within their countries. In doing so, they greatly weakened the neo-colonial threat. That was a compensation they could set against the sufferings of colonial warfare.

Inherited problems

Africa's struggles for liberation produced, in any case, great and irreversible changes. They signalled the continent's entry into the modern world. They brought memorable victories, even if they also brought setbacks and defeats.

The setbacks and defeats have been caused, for the most part, by inherited problems that could not be avoided. Part Four will discuss these problems. They were partly the legacy of the colonial systems, and, in lesser degree, the legacy of Africa's own history. They were partly the problems of great world factors: for example, the nature of the international economic system and its inequalities between rich countries and poor countries; the development of the multi-national corporations and their huge economic power; and the growing conflict between 'West' and 'East' (that is, between the capitalist world-bloc and the socialist world-bloc). All these factors affected the amount of independence that could be won. They cannot be discussed in detail here; but they should be kept in mind.

Two partial exceptions

In the history of decolonisation there were two partial African exceptions: two countries which were not colonies. Some mention of them can best be made here.

Liberia

Liberia had long enjoyed a political independence much limited by direct economic dependence on rubber and other raw-material exports. This dependence was reinforced in 1926 by the arrival of the American Firestone Corporation with its concessions for very large-scale rubber plantation development. It was increased further under Liberia's most influential modern president, William Tubman (1895–1971). Introducing an 'open door' policy, Tubman aimed at bringing in as much foreign investment as possible. At the cost of strengthening the ruling group in Monrovia, the country's capital, this policy had its successes.

At the same time, Tubman pursued a 'unification policy' by giving votes and parliamentary seats to the people of the 'tribal interior' who provided most of Liberia's taxes and labour. In 1947 an amendment to the 1847 constitution gave votes to all adults, women as well as men, provided that they paid taxes and possessed some property. Other laws to enlarge the country's political life followed in 1956 and 1963.

Yet these laws did little for the cause of unification. The inferior position of the 'tribal interior' was scarcely changed. The poverty gap between the few rich people and the many poor people continued to widen. Tubman's successor, President William Tolbert, followed where his predecessor had led. There was rising popular discontent and in April 1980 a coup under Master-Sergeant Samuel Doe introduced a new, military, government.

Ethiopia

As we saw earlier in Chapter 6, the ancient kingdom and empire of Ethiopia regained its independence in 1941 during the Second World War (see p. 55). But this was independence within the structures of government and rules of land-ownership which had existed before Italy's invasion of 1935. After the war, Emperor Haile Selassie extended this system of minority rule, essentially an aristocratic system under the emperor's personal government, and failed to introduce any reforms which could meet popular demands for equality and justice. Partly provoked by severe famine in some Ethiopian provinces, a revolution began in 1974. Poor farmers took the land of the nobles. Haile Selassie was dethroned. A new ruling council, known as the *derg* (committee), declared that Ethiopia was to become a socialist state. A profound process of social revolution introduced new systems of education, health, trade and government. In 1976 command of the *derg* was assumed by Colonel Mengistu Haile Mariam, who strengthened the new regime.

CHAPTER 10
Raising national flags: north-east Africa

This chapter, and the six chapters which follow it, tell in some detail how the nationalists won through to independence and, in so doing, opened a new era in the history of all the continent's peoples.

Partly because the liberation of some of the northern countries came a little earlier in time, and partly for simple convenience in following a complex story, we begin in the north and move, in later chapters, progressively to the south.

Egypt: from the *Wafd* to Nasser

Egypt in 1922 ceased to be a British colony in name, but not in fact. In that year Egypt became what has since been called a 'neo-colony' (or 'new-colony'): that is, Egyptians could now govern themselves, but under the control of an outside power which, in this case, was Britain. The British government recognised Egyptian independence in a treaty of 1922, subject to these four conditions:

1   British armed forces continued to guard British imperial lines-of-communication through Egypt, between the Mediterranean Sea and the Red Sea, especially by way of the Suez Canal.
2   Britain continued to be responsible for defending Egypt against outside attack.
3   Britain supervised the protection of foreign interests inside Egypt.
4   Egypt continued to accept British control of the 'Anglo-Egyptian condominium' (joint government) of the Sudan.

Egyptian nationalists had to accept this partial independence. Their main party, the *Wafd* (formed in 1918 by Zaghlul Pasha), was still weak. It was also disliked by Egypt's King Fuad; he saw the *Wafd* as a rival. Yet popular discontent widened with the Great Depression. This plunged Egypt into a tremendous economic crisis. There was growing civil strife; and then came Italy's invasion of Ethiopia (1935). All this made Britain fear for her own position in the region. Attempts were made to improve Britain's relations with the

Egyptian leaders. These led to the Anglo-Egyptian Treaty of 1936 between the British imperial government and the *Wafd* government under Zaghlul's successor, Nahas Pasha (1876–1965).

The new treaty of 1936 made some concessions to Egyptian nationalism. But it altered nothing of substance: only on the third and least important of the four conditions of 1922, the protection of foreign interests, did Britain give way. Within three years there followed the Second World War. Britain used Egypt as a military base from which to fight against Italian and then German attempts to occupy the country.

Egypt's own government did not declare war against the Italians and Germans. But the *Wafd* nationalists now went over to a pro-British position because they believed that occupation by the fascist Italians and nazi Germans would be worse than continued occupation by the British. In 1942 a long-standing rivalry came to a head between King Faruk (born 1920, and king of Egypt after his father's death in 1936) with his courtiers on one side, and the *Wafd* on the other. The British settled it by forcing King Faruk to accept another *Wafd* government.

As elsewhere, the tide of Egyptian nationalism began to run more strongly after the Second World War. There was an additional reason here. This was the foundation of the State of Israel (see p. 63) despite Egyptian and other Arab attempts to prevent it. Relations with Britain, which was held responsible for handing over most of Arab Palestine to Israel, grew steadily worse. Some Egyptian guerrilla fighting against continued British occupation of the Suez Canal Zone broke out in 1952. This was unsuccessful; but now came a new development which was the opposite.

In that same year, 1952, a group of young army officers led by Lt.-Col. Gamal Abdel Nasser (1918–70) seized control of Cairo and then of the whole country. There was no bloodshed and the action was widely popular, because the old nationalists seemed unable to win a true independence or solve the country's problems. The young officers formed a new government under General Muhamed Naguib, and this government, on 10 February, 1953, declared Egypt a republic. The deposed King Faruk went quietly into exile.

Naguib was found too conservative by the young officers' movement and was ousted in 1954, when Nasser became president. In July 1954 the British agreed to evacuate their forces within twenty months. They kept this agreement, but by this time the USA and its western European partners had become strongly hostile to the Nasser regime. Meanwhile, Nasser tried to lessen this hostility by asking for American and British financial aid to build a high dam across the Nile at Aswan, so as to improve the use of the Nile waters for irrigation. At first the USA and Britain agreed, but in July 1956 the USA changed its mind, and Britain did the same. They would not help to build the dam (which was afterwards built with Soviet aid). Nasser replied to this refusal by turning the foreign-owned Suez Canal Company into Egyptian national property. Its profits, he said, could help to finance the building of the dam.

Aggression followed. In November 1956 Israeli troops invaded the Canal Zone by secret agreement with Britain and France, and were supported by the landing of British and French troops. This invasion was aimed chiefly at destroying the Nasser regime so that it could be replaced by a less patriotic one. But the aim was not realised. The aggression met with world-wide condemnation. The Israeli, British and French invaders quickly withdrew.

Egypt had suffered casualties and loss of property, but had emerged as a truly independent state for the first time in modern history.

Sudan, Somalia, Djibouti, Eritrea

Britain had long wielded all the real power in the Anglo-Egyptian Sudan, largely because of that country's strategic control over the upper waters of the Nile. In changing times, the old nationalists in Egypt had usually argued that Britain in due course should place Sudan under Egyptian control. But the new Egyptian nationalists accepted the idea of Sudanese independence. After the Naguib-Nasser revolution in Egypt of 1952, Britain accordingly said that she was ready to leave Sudan. On 11 February 1953, Britain signed an agreement with Egypt which said that Sudan should have independence within three years. President Nasser confirmed this agreement after taking power in 1954. On 1 January, 1956, British and Egyptian troops left Sudan. A new Sudanese government declared the country an independent republic.

This easy decolonisation, without a shot fired on either side, nonetheless proved unstable. A deep conflict had long divided the Muslim and Arabic-speaking peoples of the centre and north from the largely Christian and non-Arabic-speaking peoples of the south; and long British control, separating the north and centre from the south, had helped to worsen rather than ease this conflict. There was also rivalry for power between the nationalist leaders of the centre and north, organised in the Ashiqqa and Umma parties. Each of these conflicts was going to give much trouble. Yet Sudanese independence, after January 1956, was assured.

Eastward toward the Indian Ocean, the Somali people were divided by the colonial partition into four colonies. These were Italian Somalia, British Somaliland, French Djibouti – a very small colony consisting of Somali (Issa) and Danakil (Afar) peoples – and Ethiopian Ogaden. The last, although almost entirely Somali in population, had been enclosed within the Ethiopian empire, as part of the colonial 'share-out' in the 1890s. Ethiopia regained control of it after Italy's defeat in 1941. In addition, Somalis also lived in the Northern Frontier District of colonial Kenya, and claimed this district from Britain (and then, after 1963 when Kenya became independent, from Kenya).

After 1943, the newly-founded Somali Youth League (SYL) campaigned for the independence and union of all five territories noted above. For a long time, they had no success. But the defeated Italians were restored in 1950 to control of Somalia, their former colony, only for a ten-year UN trusteeship. In 1960, they left Somalia. At the same time, the British withdrew from Somaliland, and that territory was at once united with Somalia. Both were merged to form the independent republic of that name.

This brought most Somalis together. But Ethiopia retained Ogaden, and France retained Djibouti, while the Northern Frontier District of Kenya remained as part of that country. Somali guerrilla fighting against Kenya control broke out in 1963, and continued until a settlement of 1967 confirmed the district as part of Kenya. Much more serious Somali fighting against Ethiopian control began in Ogaden in 1976, but failed again. Djibouti won its political independence from France in June 1977.

Italy's Red Sea colony of Eritrea passed under British military government in 1941, when Italy was ousted from the whole region of the Horn. In 1945 the United Nations agreed to put Eritrea under its own supervision, but that British military government should continue there until the country's future could be decided.

Eritrean nationalism was still weak at that time, while the Ethiopian emperor, Haile Selassie, put in a strong claim to the former Italian colony. His claim being partly accepted by the UN, the British withdrew in 1952, when Eritrea became a federated state within the Ethiopian empire. This arrangement was meant to give Eritrea a wide measure of internal self-government while foreign policy, defence, and financial control passed into Ethiopian hands. It satisfied the Eritrean nationalist leaders of that time. Most of them were merchants, lawyers or chiefs, who thought that their interests would be better served within the Ethiopian empire than within an independent Eritrea.

But the arrangement failed to satisfy Haile Selassie and his court. They wanted complete control of Eritrea. In 1962, Haile Selassie managed to induce the Eritrean state assembly to give up self-government. In defiance of UN promises, Eritrea was absorbed into the Ethiopian empire as a mere province with no powers of its own. Trouble followed at once. Eritrean nationalism had grown much stronger and more popular by now. Challenging this forced union, young Eritrean nationalists began a guerrilla war for independence. Many years of bitter fighting followed, continuing into the 1980s.

While all these events were taking place, others of the same kind were on the way in British West Africa. In 1951 the Gold Coast won internal self-government as a prelude to its full independence as Ghana. Soon after, the same advance was made in the southern regions of Nigeria, and later in the northern region. But we shall find it more convenient if, next, we turn to North Africa where, apart from Egypt, three countries were already independent by 1956.

CHAPTER 11
Libya and the Maghrib

Libya became independent quite quickly after the Second World War. This was because the big powers could not agree on which of them should have the UN trusteeship of this former Italian colony. In 1951 the territories of Cyrenaica and Tripolitania were removed from British and American military government, and, with Fezzan, united as the kingdom of Libya under King Idris al-Sanusi.

But this independence was only partial, with British and American control behind the scenes. Younger nationalists soon called for more independence, and more modern methods of government. Yet the king's power held firm till September 1969. He was then overthrown by young army officers; and a new Islamic republic was declared under Colonel Muammar Gadafi. This new government set about bringing the three provinces of Cyrenaica, Tripolitania and Fezzan into a closer unity. It also set about exploiting large oil deposits found by foreign investors in the 1950s.

Further to the west, in the Maghrib (Tunisia, Algeria, Morocco), the struggle for independence had to be both long and violent. For these were all settler colonies; in 1945, there were about 250,000 Europeans settled in Tunisia, more than a million in Algeria, and about 300,000 in Morocco. These settler communities were minorities, but large ones and violently racist. They were determined to stay on top. And while France ruled Morocco and Tunisia as protectorates which might at some distant time become free to rule themselves, Algeria was ruled as part of the motherland. Its fertile northern regions, between the Sahara Desert and the Mediterranean Sea, were administered as departments of France itself. All this ensured great trouble for the future.

Tunisia and Morocco

Formed in 1934 under Habib Bourghiba, the New-Destour (see p. 71) could make little progress in the late 1930s, and was soon suppressed by the French colonial authorities. In 1938 Bourghiba himself was imprisoned in France, and released only in 1942 by the nazi-German occupying forces, in France, because they wanted him

103

to work for them. Bourghiba refused; after the war was over, he was able to return to Tunisia. At that point the national demands of the New-Destour, till then a rather weak party of the educated few, were being strengthened by mass support.

To this stronger pressure of Tunisian nationalism, the French answered with renewed violence. Finally, in 1952, they banned the New-Destour once more, and again imprisoned Bourghiba, as well as using their army against Tunisia's new trade unions. But already the cause of nationalism was winning wide support. It became clear that many rural people, as well as poor people in the towns, believed now that national independence was going to be the only way for them to live better. They had to care very much about living better, even if, perhaps, they cared very little about the theory of nationalism.

They showed that they were ready to fight for their chance of living better. They began a guerrilla war against the French forces. Their fighting bands were small and few; but they were strong enough, by 1952, to have made the French bring in 70,000 troops against them.

Fighting to regain control, the French saw that they would be wise to reach an agreement with the leading nationalists. For now they had another fear in mind. This was that the young men in the guerrilla bands would cut the political ground from under the feet of Bourghiba and other moderate leaders of the New-Destour. If that should happen, France might be unable to reach an agreement that would leave the French with any control behind the scenes. In March 1954 they let Bourghiba out of prison, and began to manoeuvre for the kind of agreement they wanted.

But another event pushed them further. It happened far away in Vietnam. There, a big French army had long been fighting to regain French colonial control of the Vietnamese, a control which they had lost to Japan during the Second World War. Now the Vietnamese proved too strong; in May 1954, they defeated the French in a great battle at Dien Bien-phu.

Shocked by this disaster, and therefore compelled to think again about the extent of their colonial commitments, the French government decided to make peace in Tunisia. In August they allowed the New-Destour under Bourghiba's leadership to become legal and active, and agreed to Tunisian independence. With this promise, the guerrilla bands laid down their arms. In April 1955, the Tunisians were able to form their own government. In March 1956, Bourghiba led the country to independence. This was a victory for the educated men who led the New-Destour. But it was a victory, too, for the mass pressures without which the French would not have given in.

Much the same kind of 'double thrust' produced a similar victory in Morocco. Here, too, economic depression had widened support for nationalist demands, much strengthened in 1934 and after by Moroccan loyalty to Islam. There was hunger and unemployment, while better-off Moroccan merchants and professional men found themselves pushed aside by French settlers and businessmen. Then came the war, and French defeat in France; and then, in 1942, an American and British army landed in North Africa to chase out the nazi-fascists.

All this ripened the cause of Moroccan nationalism. In December 1943, a strong group of professional men and merchants founded a party called *Istiqlal* (Independence). This marked two steps forward. First, as its name said, *Istiqlal* did not demand better colonial government; it demanded an end to colonial government. Nobody in Morocco had done that since the days of Abd al-Krim. Secondly, the *Istiqlal* leaders looked around for mass support. They appealed to the people to come in with them, just as the New-Destour was doing (if then illegally) in Tunisia.

Here, too, the French answered with new repression. In 1953 they even went so far as to depose the traditional Muslim ruler of Morocco, King Muhamed V, and put a 'puppet king' called Ben Arafa on his throne. This gave fresh fuel to the nationalist cause. Mass demonstrations of protest shook Moroccan towns where new trade unions were now in the lead. Many died in clashes with French troops. Then in 1955, in the moment when one guerilla war had shown its power in Tunisia, and a second (as we shall see) was exploding in Algeria, a third guerrilla war began in Morocco. Acting on the old inspiration of Abd al-Krim, thirty years earlier, a people's army of guerrilla bands became active in the hills.

Faced with this, the French found themselves with no useful friends in Morocco. They had counted on the anti-nationalist support of several Berber chiefs, notably al-Glaoui of Marrakesh. But these men proved to be broken reeds; their following withered away. Giving in, the French restored King Muhamed to his throne and opened negotiations with *Istiqlal*. Morocco became independent on 2 March, 1956, just eighteen days before Tunisia.

Algeria: the harshest struggle

Like the British in South Africa and Rhodesia, the French in Algeria had always acted as though the whole country was for them as settlers. They remained deaf to Algerian demands for equality of treatment and of rights. Stiffly racist, they allowed Algerians to use their chief language, Arabic, only in religious schools. All privileges went to the settlers; all power of government stayed with them, or with Paris and its governor-general in Algiers.

Against that situation, the leaders of Algerian nationalism such as Messali Hadj had campaigned in vain. They achieved nothing in the ten years after 1945: nothing, that is, except a stronger colonial repression. Believing that no progress could be made by peaceful means, a younger generation of nationalists decided to adopt violent means. After some failures, they formed a secret Front of National Liberation (in French: FLN), and launched a war of independence from the Algerian Aurès mountains during November 1954.

To begin with, they had only some 300 Italian rifles bought from war dumps in Libya, and their rising spread slowly. But it was well led by men, such as Ahmed Ben Bella, who had fought against the nazi-fascists in units of the Allied armies during 1943–45. Gradually, the revolt found mass support in every region. Once the revolt had won this mass support, volunteers flocked to it.

All through 1955–56 the fighting rose in ferocity and power: but, largely, to Algerian advantage. With some 15,000 fighters in the field, the army of the FLN held its own against a French army of some 200,000 men that was divided into some 530 garrisons and fortified camps. Meanwhile the FLN began to work out its political plans for independence.

But late in 1956 the fighting went against the Algerians. Partly, this was because the French brought in many more troops from France, and French generals began to adopt better anti-guerrilla tactics. Partly, it was because some of the Algerian leaders, in order to escape capture by the French, were obliged to take refuge in Tunisia during September 1956.

After that withdrawal, a gap widened between the Algerian political leaders and armed forces outside Algeria, mostly in Tunisia, and the fighting units and their political supporters inside Algeria. Seeing this gap, the French set about breaking all contact between the 'outside' and the 'inside', thinking that in this way they would be able to destroy popular support for the liberation war. They built electrified fences up and down the Algerian side of the frontier with Tunisia, laid more than a million land-mines along the fencing, and placed strong forces to prevent men and supplies from getting into Algeria from outside. At the same time, learning the military lessons of anti-guerilla warfare, the French generals stopped trying to control every small district with fixed garrisons. They combined their very strong forces into 'hunt-and-destroy' units, backed up by helicopters and big support units. These had much success.

By 1960 the French had about 700,000 troops in Algeria, an enormous army, and had driven the army of the FLN nearly to defeat. But now the French had to swallow another hard lesson. They found that in this kind of warfare a win on the battlefield cannot be decisive, unless it goes together with a win in politics. This second success would have to mean that the FLN lost mass support. It did not happen. Great pro-FLN demonstrations in the cities proved, even now, that the FLN still held the loyalty of the people.

Meanwhile, across the Mediterranean, great disputes about the war were tearing France apart. Taking power in 1958, General Charles de Gaulle became president and decided that he must negotiate an end to the war. He still thought that he could do this in such a way as to keep French control. In June 1959 he offered a cease-fire to the FLN, but with no promise of independence. The FLN refused.

The war continued, but now the settlers in Algeria were convinced that de Gaulle meant to desert their cause. They organised a settlers' rebellion against France, rather in the same way as the Rhodesian settlers were going to rebel against Britain six years later: but, unlike the Rhodesian settlers, they failed. On the contrary, their terrorist actions inside France, where they murdered opponents and blew up buildings, hastened President de Gaulle's willingness to make peace. He reopened negotiations with the FLN.

A cease-fire followed in March 1962, and Algeria became independent in July 1962. More than a million Algerians had died. Much of the country was a smoking ruin. Yet in that July, before the French left, the FLN won its biggest victory. The whole population was asked to vote for what they wanted. Among the Algerians, exactly 16,478 votes were cast against independence: but 5,993,754 votes were cast in favour.

CHAPTER 12

South of the Sahara: French colonies

Even before Sudan, Morocco, and Tunisia had become independent, big advances in the same direction were being made by nationalists in the Gold Coast and Nigeria. Kenya was shaken by the rising of the 'Land and Freedom' armies. And the tide of popular pressure was gathering strength elsewhere. In this chapter we continue with the history of decolonisation in the French empire.

The peoples of French colonies south of the Sahara had the same problems as those to the north of it. They had to face the French policy of regarding all French colonies as part of a 'greater France': that is, the policy called 'assimilation' (see p. 33). Secondly, there were aggressive settler minorities in Ivory Coast, Senegal, Cameroun and Madagascar.

African populations in these colonies were much smaller than those of the British empire south of the Sahara, but they were still large. They numbered some 16 million people in the eight colonies of French West Africa – Mauritania, Senegal, Soudan (now Mali), Guinea, Upper Volta, Ivory Coast, Dahomey, Niger; and some 4 million in the four colonies of French Equatorial Africa – Gabon, Middle Congo, Oubangui-Shari (now Central Africa), and Chad. Two old mandates of the League of Nations, and since 1946 UN trusteeship territories, were also under French colonial rule: Cameroun, with a population of some 4 million, and Togo with about one million. Lastly, there was the great island of Madagascar, with more than 4 million in 1945, and a scatter of small Indian Ocean islands. Altogether, this added up to some 30 million people.

What future did these peoples now want? What did France mean to do? Was there to be a struggle for independence, and, if so, how was it going to be settled? For some years after 1945, the answers stayed mixed and uncertain.

Change and reaction

The Brazzaville Declaration

While the war lasted, France gave no sign of being willing for any change. Up to 1942 its governors and generals in French West Africa all stayed loyal to the racist ideas of the wartime Vichy government in southern France, a puppet of the German nazi conquerors. They increased the use of forced labour; they filled their prisons with any who protested. In French Equatorial Africa, however, it was a little different. Leading French governors and others, there, decided to go against the Vichy government and support the 'Free French' movement of General Charles de Gaulle, who backed the Allies. There was talk of a 'new deal' for the colonies after the war.

But there was little more than talk. In February 1944, with de Gaulle's approval, a conference of 'Free French' colonial governors met at Brazzaville and discussed the future. Their Declaration of Brazzaville spoke of the need for new policies of respect for African rights and dignity. But it also spoke against any real concessions. Its key passage said:

the colonising work of France makes it impossible to accept any idea of autonomy for the colonies, or any possibility of development outside the French empire. Even at a distant date, there will be no self-government in the colonies.

There might be new words about 'union and friendship'; yet that, it seemed, was all. In fact those governors, like de Gaulle himself, misread the future. They counted without the wider effects of the Second World War.

Africans in the French parliament:
RDA and other parties

When France regained its own independence, after its liberation by British and American armies in 1944, the people of France also needed a 'new deal'. All their old conservative and middle-of-the-road parties – those that had made the empire – had gone down in defeat. Many were badly stained by collaboration with the nazi occupiers of their country. Liberal and left-wing parties came to power, and some of them were anti-colonial. They shaped a new constitution for France and its empire.

Rather like the Brazzaville Declaration, this constitution seemed at first to make little change. The colonies remained colonies in fact; in name only, they were changed to become members of a sort of commonwealth called the French Union (*Union Française*). But the new constitution went further in one important respect.

Thanks to liberal leadership in Paris, the constitution (agreed by national referendum in October 1946) provided for many colonial Africans to vote in elections for the French National Assembly.

These were able to elect about 20 Africans to that assembly; while other Africans were elected to a less important but still useful platform of opinion, in Paris – the Assembly of the French Union. These African members of the French parliament came from several new parties. Some of these parties were colonial offshoots of French ones; but some were not, and the biggest among those was entirely African. This was the *Rassemblement Démocratique Africain* (RDA), or African Democratic Rally, formed in 1946 at Bamako (then capital of French Soudan, now of Mali) by go-ahead leaders of African opinion in many of the twelve colonies of French West and Equatorial Africa. Among these men were Félix Houphouët-Boigny of Ivory Coast, Mamadu Konaté of French Soudan (Mali), and Gabriel d'Arboussier of Senegal. Others who now took a lead were Léopold Sedar Senghor of Senegal, Sékou Touré of Guinea, and Barthelèmy Boganda of Oubangui-Shari (Central African Republic).

These men did not press for the separate national independence of each of their countries. They had to work inside the framework of French ideas about assimilation and 'greater France'. So they pressed for progress in winning rights for Africans, and in abolishing the worst of the colonial laws. They made some progress. A law of 1946, especially the work of the Senegalese Lamine Guèye, successfully abolished forced labour in French colonies, and, at least in name, greatly extended the rights of French citizenship. The future for 'French Africans' south of the Sahara began to look brighter.

Colonial backlash

These moves towards equality between French and Africans in the colonies were opposed by French settlers and businessmen who feared a loss of privilege and profit. And now, after 1947, these businessmen and settlers were reinforced by a swing back, in French politics, to conservative ideas and parties. New French ministers began a campaign to cancel out the gains won by Africans.

The first target of this colonialist fight-back was the strongest of the new territorial parties, the Democratic Party of Ivory Coast (in French: PDCI) led by Houphouët-Boigny. As Nkrumah's Convention People's Party in the Gold Coast, next-door, was about to do, the PDCI had won wide popular support. In 1949 the French government in Paris sent out a new governor, Péchoux, with orders to destroy the PDCI. He failed, but his repression was severe. Several dozen African members of the PDCI lost their lives, hundreds went to prison. Elsewhere, too, there came the same administrative violence. It seemed for a while that settler and business interests had won the day.

But the tide of history proved too strong for them. The rights won by Africans – in their new political parties and trade unions, in the launching of their own newspapers, in other cultural and social fields – were defended; they remained in force. Now, too, 'French Africans' saw that other Africans were winning fresh advances, especially in the Gold Coast and Nigeria. Skilfully playing the game of the French Union, their leaders took fresh courage. Those of the RDA pressed for the formation of two self-governing federations, one composed of the eight territories of French West Africa, and the other of the four territories of French Equatorial Africa. They wanted each federation to have its own central government, forming two big states inside the French Union. They believed that two big states would afterwards be able to win a real control over their future.

But the French were against this for the same reason as the Africans were for it: they believed that twelve small states would be much easier for the French to control than two big ones. So the French moved towards the idea of self-government for twelve weak states. This idea was then accepted by Houphouët-Boigny, who became a junior minister in the French government of 1952.

In 1956, moving further towards this division of the two colonial 'federations' (West and Equatorial) into twelve self-governing states, the French parliament passed an important Act, the *loi cadre* or 'enabling Act'. This took power away from the two big colonial governments (in Dakar and Brazzaville), and gave this power to the twelve territorial governments. The power thus transferred was, as yet, only for local affairs; the big colonial governments in Dakar and Brazzaville still had control over finance, foreign policy, police and army. Yet this partial transfer proved decisive; it shaped the future.

In fact, a French plan for indirect control had now taken over from old colonial ideas. It opened against a wide background of change. In that same year of the *loi cadre*, 1956, Morocco and Tunisia became independent. The Gold Coast was about to become Ghana; similar moves towards independence were far advanced in Nigeria. In Kenya the anti-Mau Mau Emergency ended, leaving Kenya's nationalists with a good hope of political progress. Then came the French internal crisis over Algeria, and de Gaulle's return to power in 1958. What could the French still save for themselves?

A limited independence

De Gaulle and Sékou Touré

De Gaulle saw at once that French direct control south of the Sahara was no longer possible, and that he would have to move fast if France were to keep an indirect control. He accepted the idea of self-government for the twelve territories: each, he said, was to become an associated state within a new sort of union, this time called the French Community (*Communauté Française*). Each would have large local powers; but France would remain the 'motherland' in command of finance, foreign policy and military affairs. Each would have its parliament, government, flag and national anthem; but each would follow France in all big decisions. The horse would certainly be African; but the rider, just as surely, would be French.

De Gaulle's plan succeeded. By this time the leaders of African opinion were divided about what best to do. A few were solidly against the plan, and ready to oppose it. A few eagerly accepted the plan, for it gave local power into African hands, and some could benefit from that. Others disliked the plan, but felt that they and their parties were too weak to oppose it. All were beginning now to think as nationalists, outside the framework of assimilation. But many still believed they could be nationalists only as junior partners in the French Community.

De Gaulle set about isolating and defeating the opponents of his plan. He offered a referendum to each of the twelve colonies. The people had to vote 'yes' or 'no'. If they voted 'yes', they accepted the plan; if 'no', they could have full national independence, but in that case France would at once stop all aid and support. Appealing for a 'yes' vote, de Gaulle himself toured the colonies. He was sure that each of the colonies would vote 'yes', because each depended on French aid and support. Of course the French could also depend on their control of the voting machinery, yet mostly it was a kind of blackmail, and it worked. All gave 'yes' majorities: except one.

That was Guinea. Under Sékou Touré's strong leadership, the Democratic Party of Guinea (in French: PDG) not only won wide popular support; it also succeeded in undermining the influence of French-appointed chiefs. Not even French control of the voting machinery could help de Gaulle here. To his dismay and anger, 95 per cent of the votes in Guinea went against his plan. He cut off all aid at once, but it made no difference to the decision. Guinea became independent under a PDG government.

Another colony almost did the same. The biggest local party in Niger, Sawaba, led by Djibo Bakary, also campaigned for a 'no' vote. They failed; but there seems little doubt that the true voting returns were falsified by administrative action. The published results showed that about 100,000 had voted 'no' while 370,000 voted 'yes'. But no less than 62 per cent of the voters were said to have abstained.

With Guinea winning independence in 1958, the whole outlook was in any case dramatically changed. It became clear that nothing could now stop the other eleven colonies from moving in the same direction. Yet if de Gaulle's plan for twelve associated states was in ruins, the further plan for French indirect control was not.

1960: a fresh start?

Apart from Guinea, already independent, all the French West and Equatorial colonies, as well as the trusteeships of Cameroun and Togo, became national republics in 1960. All, except Guinea, had to accept French indirect control. Only the relatively rich Ivory Coast, Gabon, and to some extent Senegal, proved able to pay this price and still make overall progress.

Each of these neo-colonial states (again, except for Guinea) had to enter into agreements with France which placed their finance, foreign policy, and even national defence under strong French supervision. Through the Bank of France, the old 'motherland' continued to manage their finances by means of the so-called 'colonial franc'. Through various business interests, Paris continued to dominate their economic policies. Through military treaties, French armed forces stayed on their national soil. Through a host of links and habits, France remained their 'heart of civilisation'.

The grand vision of two strong federations, groundwork for a pan-African future, had faded away. The old colonial policy of 'divide and rule', though under a new guise, had stepped back into place.

Togo and Cameroun

Though in name a trusteeship territory and not a colony, Togo was governed by France in the same way as the rest of French West Africa. Togo shared the same road to independence in 1960, when Sylvanus Olympio became its first president. Meanwhile, in 1956, a referendum in British Togo (the western sector of the former German colony) had showed a majority in favour of its integration with Ghana; this duly occurred in 1957.

Cameroun was covered by another League of Nations mandate converted in 1946 to a UN trusteeship, but governed as a colony like all the other trusteeships: in this case, as a French colony. Yet this special status was not without its value to anti-colonial Africans. It enabled them to argue that France (in the case of Cameroun) should carry out its 'missionary trust' and agree to the country's independence. Of course, before the Second World War Camerounians could not argue like this, at least publicly, inside Cameroun. But Camerounians in Paris could do it. And we find them doing it as early as 1933 in the columns of the anti-colonial *Cris des Nègres*:

> Cameroun demands its independence, and an end to a mandate which has done the country no good.

With the new French constitution of 1946, demands for Camerounian independence were heard more strongly; but now they were heard inside Cameroun. Local settler and business interests quickly mobilised against these demands. As in Kenya on the other side of Africa, settler interests were strengthened by the Second World War. They meant to command the country's future. Again like the Kenya settlers, they had powerful support in the 'motherland'.

If the majority interests of Camerounian Africans were to succeed against the settlers, they clearly needed the support of a political party. And if this party were to do any good, it must just as clearly stand for national union against tribal disunion. This was going to be difficult, because there were many different peoples in Cameroun, and the French, like other colonial rulers, had promoted the idea of 'modern tribalism' (see Chapter 7).

In 1948 a group of young nationalists, led by a trade union organiser called Reuben Um Nyobé, decided to tackle this difficult task. They formed the Union of the Populations of Cameroun (UPC). Um Nyobé proved a far-seeing leader. The UPC was among the earliest parties of African nationalism to show that the enemy to be fought was not only direct colonialism, but also its indirect form of neo-colonialism.

The UPC became a main target of the French colonial fight-back, just like the PDCI in Ivory Coast. Harried by the colonial authorities, leaders and rank-and-file supporters of the UPC had to face much repression. Finally, in 1954, Governor Pré was sent out to destroy the UPC, as Péchoux had tried to destroy the PDCI in the Ivory Coast some years before. Pré banned all UPC meetings, set his police to harass Um Nyobé and others, and then declared the UPC illegal. But Um Nyobé and others managed to escape arrest.

Peaceful political action having got nowhere, the UPC responded with guerrilla action. Based in southern forests protected by UPC fighters, their liberation movement defied the French and began to build an independent life. But tribal disunity defeated them. While the people of two large areas supported UPC, the rest stayed inactive or sided with the French. In 1958 Um Nyobé was killed by a military patrol. Two years later, his successor Félix Moumié was murdered by rightwing extremists in Europe. Gradually, the UPC was destroyed.

The French, meanwhile, found other Camerounian parties ready to accept French plans. Chief among these anti-UPC parties was the Movement for Union of Cameroun (MUC) led by Ahmadou Ahidjo. Together with smaller parties, MUC won 60 out of 100 parliamentary seats in elections of 1960; and Ahidjo became president of a new Camerounian republic.

A peaceful Nigerian wisdom settled the future of Northern (or British) Cameroons, a UN trusteeship territory since 1945 (and before that governed under mandate of the League of Nations). The people of the northern region voted to stay inside Nigeria, and formed the Sardauna province in June 1961. The people of the southern region voted, during a UN-supervised referendum of February 1961, to become part of the Cameroun republic.

Madagascar, Comoros

Fifteen thousand French soldiers, using 7,000 Algerian and Somali porters, invaded the large island of Madagascar in 1894. Against much armed resistance, France gradually installed a system of colonial rule. By the late 1930s, this system was essentially as follows:

1 All political power was held by French officials, who governed through Malagasy clerks, interpreters, police, and so on.
2 The economy of the island became a colonial economy: that is, more and more Malagasies worked to produce crops for export, under French control of prices and wages.
3 Education and social services were provided for a few Malagasies who accepted assimilation to French culture and loyalty to France.
4 By 1939 the Malagasy population was divided into a minority of about 8,000 assimilated persons, and a majority of more than 4 million 'natives' (*indigènes*) who were subject to colonial laws on forced labour and other obligations.

As in other settler colonies, the Second World War appeared to strengthen local settler power in the short term. It brought other consequences that we have noted: a stiff repression went together with a deepening rural poverty, and Malagasy towns grew rapidly in size. But here, too, French defeat in 1940 shattered the prestige of the colonial system. A fresh hope of anti-colonial change appeared. This was spread further as some 10,000 Malagasy servicemen, returning home again, brought news of nationalist successes in Asia. Then came the changes made by the new French constitution of 1946.

Four men were elected to the French parliament in 1946. Two were settlers. But the other two were Malagasy nationalists. They represented a new party with mass support, the Democratic Movement for the Reconstruction of Madagascar (in French: MRDM). These two MRDM members of the French National Assembly, Ravoahangy and Raséta, were instructed by their electors to ask for Madagascan self-government as a step to independence. They put this demand in March 1946, but were refused, partly through the influence of some 60,000 French settlers, partly through the colonial fight-back mentioned above.

Events then moved fast. In September 1946 the French government instructed their colonial government in Madagascar to 'fight the MRDM by every means.' A new repression began. But this met widespread support for nationalism, and a big rebellion broke out against French rule. Starting in March 1947, this rebellion quickly won control of wide areas, but was smashed a year later by military force and by hunger resulting from a French blockade of rebel-held zones. Many thousands died: as many as 80,000 in French reports at the time, about 11,000 in later French estimates. By 1948, some 6,000 nationalists were in prison.

Only in 1956 did the French raise their 'state of siege', or direct military rule. Only in 1957 did they release the last of their Madagascan political prisoners. But the MRDM, together with its call for a strongly independent nationalism, was now destroyed. Here, too, the French plan succeeded. In the Gaullist referendum of 1958, about 77 per cent of voters were said to have voted 'yes' to the French Community; and Madagascar was given self-government within the Community in October 1958. Direct French control gave way to indirect control in 1960, when Madagascar became a republic.

The four inhabited islands of the Comoros became French property at various times, and were formed into a single colony in 1912. From then until 1946 they were governed from French Madagascar. During 1961 they were given some self-government. In a referendum of December 1974 the population of three islands voted overwhelmingly for independence; but that of Mayotte (Mahoré), the fourth island, cast 64 per cent of its votes against independence. In July 1975, the three islands formed the independent state of the Comoros, while Mayotte's population decided by a large majority to remain under French control.

CHAPTER 13

British West Africa

After the Second World War, decolonisation was less difficult to achieve in the four British West African colonies than in most other regions of the continent. Here there were no settler communities to get in the way of progressive change. Colonial advisers in Britain were already saying, even before 1945, that steps toward self-government for these four colonies would have to be taken. Governor Burns in the Gold Coast even appointed two Africans, in 1942, to be assistant district officers: a big step, as many thought then.

Yet it was still far from easy to push Britain into accepting African self-government, and then independence. For the British also had ideas about safeguarding British interests. These ideas were different from the French ideas inspected in the last chapter (see p. 112). The British had no policy of assimilation. They had no wish for the Africans in their colonies to become citizens of Britain. Nor did they think that their colonies should remain part of a 'greater Britain'.

But they did wish, very much, to keep a strong economic and strategic influence over these countries in the future. With that in mind, they aimed at less than the complete neo-colonial control achieved by the French in most of France's former African colonies. Their idea was that the four colonies should move towards eventual membership of the British Commonwealth of Nations. This was at that time a British-dominated 'club' of independent states, formed many years earlier with the old 'white Dominions' of Britain (Australia, Canada, New Zealand, South Africa), but enlarged, after the Second World War, to include independent India, Pakistan and Sri Lanka (Burma refused to join).

But the British wanted this movement to independence within the Commonwealth to be very slow, and by small steps. Many years must pass, the British thought, before there need be any real transfer of power. Therefore the problem for the nationalists was a double one. They had to find ways of pushing the British into agreeing to faster advance. Secondly, they had to work out how they should use the powers of independence, once these powers were transferred to them.

Neither side of this dual problem was easy to solve. And some of the solutions that were found, during those years, were to weigh heavily on the future.

Different views and priorities

The 'old nationalists' of the merchant-lawyer class in British West Africa had asked for 'colonial improvement'. Now, times were changed. New men and new parties were in the lead. Their demand was not for improvement, but for independence. Yet it remained that different kinds of people, eagerly following these new leaders, wanted different things; and this, indeed, was the case in every colony.

One important section of opinion, that of the educated few, was much larger than twenty years earlier. By 1945 or soon after, the Gold Coast had about 10,000 persons with some or much education, whether as lawyers, teachers, clergymen, or businessmen; while Nigeria, though with fewer, already had 114 lawyers, 38 medical doctors, 32 journalists, and 435 clergymen, as well as many businessmen.

All these persons, broadly, wanted political success. They looked forward to governing an independent country. The Nigerian Chief Obafemi Awolowo spoke for them when he wrote, in 1947, that they were the persons who understood modern politics, and so 'it must be realised, now and for all time, that this articulate minority are destined to rule the country'.

Yet the great majority of people, whether in village or town, had less interest in winning power than in getting a better daily life. For them, nationalism was a way to become less poor; to send their children to school; to benefit from better roads, prices, public services. They looked to nationalism for social gains, while the educated few mostly had their eyes on political gains.

Later, as Part Four will show, this difference in expectations was to become a source of much conflict; and not only in West Africa. Meanwhile, the majority of people listened to the promises of the new leaders and movements; and these promises were large and many. They had to be large and many, for this was now a time of vivid hope after the years of colonial standstill or repression. People saw the winning of independence as the gateway to a better life. Whatever troubles might come later, they were not wrong about this. They went into the campaigns for independence with stout hearts and strong hopes.

Nigeria: giant on the move

The Nigerian giant moved, in fact, even before the Second World War was over. Founded in 1944 (see p. 73), the NCNC under

Nnamdi Azikiwe took a lead in southern Nigeria. This the British had already divided into two regions, Eastern and Western. In 1950 a new party emerged in the Western Region; this was the Action Group (AG) under Obafemi Awolowo. The same year saw the formation, under Aminu Kano, of a modernising party in the vast Northern Region; the Northern Elements Progressive Union (NEPU).

But the Northern Region had been more or less cut off from the two southern Regions, by colonial rule, ever since 1922; and now its 'indirect rulers', the emirate chiefs, wished to conserve their powers. In 1951 they developed a far more influential party; this was the Northern People's Congress (NPC) under Sir Ahmadu Bello, the prestigious Sardauna of Sokoto. Other parties followed: notably, in 1955, the United Middle Belt Congress (UMBC), a merger between two earlier movements among the people of central Nigeria.

Already, as these parties showed, Nigerian politics were falling into a markedly regional pattern. Of course this must always have been hard to avoid in so big and diverse a country as Nigeria. But colonial rule had done nothing to lessen internal divisions. On the contrary, colonial rule had long isolated north from south, and strengthened regional distrust or rivalry. For all these reasons, the advance to nationalism, and to all-Nigerian unity, could never be an easy one. As things turned out, it became less easy as the leaders of this or that region came into competition with the leaders of other regions.

Small steps: from Richards to Macpherson

Following their policy of going forward slowly, the British ventured on a first small step in 1946. Governor-General Richards brought in a new constitution which, for the first time, created an all-Nigeria legislative council. This was only an advisory council, and only two Nigerians were members of it. At the same time, however, Richards provided for three regional councils, one each for the Northern, Western and Eastern Provinces (later called Regions). Once again, this reinforced the regional pattern.

The Richards constitution met immediate criticism from leading nationalists. Here we may usefully recall some words of Chief H.O. Davies. He pointed out that the constitution said a lot about discussion, but nothing about participation. In it, said H.O. Davies, 'there is neither the intention nor the pretension to secure greater participation by the Africans in the management of their own affairs'.

Under such criticism, Britain's small steps to independence began to come less slowly. Due for revision only in 1955, the Richards constitution of 1946 failed to satisfy anyone. Another was introduced by Governor-General Macpherson in 1951. This gave way to demands for more power in each region. These were strong demands because, by this time, Nigerian politics had largely become a three-way tussle between the NCNC (mainly Igbo), the AG (mainly Yoruba), and the NPC (mainly Hausa-Fulani). The Nigerian constitutional specialist Kalu Ezera has even gone so far as to say that 'from this time onwards [that is, from the end of the 1940s] tribal nationalism came to dominate the Nigerian political scene'.

The Macpherson constitution provided for an all-Nigerian federal government, seated in Lagos. But it also transformed the regional councils into regional parliaments, each of which now elected its own regional government.

One Nigerian nation

Under strong nationalist pressure, the British agreed to faster steps. In 1954, only three years after its introduction, the Macpherson constitution was scrapped. Another new constitution, named this time after Lyttleton who was British colonial minister, was brought in. This Lyttleton constitution did something to strengthen the powers of the federal parliament and government. But inter-regional rivalry was very sharp by now; and it was the regions that still dominated the situation.

In August 1957 the Western and Eastern Regions became self-governing states, while the vast Northern Region, adjusting less quickly to the pace of change, moved into self-government in March 1959. That cleared the way for the last act in the drama of colonial withdrawal. On 1 October 1960, Nigeria became independent as a federation of three self-governing states.

Was this to mean that Nigeria would be one nation, or merely a combination of separate nations? Historians, since then, have said that the greatest success of Nigeria's leaders was to keep this great country as one country, and to hold firmly to the creating of a single Nigerian nation against all the rivalries of the regional pattern. Yet the regional pattern of power and privilege for active nationalists – what Kalu Ezera called 'tribal nationalism' – still had great disruptive force behind it. This force was to be violently felt within the following ten years (see Chapter 18).

Gold Coast upheavals: Ghana takes shape

The Gold Coast also had regions. But the country is smaller than Nigeria, and its regional divisions were less developed. Here, too, strong differences developed between the ideas and aims of the educated few, including powerful traditional rulers such as the Asantehene (king of Asante), and a mass nationalist movement which soon took the lead. The former wanted to safeguard their positions; the latter worked for wider ideas and aims.

But the educated few still pressed for anti-colonial change. Under well-known men such as J.B. Danquah (1895–1965), they formed in 1947 the United Gold Coast Convention (UGCC) as an instrument of political pressure. They meant to use the UGCC as a way of pushing the British into progress towards independence. But they meant to use it carefully, and without appealing for mass action to support them. It turned out differently.

Looking for a competent secretary for the UGCC, Danquah offered the job to Kwame Nkrumah (1909–1972), then in London after returning from several years of higher education in the USA. Nkrumah came home at once and took the job. But he took it with ideas that were markedly different from those of the UGCC leaders. He believed that mass action was required, and began to organise it. Young nationalists were actively on his side. They called for a country-wide campaign of pressure for change. Soon, Nkrumah was inviting mass action through strikes and boycotts of imported goods.

At this point, the UGCC leaders began to regret their choice of secretary. But mass action now came on the scene without being invited. A minor chief and trader of Sierra Leonean origin, Nii Bonne, organised a boycott of European goods in Accra, the capital, in January 1948. It proved a success, and colonial government agreed to reduce the prices of European goods. But on 28 February, 1948, the day when prices were to come down and, as colonial government hoped, the boycott would end, there came another of history's accidents. It changed everything.

A group of ex-servicemen marched that day to the governor's castle, in a peaceful demonstration, so as to ask for a settlement of their grievances about pensions and jobs. Colonial police barred their way. An argument broke out. A British police officer shot at and killed two ex-servicemen, also wounding four or five others.

Though planned by no-one, the effect was shattering. For years the British had thought of the Gold Coast as their 'model colony', always peaceful and patient. Now, suddenly, it exploded. Down the road from the castle, in the middle of Accra, angry crowds began looting and burning European shops. From Accra the rioting spread to other towns, and it went on for days. Army and police restored order in the end, but many people were dead by then, and much property was destroyed.

Taken by surprise, the British governor arrested the 'big six' leaders of the UGCC, including Danquah and Nkrumah, although none of them had the least responsibility for the riots. As usual in those days, the police wanted to believe that they had discovered a communist plot, although, again, the UGCC was against any left-wing ideas, and above all against anything like communism. Their 'discovery' did the police no good. All six leaders had to be quickly released for lack of evidence. But five of them came out of detention determined to get rid of the sixth, who was Nkrumah. They blamed him for the bad name they were getting with the authorities. They were more than ready, now, to go slowly. But Nkrumah was not.

Nkrumah and the CPP: a breakthrough

Ousted from UGCC, Nkrumah and his followers formed their own party, the Convention People's Party (CPP), in June 1949, and prepared to use mass support to win independence without delay. Their immediate aim was to call a general strike through the trade unions. This strike began on 8 January 1950, and many joined it. The governor at once replied to their peaceful action by violence which proved decisive, though in no way that the governor had expected.

Three days after the strike began, the governor declared a state of emergency. Arrests followed, and clashes. Two policemen were killed. Arrests continued. On 21 January the police took Nkrumah and his chief aide into prison.

But now, with the country in growing ferment, the British changed their ground. Seven years before de Gaulle was going to do the same, they acted to regain control by seeking agreement with the nationalist leaders and above all with Nkrumah. Pushed on by mass pressure, they prepared for a new general election. This would lead to a constitution. And the new constitution would open the way for further steps toward self-government and independence.

In this general election of February 1951, CPP candidates won a clear majority of seats. Though still in prison, Nkrumah himself won almost all the votes in Accra Central. A newly-appointed Governor, Sir Charles Arden-Clarke, at once saw, as he said later, that 'Nkrumah and his party had the mass of the people behind them.' He released Nkrumah and asked him to become the leader of an African government with important internal powers. This was in some measure self-government; and independence, Arden-Clarke promised, would come later. In the circumstances of those days, it was a great breakthrough. Nkrumah accepted. His party and mass following gave their enthusiastic agreement.

Looking back, one sees that this was only a partial breakthrough. It was enough in the end to secure independence, but the CPP still had to struggle for another six years before the Gold Coast became independent Ghana. As in Nigeria, these were years when many of the problems of coming independence were hardened into conflict. Nkrumah and the CPP had to meet very sharp opposition from chiefs and their allies in the UGCC or successor-parties to the UGCC. They had to overcome the strong drive for a regional break-away in Asante, and they had to win the trust of the Muslim north.

All this was done, although much that was done during those six years became a matter for angry debate. Yet the greatest task was done with full success when, in 1957, the people of Ghana became the first colonial people south of the Sahara to win through to independence. Especially in their breakthrough of 1951, they gave a wide encouragement to nationalists in every part of Africa, even in the distant and very isolated colonies of Portugal. For their success taught a lesson highly valued in those times. No matter how tall and tough the colonial barriers to freedom might be, they could still be overthrown.

Sierra Leone and The Gambia

After 1950, in these vigorous though smaller colonies, the underlying pattern of events was much the same as in Nigeria and the Gold Coast. Sierra Leone also had its internal divisions: of these, the most important was a result of the slave-trade and colonial periods. It consisted in a division between the Creoles in and around Freetown, many of them the descendants of freed captives from other parts of West Africa, and the peoples of the interior, known in colonial times as 'the tribal interior'.

The British shaped their 'small steps' in line with this internal division. A new constitution of 1947 gave Sierra Leoneans an 'unofficial majority' in the colonial legislature. Elected Sierra Leoneans in this legislature were more in number than colonial officials; but colonial officials still held the power. This constitution favoured the 'tribal interior' because it was much larger than the Creole coastal neighbourhood.

In 1951, a revised constitution gave local power to African ministers drawn from the majority party in parliament. This was the newly-founded Sierra Leone People's Party (SLPP) under a medical doctor turned politician, Sir Milton Margai (1895–1964). He was from the 'tribal interior', but succeeded in making an agreement for joint action with the Creole leaders of Freetown. In 1960, the SLPP combined with other groups in a coalition called the United National Front; and this led Sierra Leone to independence in April 1961.

Here was another good breakthrough, linked also to the growth of an effective trade union movement led especially by Siaka Stevens (born in 1905 and national president from 1971), who became the first secretary of the Sierra Leone Trades Union Congress as early as 1946. Like others of its kind, this independence solved the problem of getting rid of colonial rule, but left other problems to be tackled later. Among these other problems was a big difference, as in other countries, between the expectations of the educated few and the expectations of the mass of people.

Though The Gambia had a population of only some 300,000, its nationalists were determined not to be left behind. Their first parties naturally took shape among educated groups in the capital, Bathurst (now Banjul). These were The Gambia Democratic Party and The Gambia Muslim Congress, both formed in 1945, and the United Party (UP) formed in 1951. For the most part, their leaders were the younger generation of those who had worked in the Gambian section of the National Congress of British West Africa twenty years earlier (see p. 31).

But the politics of nationalism could win in The Gambia, as elsewhere, only by calling on mass support. This, largely, had to come from the 'tribal interior'. It began to be organised in 1959, when Sir Dawda Jawara and others formed the People's Progressive Party (PPP). The PPP swept the polls in a general election of 1960, a victory which led the British, in 1962, to produce another new constitution. Under this, The Gambia won internal self-government in 1963. After combining in a coalition with the UP led by P.S. Njie, Jawara and the PPP led The Gambia to independence in February 1965. In December 1981 a Confederation of Senegambia was proclaimed, between The Gambia and Senegal, by the two governments concerned.

CHAPTER 14

East and Central Africa: British settler colonies

Harsh years led to independence in most of the British colonies of East and Central Africa. Many differences existed between them and the colonies of British West Africa. They were differences of history, culture, population, as well as of climate, land use, other natural factors. But those were not the differences that toughened the road to independence. The harshness came from the presence of white-settler minorities.

In order to see into those years, and make our way through their complexities, we can best divide these countries into two groups: first, those of British East Africa: Kenya, Tanganyika, Uganda, and Zanzibar. Secondly, those of British Central Africa: Northern Rhodesia (Zambia), Nyasaland (Malawi), and Southern Rhodesia (Zimbabwe). But in many ways their history of struggle for progress was much the same.

Background to confrontation

Except Uganda with its very few settlers, and Zanzibar with almost none, each of the British East and Central African colonies was the scene of an often sharp confrontation between settlers and Africans. On one side there were the settler minorities, determined to 'stay on top' and take over control from colonial government. On the other side, after 1945, there was the African advance from colonial tribalism to modern nationalism. And from that advance there came the formation of new parties or congresses of national union, aiming at independence under African rule.

We have already mentioned this advance (see pp. 66–67). It occurred everywhere, and proved decisive. In Kenya, for example, 1945 saw the formation of a Kikuyu General Union and of a Luo Union, and again, in 1947, there was added a Bara African Union for the benefit of other 'modern tribes'. Yet the advance from those ideas of limited union, based on old traditions of history, to new ideas of national union, of nationalism, was already overtaking these tribal unions and self-defence associations.

Thus 1944 saw the emergence of the Kenya African Union (KAU), and then, with a further advance to modern nationalism, 1960 brought the formation of the Kenya African National Union (KANU) and of the Kenya African Democratic Union (KADU). The same advance was made elsewhere. Then it was the big national parties, such as KANU in Kenya, which carried the day against settlers and colonial government alike.

Imperial policies

Confrontation between British settler minorities and African majorities was painful everywhere. But it was most violent in Kenya and Southern Rhodesia, where settlers were many. That was the same as in the French empire. Wherever French settler communities were large, above all in Algeria and Madagascar, the road to independence became stained with blood. We shall find similar features, once again, in the Portuguese empire.

Yet settlers and Africans in these east and central colonies were not the only powers on the scene. There was also the power of colonial government directed from London. Which side of the confrontation, the settlers or the Africans, was backed by imperial policy?

In East and Central Africa, British imperial policy liked to say that it backed both sides: it wanted to 'maintain a balance'. It was solemnly pledged to regard the interests of the majority – that is, of the Africans – as having first place whenever a conflict of interests arose. On the other hand, strong business and political interests, in Britain, still wanted the settlers to have first place. In practice, this meant that the settlers usually got what they wanted, later if not sooner. They got it more than ever in the aftermath of the Second World War.

Before looking at the detailed record, one other complication can be noted.

Asians in East Africa

Though few in central Africa, Asians in East Africa were an important minority. Some had long settled in the coastal ports of the Swahili, and could look back through centuries to the peace and prosperity of the old Indian Ocean trade before the coming of Europeans. Mostly, these long-settled Asians were the East African descendants of Arabian peoples. But other Asians came from the Indian sub-continent during the colonial period, either because colonial government invited them to work in East Africa, or because they saw the chance of a better life.

Immigrants from Asia grew in numbers after the Second World War. In Kenya they increased from about 50,000 in 1939 to 170,000 in 1960; they also increased in Tanganyika (about 87,000 in 1960), and in Uganda (about 75,000 in 1960). They belonged to different Asian communities. In Kenya about two-thirds were Hindus; in Tanganyika, Hindus were rather less than half the total. Apart from a small Sikh and Jain community of about 32,000, mostly in Kenya, all the Asian Muslims belonged to one or other of three Shia brotherhoods: the Ismaili Khoja, Ithna'ashri, or Bohra.

Some of these immigrants were literate in English at a time when few Africans had been able to learn to read and write. As such, they were useful to colonial government in junior civil service jobs. Other Asians used their trading skills to find a place for themselves between big European commerce and the needs of African communities. They were welcomed by colonial government in this role of intermediary traders. They often played a valuable and even necessary part in colonial trading systems.

Yet their positions and work brought them, steadily, into growing conflict with Africans. As civil servants, they were no supporters of African anti-colonial action. As intermediary traders, they were often the only traders. Africans came to resent their prices, trading habits, and command of village credit. Unhappily for these Asians, they and their leaders proved unable to adjust to the interests and needs of the overwhelming African majority of all the people in these countries. In changing times, this was bound to bring the Asians into trouble.

'Closer union': settlers attempt to join forces

We need to consider one other background point. It applies to the 1930s.

Settler politicians began pushing for the idea of closer union between Kenya and Tanganyika and also, if possible, with Uganda as well. In this way, they believed, they would be able to combine their minorities so as to strengthen their chance of governing the whole region.

The Kenya settlers took the lead. Their farmers in the so-called 'White Highlands' of Kikuyu country already numbered about 2,000 in 1934, owning just over 2 million hectares of good land. Soon, they argued in the 1930s, other settlers would start industries in Kenya. Then a white-ruled Kenya could dominate the whole East African region. It could become the central country, they hoped, of a new white-ruled Dominion of the British Commonwealth.

They failed to get this closer union, partly because imperial policy was pledged to give first place to African interests (even if, in practice, the pledge was seldom kept); and partly because the Great Depression made Britain unwilling to risk any big change. Yet the idea of white-dominated closer union was not forgotten; it emerged again after the Second World War.

Settlers in the three Central African colonies also tried for closer union in the 1930s. They argued that if four territories in South Africa could be united under white rule, as they were in 1910, then so could three territories in Central Africa. But here, too, the settlers failed until, in 1953, they succeeded with the Central African Federation (see p. 132). In the end that also failed, but only through the rise of a still more successful African nationalism.

Tanganyika and Zanzibar (Tanzania): advance to independence

Confrontation here was less severe for two reasons. One was that the settlers numbered only some 20,000 in the 1950s; besides, many were not of British origin, and had less support from political interests in Britain. Since the First World War, governors had been generally careful to protect African land and labour from white settlers in search of land to take and labour to exploit. Another but related reason, after the Second World War, was that Tanganyika became a UN trusteeship territory in 1946. As such, it could scarcely be allowed to fall under settler control, whether directly by settlers in Tanganyika or indirectly by settlers in Kenya.

Nationalism developed after 1945. Up to then, the country's many different peoples and communities had often accepted the colonial division into 'modern tribes', and had taken no part in anything but purely local politics. Even so, the forerunner of an all-Tanganyika union, the Tanganyika African Association (TAA), emerged as a discussion group among educated persons as early as 1929. Then, with all the new ideas and influences of the period of the Second World War and following years, there came the advance to national union, to nationalism.

The men of the TAA moved with this new tide. They became more and more involved in all-Tanganyika affairs. In 1953, under the skilful chairmanship of Julius Nyerere, the TAA was reorganised as a political party, leading directly to the formation of the Tanganyika African National Union (TANU) in 1954.

Other currents of action strengthened TANU. Trade unions became more active. So did strong producers' co-operatives among peoples growing crops such as coffee and cotton. Soon, with the small settler community in political retreat, TANU candidates were winning big majorities in general elections; in many constituencies, they now faced no rival candidates. This national unity had its reward. In 1961 the country became independent, with British agreement, under a TANU government with country-wide support.

Two years later, in December 1963, the island of Zanzibar (together with the smaller island of Pemba) also became independent by a peaceful process; but, this time, under a government without wide support. This was a government dominated by the Sultan of Zanzibar and a minority of land-owning local Arabs. These numbered some 50,000. But the rest of the population, consisting mostly of landless Shirazi (Swahili-speaking islanders) and recent immigrants from the mainland, totalled some 230,000.

Two months after independence, in January 1964, the Sultan's government was overthrown by local policemen, and power passed to non-Arab parties. Much violence followed; several thousand Arabs were said to have lost their lives. The new regime brought in a plan for social revolution, and received aid from East Germany and China. But Zanzibar's new leaders also wanted to keep close links with the mainland. They accepted a Tanganyika proposal for a loose kind of union. In April 1964, Tanganyika and Zanzibar joined to form the United Republic of Tanzania. But each country continued to have its own government.

Through all these events the TANU leaders, and especially Nyerere, supported the idea of an East African Federation as soon as the colonies were free. They joined with Kenya's and Uganda's leaders in forming organisations with that aim (see pp. 212–213).

Rivalries in Uganda: independence for whom?

Unity such as TANU was able to achieve among Tanganyika's many peoples proved impossible in Uganda. As in Tanganyika, there existed strong loyalties to ancient kingships and other traditional authorities. But colonial rule in Uganda greatly deepened these divisions, above all by taking the kingdom of Buganda into a 'junior partnership' with colonial government.

Buganda's leaders, including their king (*kabaka*), welcomed this opportunity of working with and for the British. It gave them privileges. They won better positions than the leaders of other old kingdoms, notably those of Buganda's traditional rival, Bunyoro. Generally, the Baganda had better chances than other Ugandan peoples of going to school, getting good jobs, and making money. This was widely resented.

There were, as well, strongly-felt religious differences. Many northerners were Muslim; but most of the educated nationalists, especially in the southern regions, were Christian. Yet some Christians were Protestant and others Catholic; and these two Christian communities in Uganda had long competed against each other.

Rivalries and resentments such as these worked against national union almost from the start. Led by competing groups of mostly educated men, two main parties during the 1950s began to struggle against each other for the powers that Britain was soon going to hand over. These parties were the Uganda National Congress (UNC), formed in 1952 with support from northerners and Protestant Christians; and the Democratic Party (DP), formed in 1956 with largely southern and Catholic Christian support.

This rivalry between the DP and UNC – and the UNC's successor party, Uganda People's Congress (UPC), formed in 1960 – was less about winning independence than about who was going to get the most benefits from independence. Instead of working together to build their new nation, they worked against each other. They built disunity instead of unity. This disunity was increased by the Baganda king (Kabaka Mutesa II) and his chiefs, who pressed hard for their own Baganda nationalism. In 1960 they even went so far as to claim that Buganda must become an independent state. The British rejected this; but Baganda separatism continued.

Against these sharpening conflicts, there was little to unite the mass of Ugandans except economic grievances: especially, a widely-felt grievance against European and Asian control of the marketing and ginning (processing) of African-grown cotton. So the internal struggle for power went on.

Finally, with none of these rivalries resolved, Uganda became independent in October 1962. This was under a government formed by the UPC, led by Milton Obote, and a Baganda nationalist party called Kabaka Yekka (meaning: 'the King alone'), with the DP in opposition. But trouble soon followed. Not only was Kabaka Mutesa the president of this Ugandan republic, but his kingdom, Buganda, enjoyed a special and separate position within the republic. And the separatist ambitions of Buganda rapidly led to wider troubles.

Kenya: a hard road to freedom

African nationalism in Kenya proved powerfully successful in winning *uhuru* (freedom) against internal divisions, against settler domination, and against colonial government. But the road was hard.

Kenya was the home of many different communities who had long lived together and traded with each other, but had known no general unity. Some of these communities were large, such as the Kikuyu and Luo; others were quite small. There were many differences of culture between them. But the pressure of settler domination, together with strong African leadership, gave them a common ground to stand on; and, after the Second World War, they stood more firmly on it than before.

When the war was over, colonial government lifted its ban on African politics. An advance to modern nationalism began. At once, it ran into sharp settler opposition.

The settlers had got more power during the war. Their 'hard core', now composed of more than 3,000 farmers owning about 2.6 million hectares of Kenya's best land, had made big economic gains. Their spokesmen were strong in the colony's legislature; and colonial government now listened to them more often than it listened to London. They were determined to win political as well as economic control, and to keep both. They decided that they must destroy the power of this new African nationalism.

Formed in 1946, the Kenya African Union's first president was the Harry Thuku of whom we have heard before (see p. 67). But a new and more effective leadership was now required. This was found in Jomo Kenyatta (1891–1978), who came home in 1946 from a long stay in England and took over the KAU leadership in 1947. Touring the country and speaking to multitudes, Kenyatta showed the way to freedom from settler and colonial dictatorship. Other notable men, such as Oginga Odinga (born in 1911), did the same. They and their message of freedom became very popular, especially among all those people, very many by now, who suffered landlessness, unemployment, or starvation wages (see pp. 79–80).

Faced with the popularity of the KAU and its leaders, the settlers became more violent. Far from seeking an agreement with the KAU, or trying to reduce African grievances, they redoubled their demands for settler control of the country. By 1950, now numbering some 60,000, this settler community was in fact ready for collision, and even wanted it, thinking that in this way they could destroy African political resistance. Giving way to settler pressure, colonial government did nothing to prevent a clash.

So collision came in 1952. Replying to sporadic acts of violence and pushed on by the settlers, colonial government declared a state of emergency, and arrested Kenyatta with other KAU leaders. Greatly fearing settler reactions, thousands of young men and women in Nairobi fled to the shelter of the Aberdare Mountains and Mount

Kenya. There they formed the 'Land and Freedom' armies, as they called themselves, although the British insisted on calling them 'Mau Mau'. Their armed groups began to attack police stations, settler farms, and other targets.

Four years of bitter warfare followed. Heavily outnumbered by colonial forces, the Land and Freedom armies held out until 1956; in the end, the British had to send 100,000 troops and armed police against them. About 10,000 Africans were killed in this war or died as a result of it.

In one sense, the great rebellion failed. Among all the peoples of Kenya, only a part of the Kikuyu and of their Embu and Meru neighbours took part in it. More than three-quarters of the colonial forces sent against it were composed of African troops from other parts of Kenya; and these were reinforced by some 30,000 Kikuyu men organised as 'home guards' in local-defence militias.

But in another sense, more important for the future, the rebellion did not fail. Though smashed, it shook the foundations of settler power. Shocked by the fighting and its cost, opinion in Britain began to favour an advance to African majority rule. At last seeing the wisdom of agreeing to some progress, the industrial and business settlers began to turn against the 'hard core' farming settlers.

Nationalism grew wider and stronger. A big national union was formed in 1960: Kenya African National Union (KANU); and a smaller one, Kenya African Democratic Union (KADU). In 1961, with Kenyatta now released from detention and their leader, KANU formed a coalition government with KADU. With the settlers politically discredited and divided, Kenyatta and his colleagues went on to win independence for Kenya in December 1963. Again, unity had its reward.

Central Africa: a settlers' federation

Similar kinds of change and drama occurred in the three Central African colonies of Britain. Here there was the same advance from ideas of tribal union to ideas of national union. There was the same resistance by white-settler communities; and in the end, in Rhodesia (Zimbabwe), there was a long war.

Before African nationalism could win, however, these colonies had to undergo ten years of settlers' federation. Here the leaders were the settlers of Southern Rhodesia, more than 200,000 by 1950 (with smaller numbers in Northern Rhodesia and Nyasaland). Britain had given them full control of the country in 1923, after which Southern

Rhodesia was a colony only in name. They proceeded to take the best land for themselves. They continued to make African farmers work for them by money-taxation or other means. They denied Africans any political rights. Their system was repressive, and much like the system in South Africa.

These settlers had long failed to win closer union with the settlers of the two other two colonies (see p. 128). But they succeeded in 1953, when Britain agreed to a Central African Federation. This was to be a 'settlers' federation' aimed at keeping government in white hands. The Southern Rhodesian settlers were going to be in control, but the settler communities in Northern Rhodesia (Zambia) and Nyasaland (Malawi) agreed to this because they accurately saw federation as a dam to stem the advancing tide of black independence.

The Southern Rhodesian settlers had the upper hand from the start. Dominated by mining companies located in Southern Rhodesia and South Africa, the new system was able to 'milk' the Northern Rhodesian economy, rich in copper, of a large part of all its mining profits. These totalled, after tax, no less than £260 million in the ten years that the Federation lasted (1953–63). That was a much bigger sum than all the money spent in those years by the colonial government of Northern Rhodesia. Little of these profits were invested in Northern Rhodesia, but a large part of them went to help white-settler development in Southern Rhodesia and South Africa.

Yet the settlers still did not have the full control they wanted. The two northern colonies stayed under colonial government. This government now had to take account of new and strong movements of African nationalism. In Northern Rhodesia these began in 1948, with the formation of the Northern Rhodesian African National Congress and then, in 1959, with the emergence of its stronger successor, the United National Independence Party (UNIP) led by Kenneth Kaunda. Organised nationalism began still earlier in Nyasaland (Malawi) with the formation, in 1944, of the Nyasaland African National Congress. This had determined leaders, and was further strengthened in 1958 with the return home, after many years abroad, of a forceful independence pioneer: Dr Hastings Kamuzu Banda. These movements of national union offered a powerful challenge to settler control and colonial government.

Malawi and Zambia: breaking the settlers' power

Their challenge in these two countries was a peaceful one. Its central claim was that parliament and government should be decided by democratic elections. If all grown-up persons had the vote, the result would be majority rule: necessarily, African majority rule. The settlers would have their share of power, but it would be a minority share because they were few.

Neither the settlers, nor at first the colonial governments, would listen to this claim. Collisions followed, though smaller than in Kenya. Both Kaunda and Banda were arrested, and many others. A state of emergency declared in Nyasaland in 1959 led to the death of 52 Africans, and many arrests. Two years later there were more collisions in Northern Rhodesia, when 27 Africans were killed in clashes and some 3,000 arrested.

But in 1961 colonial policy began to change. Under strong African pressure, Britain allowed a step-by-step advance towards democratic elections. In August 1961 a newly-formed Malawi (Nyasaland) Congress Party, with Banda again firmly in the lead, won a large majority of seats in the local parliament. In January 1963 Malawi achieved internal self-government; and in July 1964 it became an independent state. Meanwhile, the same advances were made in Northern Rhodesia, where, in January 1964, UNIP with Kaunda in the lead also won a large majority of seats in the local parliament. Northern Rhodesia became the independent state of Zambia in the following October.

By the end of 1963, these advances had utterly destroyed the settlers' federation; and it had to be dissolved.

Rhodesia: the settlers' republic

South of the Zambezi River, in Southern Rhodesia (known as Rhodesia after Northern Rhodesia became Zambia), the African majority and the settler minority had each been watching the tide of anti-colonial change as it swept south towards them. It encouraged the Africans. But it greatly worried settlers who already had all power and privilege in Rhodesia, and were determined to keep both.

By 1960, these settlers were asking the British government in London to let them become independent in name as well as in fact; then, they believed, the tide of change would never be able to cross southward over the Zambezi. But the British government, already warned by the great rebellion in Kenya and fearing other bad collisions, refused to agree. It replied that Rhodesia could have full independence only when the settlers agreed to accept African majority rule at some time in the future.

Some of the less extreme settlers did agree to this. Their government accepted a new constitution, in 1961, which gave Africans a small share in parliament. This was very little; but it proved too much for most of the settlers. A new settler government came to power in 1963, formed by an extreme racist party called the Rhodesia Front.

This government again demanded full independence, and London still refused. Faced with that refusal, the most extreme settlers took the lead. Under a government led by Ian Smith, they rebelled against Britain in November 1965. They declared that Rhodesia was independent under their minority rule. This was called UDI – unilateral (one-sided) declaration of independence.

Though a painful blow to British prestige, this rebellion was met with little more than verbal protest from London, and then, hesitatingly, by partial economic sanctions against the Smith government. These British sanctions were adopted by the UN, but the 'bite' in their blockade had many missing teeth. Unlike the sanctions applied against fascist Italy in 1935, these sanctions included oil; but that was only in theory, as in practice oil supplies continued to get through to Rhodesia. Besides that, South Africa and Portugal (then in control of neighbouring Mozambique) refused to apply the sanctions. Both of these backed the settlers' rebellion, as did some big-business interests in Britain and elsewhere.

Another war for freedom

Ian Smith's government was able to carry on. It did so by hitting still harder at all African protest of any kind. At the same time, it multiplied laws to safeguard and enlarge settler power and privilege. For most Africans, Rhodesia became a police state.

The question for African nationalists was what to do next? Their organisations were badly hit by settler repression, and found it hard to find the answer. Here, too, colonial tribalism had its dividing influence, making it difficult to build a firm unity beteeen the Shona majority and the Ndebele minority. Apart from that, some nationalists continued to think that peaceful protest was still the only way, however little it could promise. But by this time there were others who thought differently. They believed that armed resistance was necessary, as earlier in Algeria and now in the Portuguese colonies (see p. 140).

The earliest mass party, the African National Congress of Southern Rhodesia (formed 1957), had proved a failure. A more determined party, Zimbabwe African People's Union (ZAPU), had appeared in 1961. Two years later ZAPU split. A big section broke away and took the name of Zimbabwe African National Union (ZANU). It called for more determined action. Almost at once, the Smith government arrested as many of the leaders of both parties as it could find, while others, escaping, went into exile (mostly in Zambia, independent late in 1964).

Now there was no way left but armed resistance. Yet this was hard to carry out with any success, until the mass of African people inside Rhodesia (Zimbabwe) were ready to support and take part in the struggle. Time was needed to win that support and participation. Zimbabwe guerrillas sent in from Zambia made their first armed attacks in 1966–67. But all failed, as did others later.

The decisive change came only in 1972. Zimbabwe guerrillas had by then gained experience in fighting alongside Frelimo guerrillas, in north-western Mozambique, against joint Portuguese and Rhodesian forces. And when Frelimo defeated the Portuguese in 1975, Zimbabwe guerrillas were able to use Mozambique, as well as Zambia, as a base for a bigger effort. Meanwhile, African opinion inside Rhodesia began to accept the need for war. Great numbers of fighting volunteers came forward.

Mostly ZANU men, the guerrillas won control of a big part of Rhodesia by 1978. The settlers faced defeat. They tried to win over African opinion by forming a joint government of their Rhodesia Front and an African party under Bishop Abel Muzorewa. But the trick, though with backing from Britain and the USA, proved a failure. ZANU, and ZAPU on a smaller scale, continued to fight.

Their victory came in 1980. With the settlers beaten, Britain agreed to a one-man one-vote election. ZANU swept the polls; it won most of the African seats in parliament, while ZAPU took the rest. This great majority formed a new government under Robert Mugabe, leader of ZANU, and Rhodesia at once became the independent republic of Zimbabwe.

CHAPTER 15
In other empires:
Belgian, Portuguese, Spanish

Many peoples were enclosed, by partition, in the vast colonies of Belgium and Portugal. To them, the movement of liberating ideas came later than elsewhere. Various reasons explain this.

Belgian repression: unhappy outcomes

The Belgians prevented the emergence of an educated few who could lead the way to new ideas. They refused to allow any of 'their Africans' to study overseas, or even attend secondary school. The Portuguese were less repressive in this way, but more repressive in other ways.

It was exceptionally difficult for Africans in these colonies to make the advance from colonial tribalism to modern nationalism. When they made this advance, late in the 1950s, the road ahead proved exceptionally difficult to follow.

From the Belgian Congo to Zaïre

In size of territory, the Belgian Congo was huge, several times' larger than Nigeria or Kenya or Tanganyika. But its population, six times smaller than Nigeria's, was spread thinly through great forests and grasslands, and so had evolved into many communities and cultures.

These peoples were unable to combine in defence of their common interests. On the contrary, they were carefully divided from each other by colonial government. One 'tribe' was played off against another 'tribe'. Men from one region were recruited into the colonial army, the *Force Publique*, and sent to 'pacify' the people of other regions. There were many anti-colonial revolts in the 1920s and 1930s, and even during the 1940s. None gave rise to any wide resistance because each, in isolation, was defeated on its own.

But here, too, the Second World War worked its changes. With more forced labour, with a greater drive for export-crops, villages grew poorer. From about 1942, there came the beginning of a 'flight to the towns'. As we have seen earlier, small colonial towns such as Léopoldville (Kinshasa) and Elizabethville (Lubumbashi), grew into large concentrations of village people looking for food and jobs.

The Belgians tried hard to stop this flight. But they were no more successful than other colonial rulers. Village people went on coming to the towns. Often they failed to find food or jobs. But among the things they did find were new ideas about how to combine together, and why combining could help them. Soon, tribal unions were many. And then, early in the 1950s, there came the first ideas about nationalism, about national union.

At first, the Belgians put down all such ideas, and imprisoned anyone who tried to use those ideas for political action. But the times were changing in other colonies; and the Belgians, after 1955, gave a little ground. They began to allow political parties. Most of these grew out of tribal unions or associations such as the Bakongo Alliance, ABAKO; and each had a narrowly regional base.

Only two of the new parties, formed late in the 1950s, had any real loyalty to the idea of all-Congolese unity of action and aim. Of these two national parties or movements, by far the more important was the Congolese National Movement (in French: MNC), formed in 1959 under the lead of Patrice Lumumba (1925–1961).

Pressure for anti-colonial change now grew fast. In 1959, after anti-colonial rioting in Léopoldville, the Belgians at last decided to try to catch up with those pressures. Up till then, they had believed that 'their Congo' would remain theirs for many more years, perhaps for another century. Suddenly, they changed their strategy. In January 1960 they offered to give independence only six months later. However intended, this could only be a plan for confusion and disaster. The new parties had no political experience. Most were little more than tribal groups. The civil service had no Africans in senior posts. The *Force Publique* did not possess a single African officer.

Independence came in June 1960, with Lumumba as prime minister; but so did confusion and disaster. Most of the Belgian civil servants went home at once. Soldiers of the *Force Publique* mutinied. Separatist tribal parties in Katanga (now re-named Shaba) and Kasai provinces lost no time in trying to form their own separate governments. Foreign business interests, especially in mineral-rich Katanga, supported this separatism.

As the only unifying political force in the country, Lumumba and his government (MNC with some smaller partners) appealed for United Nations help against mutiny and separatism. This help came, together with UN military contingents provided by several African and other countries. It did in fact help to bring regional separatism to an end, but its outcome was a failure to support or protect Prime Minister Lumumba and his government. There were many troubles, but what made matters worse was that the affairs of the ex-Belgian

Congo, now called Zaïre, became entangled with international politics.

Power was seized in September 1960, only three months after independence and in circumstances of great confusion, by an army officer called Joseph Mobutu. He was given strong Western support, especially American, on the grounds that he was 'pro-Western' while Lumumba, it was alleged, was hostile to Western interests. But the evidence shows that Lumumba merely wished to follow policies of non-alignment and, so far as possible, of independence.

Faced with Mobutu's military take-over, and fearing what might happen next, Lumumba sought the protection of the United Nations in Léopoldville (Kinshasa), and received it. But in December he left this protection and tried to make his way to Stanleyville (Kisangani) where he had strong support. He was seized by men under Mobutu's orders, and in January 1961 was flown as a prisoner to Elisabethville (Lubumbashi), at that time still the capital of the Katanga (Shaba) separatists led by Moise Tsombe. These separatists at once murdered Lumumba.

Many upsets followed, and civil war. MNC leaders formed a government in Stanleyville to oppose a new Léopoldville government formed after Lumumba's murder; and then, in 1964, two major rebellions broke out, led by Lumumbists such as Gaston Soumialot and Pierre Mulele, against the government in Léopoldville. These spread across large regions but rapidly failed, and were put down before the end of the year by General Mobutu's army with the aid of American and Belgian paratroops and foreign mercenaries. Following upon this, General Mobutu dissolved the Léopoldville government in 1965, and declared himself the country's ruler. After that he remained in personal control of the situation, while the country's economy fell ever more deeply into corruption and dependence on Western loans. Opposition protests failed to win any wide unity of support. It was remarked, however, that the name of Lumumba and the patriotic cause for which he had stood were not forgotten. Fresh dissidence broke out from time to time. It was contained, but it continued.

Ruanda and Burundi

The fate of the Belgian trusteeship territory, for a long time, was not much less unhappy. In 1962, Ruanda-Urundi became the two independent states of Ruanda and Burundi, but once again with a legacy of sharp internal divisions.

Here the Belgians had ruled indirectly, largely through the chiefs of the Tutsi, a people who numbered about one-sixth of the population, while the rest of the population, the Hutu (with about one per cent of Twa, or 'pygmies'), provided most of the colonial labour and taxes. Parties formed in 1959 reflected these old and less old divisions. The approach to independence was a brief period of rapidly growing rivalries between Tutsi and Hutu.

Rivalries turned to violence. Soon after independence the Hutu majority in Ruanda won control at the expense of the Tutsi minority, but with much upheaval. In Burundi the Tutsi minority managed to stay in control, but at great cost. A Hutu rebellion, in 1972, was met with stiff Tutsi repression. Thousands died. Not till well into the 1970s, by which time many refugees had fled into neighbouring countries, did Burundi begin to overcome its legacy of conflict.

Wars of liberation in the Portuguese colonies

From an African point of view, Portuguese rule was much like that of Belgium. It was a particularly stiff dictatorship, with Africans divided into 'tribal' compartments. Not even the white-settler minorities were allowed to form political parties of their own. The colonial authorities ruled everything.

There were also some differences. Unlike the Belgians, the Portuguese rulers never changed their minds about refusing all African demands. They were privately sure that Portugal itself was too backward and too poor to support change. They must hold on to everything or else lose everything. While this belief was probably accurate, it unavoidably prepared the ground for violence on the scale of French-ruled Algeria.

The Portuguese, like the French, had a policy of assimilation. They were ready to allow a small number of Africans to become 'black Portuguese'. These could have some civil rights, though no political rights, and they were very few in number. By 1950, fewer than one in every hundred Africans of Angola and Mozambique, and fewer than one in every three hundred in Guiné (Guinea-Bissau), were classified as 'assimilated persons' (*assimilados*). All the rest were 'natives' (*indígenas*), subject to forced labour and other racist persecution.

Most of these rare *assimilados* joined the Portuguese system and served it. But a handful turned to anti-colonial thought and action. Among them were several brave and brilliant individuals: notably Amilcar Cabral of Guiné and Cape Verde, Agostinho Neto of Angola, Edouardo Mondlane of Mozambique. They were joined by others from the Cape Verde Islands (where, at least in theory, all the inhabitants were supposed to be Portuguese citizens); notably Aristides Pereira and Pedro Pires.

These men made the advance into modern nationalism. Their way was hard, often going through bitter persecution. But they worked towards the forming of national parties. These emerged in Guiné (Guinea-Bissau) in September 1956, with the underground formation in Bissau of the PAIGC (African Independence Party of Guiné and Cape Verde); in Angola in December 1956, with the formation of the MPLA (People's Liberation Movement of Angola); and in Mozambique in 1962, with the formation of FRELIMO (Mozambique Front of Liberation).

At first these underground movements hoped for peaceful change. They appealed to the Portuguese. They sent messages to the UN, asking for help. But the Portuguese replied with more violent repression, and the UN proved totally ineffective. Soon, the leaders of the liberation movements saw that this violence of the colonial system could only be met effectively by counter-violence. They prepared for armed struggle.

Three wars of liberation followed: from February 1961 in Angola, from January 1963 in Guiné, and from September 1964 in Mozambique. They lasted through many years of savage colonial efforts to destroy the guerilla armies and their political movements. Like the French in Algeria, the Portuguese spared no weapon of mass destruction and no torment of repression. Yet the liberation movements won a complete victory in 1974–75. They liberated their own countries, Guinea-Bissau in 1974, Angola, Mozambique, Cape Verde and São Tomé in 1975. But in doing this they also made it possible for the Portuguese people to liberate themselves from their own dictatorship in Portugal. This was a case, so far unique, where a revolution in Africa led to a revolution in Europe.

That was a long and heroic story. Here we should note two central points.

First, the underground liberation movements had to begin as 'nationalists without nations'. They had to organise and fight in ways that spread and deepened the advance to national union among peoples long divided by their own history, and then by colonial rule. They found that their liberation struggles were a great help in doing this. More and more people saw that there was no choice for them but unity or defeat; and defeat would be terrible disaster. Out of this growing unity – whether in Angola, Guiné, or Mozambique – there came the force to win these bitter wars.

Secondly, they had a different problem from most colonised peoples. For the Portuguese said: 'Either accept our system, or we shall destroy you.' So they could not take over, reform, or improve the Portuguese system: once they began to fight it, they had to destroy it or be destroyed. From top to bottom, if they wished to win, they had to make a revolution against the Portuguese system. They had to build an alternative system of their own.

And this they had to do even while the wars continued. For they liberated wide areas from Portuguese control; and the people of these areas, freed from the Portuguese system, needed a new system of their own. They needed to be led to govern themselves in new ways. Worked out first in liberated areas, these new ways of 'people's power' (*poder popular*) became the basis for independent republics. They formed a new and revolutionary trend in African political action.

The legacy of Spain

During the early years of the Second World War, the pro-nazi dictatorship of Franco in Spain hoped, if the Allies were defeated, to spread its power over Nigeria and the French equatorial colonies. But nazi defeat put an end to such dreams, and, here too, came the beginning of the end of colonial rule.

When France withdrew from Morocco in 1956, Spain had to do the same. Spain's colony in northern Morocco became part of the newly-independent state. So it was the dream of the democratic liberator, Abd al-Krim, that came true: not the dream of Spain's dictator, General Franco.

In 1975 Spain also withdrew from its occupation of the Western Sahara. A conflict over the future of this territory followed between its inhabitants, Morocco, and Mauritania (see p. 219).

Spain's other holdings were the island of Fernando Po (Bioko) off the Nigerian coast, and a small piece of the equatorial mainland, Rio Muni. In 1959 these were re-named as 'provinces of Spain'; their inhabitants were supposed to have become 'black Spaniards'. Newly-formed nationalist parties then began to work for independence. They won some self-government in 1963. In 1968 the two territories became independent as the Republic of Equatorial Guinea.

CHAPTER 16

The 1980s: unfinished business

The ending of the colonial systems had begun with Libya in 1951. Almost thirty years later, with independence for Zimbabwe, the ending was almost complete.

For meanwhile, in the far south, three other British colonies had won their independence. These were the so-called 'High Commission Territories' of Botswana (formerly Bechuanaland), Lesotho (Basutoland) and the kingdom of Swaziland. Their position was difficult, because each was heavily dependent on racist South Africa, and Lesotho, as the map shows, is right inside South Africa. Yet their leaders were determined not to be left behind. Botswana and Lesotho won their independence in 1966, and Swaziland in 1968.

Yet the far south still had unfinished business in this matter of decolonisation. Namibia remained unfree. Above all, there was racist South Africa.

South Africa: new racist plans

As we noted earlier, the Union of South Africa became an independent British Dominion in 1910; and, in 1961, a republic outside the Commonwealth. Through all that time the local whites kept and used all power and privilege, although blacks outnumbered them by four to one. Exploiting African land and labour, as well as Coloured and Asian labour, these whites were rich and arrogant.

By the end of the Second World War, their racist system was no longer based on a purely colonial economy. It had largely ceased, that is, to draw its main wealth from exporting minerals or other raw materials, and from importing manufactured goods in exchange. While its mineral exports remained important, especially gold, this economy had begun to rely on its own manufacturing industries. In short, racist South Africa had now built its own capitalist system.

Up to 1948 this system had been run by governments in which the English-speaking whites had most influence. They were racist in all matters that touched on their interests and privileges; otherwise they could sometimes be 'moderate'. But in 1948 there came a sharp change. A general election brought to power the Afrikaner National

Fig. 7 Patterns of labour migration in southern Africa in 1914, 1939 and 1980

Party; and this party was in all ways a party of extreme racism. It began at once to build a far more rigid system of racism in every field of daily life. They called this system *apartheid* ('separateness').

This was now the climax of the long white dictatorship in South Africa. It completed the building of a very repressive colonial system inside the country. At the same time, the system's new economic strength, noted above, gave these rulers a wider ambition. They began to think of building an indirect colonial system throughout southern and central Africa. Their idea was that South Africa would not need to invade newly-independent African countries to the north. Instead, using economic power and military threats, South Africa would pressure all these countries into accepting its indirect control.

Publicly, this plan was first put forward in 1964 by the then prime minister, Hendrick Verwoerd. He called for the creation of a Southern African Common Market under his government's domination. Replying, most of the member-states of the OAU denounced this plan. But a few listened to it, notably the neo-colonial government of Madagascar until 1972, and Malawi.

Then the tide of liberation surged again southward. In 1975 the two big countries of Mozambique and Angola ceased to be Portuguese colonies. Each became independent under a strongly patriotic African government, determined to refuse all indirect foreign control and to help towards further liberation in the south. Next, racist South Africa's puppet-state of Rhodesia, ruled since 1965 by the Smith government and its allies, vanished in 1980; instead, there came the independent African republic of Zimbabwe, another large setback to South Africa's plans.

Yet South Africa's rulers did not abandon their plans. Continually, they harassed or attacked their African neighbours. Further, they did their utmost to keep their control of Namibia, a country they had long ruled as a colony, although legally it had been assigned to South African 'trusteeship' after the First World War.

The conflict in Namibia

African leaders in Namibia began asking the UN for help, against Namibia's colonial status and its South African racist laws, soon after the Second World War. They asked in vain.

Then a generation of younger men, just as in other colonies earlier, began to form political movements pledged to work for independence. The earliest of these new movements was the South West African Union (SWANU), formed 1959, chiefly among the Herero, Damara and Nama. Much bigger and more determined, the South West African People's Organisation (SWAPO) was formed in 1960, with initial support from the Ovambo people in the north of Namibia. Finding that polite appeals for change made no difference, SWAPO passed to armed struggle in 1966. Its guerrillas attacked the South African occupying forces. Namibian nationalists won mass backing for this anti-colonial action, as well as for workers' strikes against low wages paid by foreign companies.

All these pressures received growing support from the OAU and the UN; and in 1971 the International Court of Justice advised that South Africa's occupation of Namibia was illegal, and said that South Africa must withdraw. Trying to evade this judgment, the South African government worked to divide Namibia into ten 'tribal homelands', and then invent a way of giving a fake independence to Namibia, while South Africa kept the real control. The aim, in short, was to promote modern tribalism against modern nationalism. Against this plan, SWAPO continued to fight for a true independence. While the Western Powers remained unwilling to act against the South African plan, the future stayed uncertain. But further progress towards Namibian liberation seemed likely during the 1980s.

Resistance in South Africa

The developments of the Second World War, and its victory over nazi-fascist racism, brought new hopes of democratic progress to black people in South Africa, as they did elsewhere. But the ruling white minority, whether of English or Afrikaner origin, had no intention of consenting to any such progress. They were determined to maintain their dictatorship over black people so as to exploit black labour and land.

Black people responded with peaceful protest. In 1946, for example, African mineworkers in the Transvaal gold mines went on strike for an improvement in their very low wages. Armed police shot them back to work; thirteen miners were killed and many others wounded. In other, though unconnected, protests, African farmers gathered in demonstrations against laws that hurt them. They achieved nothing.

Instead, life grew harder still. So far, governments formed by the English-origin minority had built up a system of anti-black discrimination which was harsh but still had some loopholes. Now the loopholes were stopped, and the system was made much harsher. A whites-only general election in 1948 gave power to a government formed by the extreme racist party of the Afrikaner-origin minority, the Afrikaner National Party. Year by year after 1948, new forms of persecution of black people were invented, made legal by Acts of the whites-only parliament, and ruthlessly enforced by the police. This was done by additional 'pass laws' (which already insisted that all blacks must carry a series of residence, work or movement permits); by the forced removal of black families from 'whites-only areas'; by the banning of even the mildest political action of protest; by the abolition of such small civic rights as black people had managed to conserve; and by much else. This much harsher form of racist dictatorship is called *apartheid*.

Black organisations launched passive (non-violent) kinds of protest. In 1952, the African National Congress (ANC) and the South African Indian National Congress joined in a campaign of mass demonstrations against the pass laws. To put them down, the government brought in new laws to punish non-violent protesters by lashing with whips or by imprisonment, or both.

Apartheid was said to mean that the two 'races', black and white, were to 'develop separately'. In truth it only meant that the whites continued to rule and exploit in any way they chose, while the blacks continued to be their servants. After the passive-protest campaign against pass laws, all black protest was declared automatically illegal. All black political action, no matter how moderate, was banned.

Even peaceful demonstrations were now met by shooting. In 1960, at the little town of Sharpeville, police fired into a crowd of black people demonstrating against the pass laws, led on this occasion by the Pan-African Congress (PAC, formed in 1959). Sixty-seven men, women and children were killed (several were found to have been shot in the back while running to escape): 186 others were wounded.

This massacre shocked the world, but to African leaders in South Africa it brought a new conviction: peaceful protest of this kind costs lives, but wins nothing. The most determined of them now turned to counter-violence. They began to organise sabotage, but to begin with were betrayed and tracked down. Some of their outstanding men, including the ANC leader Nelson Mandela, were imprisoned for life.

Mass strikes, Black consciousness, Soweto

Workers in many industries took the next step and made their protest felt. In 1972–73 they came out on mass strikes against starvation wages; and this time they were too many for the police to shoot back to work. Thousands won higher wages. Repression ruled as before, but was now met by a new spirit of resistance.

This new spirit appeared also among black students in secondary schools and colleges of higher education. The colleges were founded by the government on a 'tribal' basis: one for Zulu students, another for Sotho students, and so on. Student leaders such as Steve Biko (soon afterwards killed when in prison) saw the need to work for unity against this 'divide-and-rule' system of 'tribal' colleges. In 1969 they formed the South African Student's Organisation (SASO). Then, looking for a way of political action in spite of the repressive laws, they launched in 1970 a movement called Black Consciousness. The successful strikes of 1972–3 gave them fresh encouragement.

Black Consciousness was not a black racist answer to white racism. Its aim was to raise African self-confidence after the defeats of the 1960s. Like SASO, but more widely, it was a political way of working for unity against racist oppression.

Then, in 1975, came the overthrow of Portuguese colonial rule in Mozambique and Angola. This was followed almost at once by another defeat for South Africa's government. It sent its army into free Angola to destroy that newly-independent republic. But the invasion was thrown back. Badly mauled, the South African invaders had to withdraw in March 1976.

These defeats for racism in neighbouring countries gave new hope to South Africa's black people, especially to the younger generations. Meanwhile the strike movement of 1972–73 had grown larger; in 1974, for example, there were 374 strikes by a total of 57,656 workers, and new gains were won. Yet bigger protests now burst upon the scene, at first in the million-strong township of Soweto, near Johannesburg in the Transvaal.

In April–May 1976 the school students of Soweto declared a boycott of their schools, organising it themselves. The police replied by shooting them in the streets. Many were killed or wounded, but the students held firm under their own young leaders; they would not go to school. This was not because they did not want to learn. It was because they did not want to have to learn their lessons in the language of their oppressors, the Afrikaner rulers. But a new government order had just declared that students would have to learn half their subjects in Afrikaans.

That was the immediate reason for protest. Soon it was seen that the political ideas of Black Consciousness and of the banned ANC were also at work. Rapidly, too, the school strikes spread to other towns. They continued for months, a massive demonstration against *apartheid* oppression.

Many students escaped abroad rather than give in. They went secretly over the frontiers. They joined the ANC there. They trained for guerrilla action against the racist system. After 1976, they began returning secretly across the frontiers. Back in South Africa they

South Africa 'Native Reserves' 1913 and 1936

'Black areas' 1913
'Black areas' added by 1936

0   500 km

South Africa: 'Black Homelands' 1982

Homelands
Gazankulu
Kwazulu
Lebowa
Qwaqwa

So-called 'independent states'
Bophuthatswana   Swazi
Transkei   Venda
          Ciskei

launched actions of sabotage, attacks on police stations, railway lines, oil refineries – in other words, on instruments of state repression or targets that contributed to the system's economy. Their ANC-launched guerrilla organisation was called Umkonto wa Sizwe, Spear of the Nations.

At the same time the strike movement had won other gains besides better wages. Black factory workers, striving for unity, had succeeded for the first time in forming groupings of independent trade unions. The largest of these groupings, the Federation of South African Trade Unions (FOSATU), had won 200,000 worker members by 1981, while the racist government, retreating once again, had conceded that unions formed by black workers could be officially registered as 'non-racial' unions, open to members of all the 'races'.

A new stage?

Did all this mark the beginning of a new stage in black resistance, including armed resistance? It is a question for discussion. On their side, the white racists pretended for the benefit of world opinion that they would act more gently in the future. But in fact they introduced new methods of repression.

Claiming that it would give 'equality' to some Africans, the government turned the old 'Native Reserves' into 'Bantu Home-lands' (or 'Bantustans'). These were the tenth part of all South Africa that was 'reserved' for African ownership. They were, in fact, labour reservoirs for the 'white areas'. Desperately poor and over-crowded, they were now given some rights of local self-government, and were even said to be 'independent'. Yet nothing had really changed. The outside world refused to recognise this fake 'independence'.

Meanwhile the racist system went on piling up its armaments. It enlarged its armies. It strengthened its police forces. It multiplied its laws of repression. It continued to attack Mozambique and Angola. It threatened still more destructive aggression in the future.

But now it had to meet a new determination from independent Africa as well as new forms of African action inside South Africa. President Shagari of Nigeria spoke for this in March 1981 during a State visit to Britain. He affirmed that:

the will of the African majority in Namibia and South Africa will triumph in the end, because justice is on their side. Nigeria, therefore, will give all aid to the freedom fighters in those two countries. We shall use every means at our disposal to fight *apartheid*, and to defeat it.

SUMMARY

The struggles for independence

Success in escaping from colonial rule derived from a number of developments. Among these were:

1   The rise of mass movements of nationalism, demanding progress towards independence.
2   The weakening of Britain and France, though for different reasons, by the Second World War.
3   The effects of war experience on African opinion.
4   The rise of America to super-Power status during and as a result of the Second World War. This new America was not interested in helping to maintain the old colonial systems of monopoly. It was ready, for its own purposes, to favour African demands for an end of those systems.
5   Driven to retreat, Britain and then France became willing (in non-settler colonies) to withdraw their political controls and colonial governments. At the same time, they intended to safeguard their long-term economic and other interests. They developed a policy known as neo-colonialism. The French were especially active in promoting it.
6   African nationalists took advantage of this British and French political retreat. They pressed for political independence, believing that this advance could open the way to further advances later.
7   But in all colonies of major white settlement, a peaceful struggle for independence proved vain. The use by Africans of violence to counter the violence of the settler/colonial systems could not be avoided. Long guerrilla struggles ensued. They were painful, but all in the end succeeded.
8   In most colonies a variety of other forms of pressure were used by African organisations. These included strikes and boycotts. Wherever the colonial system would allow it, African trade unions gathered strength in this period of struggle for independence.

By the beginning of the 1980s, almost the whole continent had won free. Some of the newly-independent countries, notably among those that were formerly colonies of France, remained subject to neo-colonial kinds of foreign control, whether financial, commercial, military or administrative. Namibia was still unfree, although with a prospect of winning freedom in the near future. The black communities of South Africa were still subject to the oppressions of South Africa's racist system, called *apartheid*.

PART FOUR

New nations:
progress and problems

Nelson Mandela (1918–) Leader of the African National Congress of South Africa in the 1950s and after. He opposed racist rule by non-violent means until oppression proved these useless. Sentenced to life imprisonment in 1963 he was still in prison in 1982.

Dr T A Lambo Nigerian medical doctor and psychiatric specialist of worldwide reputation. A pioneer in the field of medical health, he became Deputy Director-General of the World Health Organisation in 1973.

Dr Annie Jiagge Ghanaian educationist and high court judge, actively concerned with women's rights. She has held high positions at the UN and, in 1975, became vice-president of the World Council of Churches.

Jeanne Martin Cissé Leading Guinean diplomat and activist for women's rights. Secretary-General of the Conference of African Women, 1962–72, she has held high positions at the UN and in her own country.

Amadou Mahtar M'Bow Senegalese historian and anti-colonial leader, served his country in the field of basic education in 1953–57. In 1974 he became Director-General of the UN Educational, Scientific and Cultural Organisation.

Angie Brooks A distinguished lawyer and diplomat, she was Liberia's permanent representative to the General Assembly of the United Nations from 1954 and served as its President in the 1969 session.

Kip Keino Brilliant success for African athletics has been another of the gains of independence. At the 1972 Olympics the Kenyan runner Kip Keino took the silver medal for 1500 metres, and won the steeplechase.

Justin Fashanu Nigerian-born footballer who has been a prolific goal-scorer for his English football clubs. In 1981 he was transferred from Norwich City F.C. to Nottingham Forest F.C. in a £1 million deal.

Part Four is concerned with questions about the gains, and the problems, of African independence, largely in the years 1960–1980.

Chapter 17   History begins anew
How did independence affect Africa's place in world affairs?
What educational changes came after independence?
What were literacy campaigns? Why were they necessary?
In what ways did business expand?
What are the chief gains of independence?

Chapter 18   Questions about national stability
What was, or is, 'neo-colonialism'?
How was political stability threatened by regionalism? By separatism? By tribalism? By élitism?
How and why did foreign interventions occur?
What were the reasons for military government? Were all military governments of the same kind? If not, how did they differ?
What party systems took shape after independence?
What are *fokolona*? What is 'people's power'?

Chapter 19   Questions about development
What was the colonial economic legacy? What was or is its 'machinery of control'?
Why did food imports increase? What happened to cause growth in the number of Africa's people?
What were the basic requirements of national development?
How did the strategy of private enterprise (capitalism) differ from the strategy of collective enterprise (socialism)?
What were the advantages and disadvantages of each strategy?
What were some of the basic problems of rural development?
What were the advantages and disadvantages of foreign aid?
What was UNCTAD?

Chapter 20   Questions about unity
How did the ideas of pan-Africanism develop after independence?
What were the Mali Federation and the Ghana-Guinea Union?
What were the groupings called Casablanca, Monrovia, Brazzaville?
What is the OAU? When was it founded, and by whom? What does its Charter declare?
What was OCAM?
How did the OAU deal with frontier disputes?
What new steps towards regional co-operation began to appear, and when?

CHAPTER 17

History begins anew

Since achieving independence, Africa's new nations now look back upon years of experiment and change, of upheaval and renewal, of new progress and its problems. Many difficulties have held up their advance to justice and stability. Much remains to be done before the promises of independence can be fully met. Poverty is widespread. A number of governments have failed. Yet none of these troubles has lessened the great fact of anti-colonial liberation. Independence gave Africans the keys to their own future, and the chance to use these keys. They could study their own continent, search for their own solutions, stand free and equal with all mankind.

The time since independence has been a time of development in small things as well as in big. When independence came, cars and trucks and radios, even shoes and bicycles, were for the chosen few. Now they are part of the daily scene, like the industry and science that made them.

Few Africans travelled before independence came. Now thousands travel every week. They are at home when overseas. They have friends in every continent.

The years since independence have been the most important time of change in all of Africa's long history. This time of change has happened very fast. In 1985, every Nigerian born since independence was still under 25; every Kenyan under 22; every Zambian under 21; and every Angolan under 10. Never have young Africans had the privilege of living through so great a time of change and challenge.

We shall look at the troubles and difficulties. But first we shall look at something far more important. We shall look at the gains of independence. They were large, and many.

Citizens of the world

When independence came, the men and women of those days took none of the gains for granted. They had to struggle for them, often meeting violence or persecution; and then they had to struggle to keep them. Rightly, they saw the gains of independence as victories for progress.

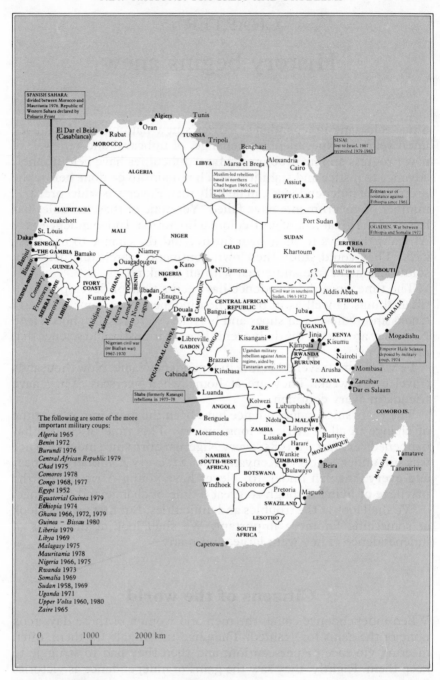

Fig. 9 Independent Africa, 1980. South Africa remains a white-ruled state

The racism of the colonial rulers gripped them at every stage. All the colonial systems, as we have seen, used the weapon of racism. They used it to keep Africans at the bottom of the ladder of development. They used it to teach Africans that the bottom of the ladder was their proper place. Consider again, for a moment, what this really meant.

In Zambia, before independence came, no African worker was allowed to drive a railway train; he could only shovel coal for the white-settler driver. In Kenya, for many years, no African farmer could share in the profits of growing coffee; that was a 'white man's crop'. No Ugandan could gin the cotton he had grown. In the Belgian Congo, no African could move from one place to another without permission from the police. In the Portuguese colonies, many farmers could not even decide which crops they would grow. Even in more advanced colonies, such as Nigeria, all banking and big business were long barred to African enterprise, or, if a few Africans could enter those fields in West Africa, their operations were severely restricted. Only a handful of Africans, no matter how talented, could hope for reasonable jobs in public service or academic work. Beyond all such handicaps, no Africans could determine the policies of governing their own countries. They could not even study long enough to learn the facts and figures that were needed in order to govern.

This all-powerful weapon of colonial racism could be destroyed when independence came. Free of its oppression, Africans could begin to develop their talents and energies. A new confidence flowed from this freedom, a new self-respect, as well as openings for every kind of job or duty. There came a revolution in Africa's chances, a revolution in Africa's standing in the world.

Africans could begin to know their own continent. Before independence came, even the few Africans in secondary schools could know little about countries outside the colony they were in. 'French Africans' could learn something about 'French Africa', and more about France. But they could learn nothing about the rest of Africa. 'British West Africans' might learn about British history or geography, but little or nothing about the history or geography of their own countries.

Now the gates of knowledge were opened. Africans could learn about other continents and peoples. They could become citizens of the world as well as of their own countries. They could take their place in the councils of the world: in the assemblies and organisations of the United Nations as well as in world-wide meetings of the non-aligned movement and other such bodies.

A revolution in education

Knowledge is the way to understanding; and understanding is the way to power. The colonial systems blocked each of these ways. The systems were there to keep power for the colonial rulers.

Missionary schools and government schools existed before independence. But most of them were colonial schools; they taught colonial values. Basically, as we have seen, these were racist values (see Chapter 8). Such schools provided an inferior education for people who were said to be inferior; they were also not many. Even in the least backward colonies, by 1960, no more than ten children in every hundred could hope for a place in a primary school. In the most backward colonies only one in every hundred, or fewer still, could hope for such a place.

When independence came, a revolution in education was therefore needed. Independent governments had to provide many more schools and teachers. This need in quantity was all the more urgent because the size of African populations was now growing fast. From the 1950s, Africa became a very youthful continent compared with Europe or North America. By 1975, for example, 442 Africans in every 1,000 were under 15: whereas the corresponding proportion for the industrialised countries was only 260 in every 1,000.

But quantity was not the only need. There was also need for a new quality in education. Consider three statements about the kind of education provided by the colonial systems. The first is by the Nigerian historian J.F. Ade Ajayi. He wrote that the colonial education of the black student had been controlled:

> not only through the prejudices of the white teacher and the white textbook author, but also sometimes by actual directives of the administrations in laws said to be designed for the best interests of the black man.

Discussing the same subject in 1967, the President of Tanzania Julius Nyerere wrote:

> [colonial education] was not designed to prepare young people for the service of their country. Instead, it was motivated by a desire to inculcate the values of the colonial society, and to train individuals for the service of the colonial state. . . . This meant that colonial education induced attitudes of human inequality, and, in practice, underpinned the domination of the weak by the strong, especially in the economic field.

This meant, in practice, that colonial education for Africans was education for inferiority. In their franker moments, the colonial rulers said as much. Here is what the Patriarch of Lisbon, Cardinal Cerejeira, told 'Portuguese Africa' in a Christmas message of 1960:

> We need schools in Africa, but schools in which we show the native the way to the dignity of man and the glory of the nation (Portugal) which protects him. We want to teach the natives to write, to read, and to count, but not to make them learned men.

Improving the quality of education, after independence, proved more difficult than increasing the quantity. And wherever countries became independent under indirect foreign control, as usually by the French plan (see pp. 112–113), the quality scarcely improved. Madagascar was an example. It became independent under indirect French control in 1960, and won a real independence after 1972. Its new leaders then said that Madagascan education, up till then, had been totally inadequate:

> a system of teaching which is out-of-date and out-of-touch with real life and with the country's needs; it has done nothing but increase joblessness and under-employment.

Faced with these needs for improvement, both in quality and quantity, strongly independent governments acted with vigour and success. In quantity, at least, the expansion was general throughout the continent. In 44 African countries, between 1960 and 1972, the number of students attending school at the three levels – primary, secondary, higher – rose from 17.8 million to 37.6 million. In twelve years of effort, school attendances more than doubled.

Another part of the colonial legacy in education was the inferior position of girls, reflecting the inferior position of women. Many fewer girls got to school than boys. Some effort was begun to be made towards righting this. The proportion of African girls and young women who were getting education, between the ages of 6 and 19, became a little larger. In 1960 this proportion was 33.7 per cent of all students then at school; in 1972 it was 37.6 per cent of double the total of students. The proportion of girls and young women getting education in Africa was still lower than in Asia, and much lower than in Latin America. Yet it was also true that the actual number of girls and young women in education had more than doubled since 1960.

At the same time, new lessons and classes aimed at giving students a 'decolonised' education. Generally, syllabuses and textbooks were

Africanised: that is, they were redesigned to meet the realities and needs of Africa, not of Europe. This was done, with much success, in two ways: first, in terms of what was taught; secondly, in providing different types of education after the primary level.

In terms of syllabus, for example, students now began to be taught the history of their own peoples, instead of the history of Europe's peoples. As never before, students could learn about the past development of their own countries and regions, instead of being taught that all development came from Europe. In terms of different types of education, new kinds of schools and colleges were opened with specially trained staffs: vocational schools for practical training, agricultural schools, medical schools, colleges of various kinds. New universities were founded to give African students a wider chance of standing level with highly educated persons overseas. More African scholars could take their place in countless meetings and conferences of learned people in other continents. In these ways, too, Africans became citizens of the world.

A pointer to the aims of independent Africa, in this great matter of education, was found in 1965, at a conference of African educational authorities in Addis Ababa, the capital of Ethiopia. Drawing up a charter for further development, they laid down the following conditions:

1 Primary education shall be universal, compulsory, and free.
2 Education at the secondary level shall be provided for 30 per cent of the children who complete primary school.
3 Higher education shall be provided, mostly in Africa itself, for 20 per cent of those who complete secondary education.
4 The improvement of the quality of African schools and universities shall be a constant aim.

If we summarise the gains that were made by the 1970s, we shall see that they were of great importance. There was huge expansion in quantity in all but the poorest countries; there was some expansion even in those. This often went together with a 'cultural revolution' in what was taught. Students in new schools could learn about the worth and dignity of African traditions and beliefs. They could open their minds to the science of the modern world. They could reinforce their understanding of the need for national unity in facing common problems.

Kenya, for example, had many different peoples formed by a long history, each with different traditions and beliefs. The new Kenya educational system did not deny those differences. But it gave all

Kenya students a common ground to stand on: all could learn the same lessons of national unity, all could feel gathered into the same nation. And so it was, often, in other countries too.

Along with these gains, there were others. In the less backward countries there were important advances in the field of social hygiene, and the provision of nurses, doctors, clinics, hospitals.

The best of the independent governments fully recognised that this expansion must continue. There were more schools and teachers by the 1970s; in the stronger countries, many more. But the size of populations was still outgrowing them. A race developed between growing numbers of young people and growing numbers of school places. Lack of resources, or bad government in the weaker countries, meant that the first could overtake the second.

African educational pioneers saw this problem. Between 1960 and 1972, for example, independent governments provided more than 16 million new primary school places. But the growth of population, during those same years, provided almost as many more children between six and eleven years of age; and this growth was still rising fast. Soon it was also seen that the target for secondary school places – 30 per cent, as the 1965 charter urged, of all children completing primary school – could not be reached by 1980. Only in higher education was the target reached and even passed. By 1972, for the whole continent, there were three African students in higher education for every two in 1965.

Apart from a shortfall in primary and secondary places, there were wide differences between countries. By the middle 1970s, for example, Ghana had found primary school places for about 70 per cent of all Ghanaian children in the primary age-group. Yet neighbouring Upper Volta, much poorer and less independent, had found places for only 10 per cent. Then in some countries, perhaps in most, the standards of teaching and examination-passing fell away as rapid expansion continued. That could not be avoided, but more time and fresh effort were needed to put it right. Another result of very rapid expansion was that the number of 'drop-outs' in or after primary school became disturbingly high; it proved hard to reduce.

As elsewhere in the world, the conclusion was that progress and new problems went hand-in-hand. Great advances were made; and on a scale never even thinkable before. Just as surely, tough problems arose in line with this progress. Yet here, too, there was another difference from the colonial past. In the truly independent countries, and sometimes even in the nominally independent ones (chiefly of the former French empire), these problems could now be understood, discussed, and tackled.

Language and literacy:
Swahili and Somali examples

Africa has more than 700 languages. Many are spoken by small communities. Some are spoken by numerous peoples, though often in different dialects: such is the case with the Yoruba language in Nigeria, and the various branches of Akan or Twi in Ghana. A few are spoken by several or many neighbouring peoples. Important among the last are Arabic in North Africa and Sudan; Swahili in East Africa; and Hausa in West Africa.

When independence came, a number of African peoples had long used a 'common language' between each other such as Arabic, Swahili, or Hausa, for purposes of trade and discussion. But because most countries had many languages, most new states had to continue using the European language of their former colonial rulers. Perhaps the future would change this situation. Meanwhile most students, at least after primary school (and often during primary school), had to learn their lessons in a European language. In some cases, however, there could be progress towards a different solution. That was so, for example, with Swahili and Somali.

Used for centuries along the eastern coast of Africa, Swahili is a large and flexible African language with an intake of Arabic forms and words. Its very name indicates this, for it derives from the Arabic word for coastland. Gradually, spreading inland, Swahili became the second language of many peoples in Kenya and Tanzania. When independence came, the new governments of those countries could almost at once decide to adopt Swahili as a national language. Progress could be made towards using Swahili as the language of instruction in schools.

Like Arabic in North Africa (and elsewhere in Muslim regions), Swahili had long possessed its own way of being written. Arabic writing dates from the earliest times of Islam. Swahili began to be written, several centuries ago, in a form of Arabic writing; afterwards, in the colonial period, it began to be written in the western (Latin) alphabet. So the use of Swahili as a national language raised no problem about how to write it.

Somali was an interestingly different case. When Somalia became independent in 1960, there was no difficulty about deciding that Somali should be the national language, for nearly all the people of Somalia are Somalis. The difficulty came in knowing how to write Somali. The colonial rulers had mostly ignored the Somali language: the Italians had ruled in Italian, and the British had ruled in English.

Learned Somali Muslims had tried to write their language in an Arabic script, but this proved inefficient because of the linguistic differences between Somali and Arabic. How else could they write it? At last, in 1972, Somalia's government and academics agreed to write Somali in the western (Latin) alphabet. They found this worked well. Somali became a national written language as well as a spoken one, and here again progress could be launched in using Somali as the language of instruction in schools.

Yet writing a language is not much use unless many people can read it. The knowledge of how to read and write, *literacy*, was very rare in the colonial period; only the educated few possessed it. Independence brought the need, but also the possibility, of changing that. Many literacy campaigns were launched, often linked with the teaching of elementary arithmetic.

Given all the difficulties, the results of these campaigns were impressive. Between 1961 and 1970, the proportion of illiterate persons – people knowing neither how to read nor how to write – fell steadily throughout most of the continent. But of course the number of illiterates remained high. For the problem of literacy was not only how to teach people to read and write. It was also how to produce conditions in which people form the habit of reading and writing, and go on doing both.

By 1970 it seemed likely that only about 27 per cent of Africans had achieved a firm grasp of literacy; large territories such as Angola and Mozambique had still, at that time, to be liberated from colonial ignorance. After this, the growth of population began to outrun the literacy campaigns, and fresh efforts were needed.

Education: a summary

By 1980, to sum up, the results of educational and literacy expansion were already much better than anything ever achieved before. Sometimes, as in Nigeria and Ghana, or in East and Central Africa, they were sensationally better. In Angola, to quote another example, fewer than 350,000 Africans were in colonial primary schools before independence in 1975. By 1980 about 1,500,000 Angolans were in primary schools with new syllabuses and new textbooks.

Were women helped as much as men, girls as much as boys? Here again the legacy of the past laid on a heavy handicap. In general, the colonial period worsened the position of most women, whether in daily life or work. They were more exploited even than before. When husbands and brothers had to leave home on forced labour, or as migrants seeking the money to pay tax and to buy useful things such as farming tools, wives and sisters were left with more work than before: in gardens, in the fields, in the home. Through all the long social crisis of the Great Depression and the Second World War, women had to bear the heaviest burdens of poverty.

This injustice began to be removed after independence. More girls and young women went to school. Adult women joined literacy classes. A wider range of jobs was opened to women in towns. Women began to speak for themselves: they said that they were still second-class citizens in their own countries. After about 1970, they began to unite in women's organisations with the aim of struggling for more equality and respect. They began to form their own assemblies and committees, and frame their own plans for improvement. Here was another gain from independence.

New artists, new arts, journalism

Freedoms came, with independence, that were valuable across the whole field of culture. Growing from many seeds, a new harvest of the arts began to ripen.

The older arts of Africa, as everyone knows, had long been famous up and down the world. Many countries had museums which honoured African sculpture in wood and metal, cloth-weaving, jewel-making, and much else that was done in the past. But most of those old arts died during the colonial period. Then the 'world outside Africa' said that Africa had no more makers of art.

But independence showed that the 'world outside Africa' was wrong about this. The old skills were now revived in new skills. Aside from drumming and dancing, which of course had never stopped, Africa's peoples began to reveal a new originality and inspiration. New kinds of sculpture won praise at home and overseas: work of high quality in wood or stone or metal, whether in Nigeria or Ghana, Zimbabwe or Zambia, Tanzania or Kenya, or elsewhere. New kinds of dramatic art came to the fore: with new theatre groups and plays, new dances and rhythms, new displays of mime and comedy. Once again the genius of Africa was free to move and speak.

Many 'popular arts' began to flourish: those of sign-writing, of painting scenes on transport-trucks, of decorating the walls of houses, of cloth-weaving in fresh designs and colours. All these sang a song of freedom: of the new freedom for artists to depict the way we live today in all its sorrows and its joys.

Other arts were added: arts of the modern world such as writing for publication in poetry and prose. As early as the 1960s, the novels and verse of new African writers began to make their mark in many countries. Gradually, as literacy grew in the 1970s, these written arts began to have a wider audience at home as well as overseas.

Another development added to this cultural revolution. This was the rapid growth of bigger and better means of public information: by national news agencies, many newspapers, broadcasting, book-publishing, cinema, television.

African·journalism was far from new when independence came. Sierra Leone had its first African owner-editor as early as 1855, while the Gold Coast had another, Charles Bannerman, as early as 1857. During colonial times, British West Africa possessed an exciting range of lively African newspapers, sometimes edited by outstanding journalists such as Thomas Horatio Jackson of Nigeria. But there were few African newspapers anywhere else; in many colonies there was none at all.

After independence, this also began to change. In the more advanced countries, African newspapers enormously expanded their circulations; even the poorest country now had some kind of newspaper. Here too, of course, there were big contrasts. Writing of the 1960s, the Ghanaian scholar Jones-Quartey has noted that the English-speaking countries, in West Africa, were ahead of the French-speaking countries. Even by 1967, Nigeria was far in advance of others with 18 daily newspapers, 15 weeklies, and 22 periodicals, several with very big daily sales; as well as 17 radio-transmitters broadcasting in many languages to nearly 700,000 radio-receiving sets; and five television stations. Compared with that, the richest of the ex-French West African countries, Ivory Coast, was a long way behind.

Progress again brought its problems. All this vast expansion in the news media raised tough questions about censorship and government control. Critics tackled these questions. Summing up the publishing scene in West Africa (but the same was true in other regions), Jones-Quartey found much to criticise. He said that this was:

> all in all, and everywhere, a period of uneven struggle for the West African press, and one also of monumental misconceiving of role and responsibility on the part of fast-changing, mostly authoritarian governments.

In this, however, Africa was again no exception in the world.

Business expansion

With independence, Africa's peoples won the opportunity not only to govern themselves but also to speak for themselves, and, through their many arts and media, to display the strength and fertility of their cultures. There were comparable gains in other fields. African businessmen, at last, could move into many fields of enterprise and profit-making from which, during colonial times, they were debarred by foreign monopoly or racist bans.

How far they could do this depended on the degree of economic or other indirect control still kept by outside powers and business interests. In the weakest countries, African businessmen could often do little more, even now, than serve as junior agents of foreign businessmen. By the 1970s, however, there were strong countries where Africans had taken over a wide field of managerial and business enterprises. Here we should note some central points of change.

First, it was possible to take national control over money, credit, banking and investment across a wide area of business activity. It was possible to nationalise foreign banking and insurance interests, as well as promoting the interests of African banks and companies. As understanding of economic matters widened, it was possible to construct national plans for the development of national resources. All this meant that the stronger countries could begin to decolonise their economies: that is, chiefly, to cut down the amount of their wealth that had always gone overseas during the colonial period.

In another field of progress, it was possible to introduce crash programmes for the rapid training of men and women who could take the place of European or other foreign technicians, managers, civil servants, and professional persons. Even the weakest of the newly-independent countries were able to make some progress in this Africanising of their managerial and professional jobs.

The gains of independence: an overview

These were made in every field of national life. They were political, cultural, social and economic.

Political gains included the power to build national political systems capable of making national decisions, and shaping national policies, for the present and the future. The power to reduce, or remove, foreign political controls. The power to experiment with different policies, solutions, constitutions and new ideas across the whole range of self-government. The power to work towards new forms of unity within, and between, African nations. In all these ways, the political gains of independence gave another power: they restored to Africans the power to make their own mistakes in policy and government, and, therefore, the power to learn how not to make mistakes.

Cultural gains included the destruction of the colonial weapon of racism. They reinforced the right of Africans, now recognised by all the world, to stand equal with the rest of mankind after long colonial subjection. These cultural gains broke through the isolation of Africa's peoples; through their ignorance of their own continent and of the world; through all the barriers erected by colonial rule against Africa's self-expression and intellectual development.

Social gains included the opportunity to build modern services in public health as well as public education; to bring the benefits of modern science to the work of improving everyday conditions of life; to train qualified men and women for all such services; to overcome ignorance or superstition about the causes of bad health and social conflict. Not least, social gains gave the power to reduce the many inequalities suffered by women.

Economic gains included the power to build national plans for national development, to command national resources, and to own and manage all kinds of business enterprise. They also included the power to experiment with new kinds of economic policy, organis-ation, and control; and the opportunity to join, whenever desirable, with other African countries in joint plans or enterprises. Above all, these economic gains gave independent countries the power to cut down, and step-by-step cut out, the transfer of Africa's wealth to countries overseas; and to use Africa's wealth, more and more, for Africa's own benefit.

The challenge of independence

But how far, in practice, was it possible for the new states to *defend* these gains of independence, and build them into everyday life? How far, in practice, could the new states *use* these powers for the good of their peoples?

All of the new states, in these early years after independence came, had to face the same real challenge. This challenge was how best to strengthen their internal stability, their drive for development, and their unity of action.

Yet the new states were not all in the same situation. Some of them suffered from much bigger problems than others. Some were much poorer than others. So the story of what happened to them, after independence, greatly differed. Some succeeded very well, others very little. A few failed altogether.

The next three chapters discuss the reasons for these differences, and the problems which the new states had to meet.

CHAPTER 18
Questions about national stability

All peoples, winning their freedom, have had to go on wrestling with the handicaps of their own history: with the legacy left to them by the past. The gains of independence, and the powers these have given, have had to be measured against the weight and drag of those handicaps. So the questions we need to ask, when looking at the years since independence, have to refer to the struggle between old handicaps and new powers.

This struggle can be examined from many points of view. We shall examine it in three main fields of effort and experiment: the struggle for political stability, the struggle for economic development, and the struggle for unity both within and beyond national frontiers. Each has a chapter to itself.

How much independence? Neo-colonialism

A first and general point to keep in mind in this chapter, but also in the next two chapters, is that independence could not be complete (see also chapter 9). There were limits placed around the powers it gave. The width of these limits varied from country to country. What could be done within those limits also varied.

In the economic field, as will be seen in the next chapter, limits on the powers given by independence were often narrow. Each new nation, becoming independent, found itself tied to a whole system or network of economic controls and conditions. Partly these controls and conditions were exercised and imposed by the world economic system; and no country could escape from them. Partly they were a carry-over, or a continuation, of the controls and conditions of this or that colonial system. New nations could escape from these, but not at once or easily.

Other limits were in the field of culture and education. Here, too, there was a big carry-over from colonial ideas and colonial schools and teaching. We discussed some aspects of this cultural carry-over, and what was done to escape from it, in the last chapter.

There were also limits on the powers of independence in the political field, in the degree to which new nations were really free to govern themselves and settle their own affairs in their own way. Narrowest in the new nations of the former French empire, these limits were an attempt by the former colonial powers to keep an indirect control; to govern indirectly through 'convenient partners'; to undermine a true independence of thought and action.

This attempt at continued overseas control, by indirect means, became a frequent feature of the African scene after the colonial flags were lowered. It came to be called 'neo-colonialism', or new-colonialism, meaning a many-sided attempt by outside powers to tie the new nations closely to the interests and needs of those outside powers. Sometimes this neo-colonial attempt was easy to see, as when France imposed military agreements on its former colonies, so that many of them, when becoming independent, had still to accept the presence of French troops. At other times, when economic pressures were used, the attempt was more difficult to see, as in the treatment of interest-payment on national debts to foreign lenders, or in the refusal to agree to better prices for exports.

Some leaders of modern Africa were unable or unwilling to oppose this neo-colonialism. Others set themselves to defeat it. Their struggle for greater independence, and the struggle of the governments they led and the peoples who followed them, hold a central place in the history of the years since independence.

The legacy of division

Other aspects of the struggle for a fresh start, for a greater independence of thought and action, added to the dramas of that time. We have already touched on this subject. These aspects arose partly from Africa's own history before colonial times, but even more from colonial history.

Africa's own history had produced many independent communities or states. These had developed their own political systems. Often, they had built wide networks of regional trade, and other ways of living and working together. The colonial partition had then taken all these, and reassembled them into some fifty colonies.

Colonial rule destroyed the regional networks of trade and agreement, and, instead, imposed quite different ones. These new colonial networks were designed, primarily, to make African labour and land serve the interests and profit of the colony-owning powers. Colonial governments used force to do this. Afterwards, they used policies of division. They used the instrument of divide-and-rule that we have called 'colonial tribalism.'

The great struggle of the nationalists, before independence, was to overcome this 'colonial tribalism' and to unite peoples into nations.

We have followed some of the achievements of that difficult but necessary struggle.

Nationalism proved strong enough to win the unity that was required to end colonial rule. But it was not strong enough to end the legacy of internal division. It could not be strong enough to do that. Ending the legacy of internal division had to call for years of work and experiment by independent peoples. So this part of the legacy was bound to cause trouble; and it did.

Three periods of effort

The detailed history of the years after independence fills many books on separate national histories. Here we can try to make a summary. Generally, but above all in the countries coming out of the British and French empires, the years after independence passed through three periods or phases of effort, experiment, and renewal.

The first of these periods was rather short. It was when the new nations tried to govern themselves by the means and methods left to them by the departing colonial governments. Mostly, these means and methods were set in place on the day of independence, or shortly before that date. They were constitutions and parliamentary systems on the British or the French or some other European model. They were drawn, that is, from the history and conditions of modern Europe, and not from the history and conditions of modern Africa.

The second period was longer. It was when the new nations found that these means and methods, these institutions of government drawn from Europe's history and conditions, did not work. Often painfully, they broke down. The reasons for these breakdowns were not in the least that Africans were less able to govern themselves, in peace and justice, than Europeans. The inherited means and methods broke down for two quite different reasons.

One reason was that these means and methods, left behind by colonial rule, proved a poor weapon against the legacy of tribalism or other divisions of the past. The other reason for breakdown was a sharp contradiction. On the one hand, the new nations took over laws and habits of colonial dictatorship. On the other hand, they acquired parliaments which were supposed to be democratic. Old laws or habits, and new laws or habits, came into conflict.

With breakdown of the means and methods of government left behind by colonial rule, there was an urgent need to fill the resulting vacuum or absence of political power. This was when one or another kind of military government stepped in.

The third period began during the 1970s. This was when new nations began to search for their own answers to the problems of government and development, and to experiment with their own ways of finding justice and peace.

The whole story has been rich and various. It has indeed reflected the problems of the modern world in all countries everywhere. The influence of the colonial legacy, or of neo-colonialism, or of too little independence, has led to disasters and defeats. But the struggle against those weaknesses has also led to solutions of success. More and more, as Africans came to grips with their real problems, these successes revealed the work of creative minds and talents. They proved that a better life is possible.

We turn now to some of the major situations met with after independence, and to some examples.

The situation after independence

Overcoming regionalism, separatism

The means and methods of government left behind by the departing colonial rulers did not work. Why was that? Nigeria, Kenya, and Sudan offer three examples from the British model.

As was explained in Chapter 13, Nigeria began independence under a constitution which divided this very large country, and its very numerous population, into three regions. Each was governed by a party representing the majority people in each region: Hausa-Fulani, Yoruba, Igbo; while smaller parties represented other peoples or ethnic groups. Each region also elected members of a federal parliament based in Lagos, the country's capital; and this had power over all-Nigerian matters such as foreign policy and national defence.

There were several reasons why this failed to work. One was that each leading party and its politicians, in each region, tended more and more to govern as though, in fact, its region was a separate country. Each regional government claimed more and more power to take decisions in matters such as commerce and industry; and there were politicians who played this game in order to help their personal careers. For these and for other reasons, there came a sharp rivalry between the regions. The idea of an all-Nigerian unity began to fade.

Another reason for dispute grew out of that rivalry. Who should control the all-Nigerian federal parliament in Lagos? This became a serious source of dispute. As things turned out, the Northern Region's chief party, the NPC, dominated the federal parliament because it had more voters, and therefore more members, than two other big parties in the east and west, the NCNC and AG. So these two parties had to be 'junior partners' in a federal government dominated by the NPC, or else go into opposition. As things turned out, this put the AG into isolation.

Tensions came quickly to breaking-point. A first explosion occurred in the Western Region during 1962, only two years after independence. A split in the AG led to violent strife. The federal government under NPC control tried to end this conflict by further undermining the AG. It imposed a state of emergency in the Western Region, and ruled there through a federal administrator until the beginning of 1963. But this really solved nothing.

Regional rivalries continued to sharpen, especially after a national census of 1964. This produced returns which gave the Northern Region a voting force so big that northern control of the federal parliament seemed bound to continue. On top of that reason for southern dissatisfaction, the Western Region exploded again during a campaign for new general elections in November 1965. By this time there was great bitterness among large sectors of Nigerian public opinion. To make matters worse, some important politicians were widely accused of gross dishonesty and corruption. With continuing violence in the west, and more threatened elsewhere, the politicians now seemed helpless or discredited. In January 1966 the military stepped in and took over national government. For Nigeria, the first period of independence had ended.

What had happened? The answer is that the means and methods left behind by colonial government had encouraged regional rivalries, and personal ambitions, to the point where everything was in confusion. New experiments were urgently required. Nigeria must find its own way to peace and progress.

This proved difficult. A complete collapse of Nigeria into three separate nation-states now threatened. The military were ready to prevent this, but they still had to lead towards long-term solutions. Inflamed regionalism in the north meanwhile brought death and persecution to Igbo living there. In response, Igbo people flocked to the shelter of their Eastern Region. There was now practically a state of war.

In May 1967 a new military president, General Yakubu Gowon, opened a new initiative. He declared that Nigeria was to be divided into twelve federated states, thus dissolving the solid blocks represented by Hausa-Fulani, Igbo, and Yoruba parties. This came too late to prevent bigger trouble. The Igbo leadership in the Eastern Region declared a separate republic of Biafra.

A bitter civil war ensued, with the rest of Nigeria united against the Igbo leadership and its people. With the additional support of the non-Igbo peoples of the Eastern Region (Biafra), Federal Nigeria won this war by the beginning of 1970, and made a tolerant and generous peace.

Nigeria could resume its necessary experiments in finding new means and methods of government. These were carried forward with growing success, at first under General Murtala Muhamed and then under General Oluṣẹgun Ọbasanjọ. The Gowon plan of 1967 for twelve federated states was extended. Nigeria was divided into nineteen federated states. Each had its own government. But strong federal leadership continued at the centre. With regional power thus reorganised, old rivalries could be overcome and progressively thrust aside. Confident in this long-term solution, the Nigerian military stepped back from power in 1979. In 1980 the whole country advanced to a new form of parliamentary government under President Shehu Shagari.

Success by KANU

Kenya was another country which had to find its own way to a system and constitution which fitted its own needs. Kenya was fortunate in being able to do this without violent strife. Though smaller than Nigeria, and with a much smaller population, Kenya was left with a constitution which divided the country into no fewer than seven federated regions, each with its own local government, parliament, civil service, police force, judiciary, border controls and other public services. In the circumstances, different from Nigeria's, this was a way to create the very disunity which Kenya nationalism had striven so hard to overcome. Besides this, critics saw that it would leave the richest region, centred on Nairobi, under powerful white-settler influence, and, perhaps, under white-settler control.

Accepting independence in 1963 with this British constitution, the ruling majority party, KANU under President Jomo Kenyatta, at once set about removing the regionalist threat to national unity. It introduced a new constitution with a single parliament and government for the whole country. This came into force in 1964; and Kenya could then move into a period of political renewal. Many problems of the colonial legacy remained. But the threat to the country's unity was gone.

Sudanese divisions

Another problem of regionalism and separatism, once more arising from past history and the legacy of colonial rule, brought much trouble to the republic of Sudan. Here, acute cultural differences were combined with a legacy of acute colonial division. About four-fifths of all the people of this large country were Muslims, as they are today. They live in the north, centre and west of the Sudan; and most of them speak Arabic. The remaining fifth live in the distant south. Few of these southerners are Muslims; many are Christians. They speak Dinka, Nuer, Shilluk, and other languages.

A North-South confrontation

These differences in culture and history are very old. They go back to the early times of Islam and its penetration into the lands of the middle Nile. They were sharpened by conflict at many times in the past, and especially during the period of Egyptian control in the nineteenth century. And when the British took over, after their defeat of the Mahdia, they gradually built a colonial system which more or less completely divided Arabic-speaking Sudanese from the peoples in the far south. Instead of being able to get to know and trust each other, these two populations were kept severely apart.

When independence came in 1956, the Muslim Sudanese naturally took control because they were far more numerous than the southern peoples. They were left with institutions, with means and methods of government, which they proceeded to use. Instead of helping the southern peoples to share in government on a federal basis, the northern Sudanese sent down officials to take the place of the British.

Yet here was a case, different from Kenya's, where agreeing to some regionalism could help to avoid conflict and separation. If the southerners could run their own affairs within a federal Sudan, the old distrusts and differences between south and north might gradually be overcome.

As it was, the southerners believed they had good reason to fear northern domination. An 'army of liberation', called *Anyanya*, took the field against the central government's police and army. Only years later, in 1972, could the fighting be ended. This was when, in that year, the Sudanese government gave southerners their own parliament and government. *Anyanya* withdrew its demand for a separate southern state. The way to Sudanese federal unity was open. Once again, after the means and methods left by colonial government had broken down, a time of experiment and renewal had proved necessary. The need for this has continued.

Facing 'élitism' and 'tribalism'

Another big problem arose, after independence came, when new national leaders lost touch with the lives and interests of their peoples. This opened a gap between the leaders, who now enjoyed power and privilege, and the mass of voters who were living in the same way as before. Into that poverty gap, many troubles flowed.

Here was another part of the colonial legacy at work. For the colonial rulers had always behaved as an élite, as a 'chosen few', who had no need or wish to keep in touch with the lives and interests of ordinary people. Taking over power by the means and methods left to them by colonial rulers, new national leaders found it easy to behave as an élite. They found it difficult to behave in a different way.

This problem of élitist government by a small privileged group was not of course confined to Africa. It has brought trouble to all nations everywhere. But in Africa it was linked to another part of the colonial legacy; and this made the problem worse. 'Elitism' became linked with 'tribalism' – with all that part of colonial influence which had pushed the idea of tribes. And the two together – élitism *plus* tribalism – could be very destructive.

How, in practice, did this happen? Let us take a little-known example, but a very clear one: that of Somalia after its independence in 1960.

Departing, the Italians gave Somalia a parliamentary system modelled on that of Italy. This parliament was elected by 'proportional representation': meaning, in brief, that each class in society could have a party with seats in parliament. Landowners, businessmen, farmers, city workers: each could have their own party. Now this might work well in Italy, where people were divided into classes. But it could not work well in Somalia.

Nearly all Somalis were farmers or cattle people. They were not divided into classes. They were divided into clans. These clan divisions were very old, but colonial rule had deepened them. We saw in Chapter 3 (p. 21) how the colonial partition first divided Somalis into four different colonies, and then destroyed the unifying work of the Sayyid Muhamed. Repeatedly after that, colonial rule used the old clan divisions as a way of preventing Somalis from uniting together, while Somali habits of thought reinforced disunity.

Even so, the Somali Youth League (founded in 1943) was able to win sufficient unity to take power in 1960. But the constitution left to them began, at once, to make disunity. It turned all politics into tribalism. Each big clan, and then each small clan or sub-clan, used the system of proportional representation so as to form its own 'party' and send its own man or men to parliament. A reckless competition for the fruits of power and privilege was soon under way.

Five Somali parties contested the first general election at the time of independence. But by 1964, this people of only three millions had produced 21 competing parties; and by 1969 there were no fewer than 62 competing parties. That was bad enough at a time when every united effort was needed in order to overcome Somalia's desperate poverty and backwardness. But élitism, joined to this tribalism, made things much worse.

To govern Somalia, at that time, it was necessary to know the English and Italian languages, because Somali, as we have noted, was not then written down. Very few Somalis could speak those languages. Still fewer could read and write them. So the great majority of Somalis had no chance of any share in the responsibilities of public life and government.

Having all the power and privilege, a small élite at the top fought personal battles for their own interests. Whenever elections came, they went back to their clans, whether big or small, and drummed up support against their rivals. Once back in power again, they returned to their dog-fights and squabbles over sharing the spoils of office. This disunity and personal rivalry led directly to bad government and corruption.

Somali farmers and cattle folk began to hate their rulers. They began to say that independence had brought them nothing but dishonesty, lies, and broken promises. Yet nothing got better. So great was the corruption at the top that the prime minister of 1969 was believed to have paid out £500,000 from public money in order to buy the votes of newly-elected members of parliament.

The gap between these rulers and the majority of ordinary people was now wide and filled with anger. People longed for a change. It came at the end of 1969. With general rejoicing, and without a shot being fired, the system left by colonial government was swept away. A group of patriotic officers under General Siad Barre took over. Not long after, they began to experiment with new ways of governing Somalia, of promoting Somali unity of effort, of using that effort to tackle the country's real needs.

Troubles in Uganda

This type of experiment was needed almost everywhere. There were countries which found their way, after many troubles, to renewed stability, to new means and methods of government, to better paths for progress. There were notable successes; and we have looked at one or two of them. Other countries marked up failures; with them, the time of necessary experiment had to continue. Uganda was among these.

We saw in Chapter 14 how Ugandan stability was undermined by internal divisions which were not overcome. After independence in

1962, these divisions continued. They even grew worse. The problems of élitism *plus* tribalism became acute. National politics, more and more, were little more than a rivalry between personal or group interests.

A determined effort to impose unity began in 1966. Prime Minister Milton Obote suspended the independence constitution of 1962, and assumed state power. In April he proclaimed a new constitution under the slogan of 'one country, one parliament, one government, one people', with himself as executive president. This was quite widely welcomed, especially by the northern peoples. But it was entirely rejected by the Baganda kingdom and its separate parliament (see . 129). In May Obote sent in troops who occupied the Baganda king's palace. The king escaped to England, and Buganda was divided into four administrative districts. In 1967 another constitution abolished all the traditional kingdoms, and gave more power to the central government.

Yet this was 'unity imposed from above'. Popular discontents as well as new internal rivalries soon led to trouble. In 1969, trying to win popular support by reducing the economic inequalities between Uganda's 'haves', who were few and were mostly in the towns, and its 'have-nots', who were many and mostly in the rural areas, Obote introduced an equalising programme called 'The Common Man's Charter'. This inflamed political opposition led by the 'haves'. Obote replied by banning the opposition parties. In this situation, his government had to rely, more and more, on its troops and police. That proved fatal.

In 1971 President Obote was overthrown by his army commander, General Idi Amin, with the initial support of Britain and other foreign interests who feared Obote's 'left-wing turn'. Uganda then passed under a military dictatorship. This became ever more harsh. Soon it was seen that Amin, by means of terror, could secure no more than a 'unity of silence'.

In October 1978, with none of Uganda's internal problems solved, Amin began to attack neighbouring Tanzania, to which Tanzania responded by sending troops into Uganda. Aided by these troops, Amin's surviving opponents drove him out. Their task now was to try once again for stability and united effort.

Many other experiments were made. Some are very well-known. Ghana passed from multi-party rule to one-party rule under Kwame Nkrumah, then to military rule in 1966, back to civilian rule in 1969, again into military rule in 1971, and then once more to civilian rule. Why so many experiments? The failure of leaders, especially when arising from élitism or tribalism, was one explanation. But, as elsewhere in the world, this was not the whole explanation. The rest of it lay in the sheer difficulty of overcoming the divisions of the past, and of tracing a road to progress in which all could have their share.

Many lessons had to be learned after independence came. Many new things had to be understood. Seen from this angle, the time of experiment has been rich in valuable experience, and in the determination of Africans to find out how to solve their national problems. We have looked at some of the internal obstacles. There were external obstacles as well.

Cases of foreign intervention

Various forms of foreign intervention, from the day of independence, had to do with neo-colonialism, or the effort to keep an indirect control in foreign hands. Some of these forms were economic, and will be discussed in the next chapter. Political and military intervention was mostly in the weakest of the new countries; or else in large states, notably Zaïre, which failed to find the way to national agreement and unity of effort. The general result of all such intervention was to inflame existing conflicts, and make stability still more difficult to reach. Sometimes, as in the case of France and the Central African Republic, foreign intervention helped local dictators into power, and then gave them enough support to stay in power. In exchange, such dictators served the interests of the intervening power and its foreign partners.

Strong countries, with patriotic leaders, could and did stop foreign intervention. Other countries failed, and paid a high price. Chad was a particularly sad example. That vast country came to independence, in 1960, with fewer than four million people, mostly in the centre and south but otherwise scattered through northern plains and hills in the Sahara. Though small, this population was sorely divided. Elitism and tribalism worked against unity; but the chief division was between the (mostly Christian) southerners and the (mostly Muslim) northerners. Reversing the situation we looked at in the Sudan, independence gave control to the southerners. But this was a very limited or neo-colonial independence. France kept strict economic controls, and stationed French troops in much of the territory.

No progress was made in overcoming internal divisions. Soon after 1960, on the contrary, these were deepened by actions of the southern-led government of President Tombalbaye, heavily supported by France. Northern rebellions began in 1968, and grew rapidly into civil war. Tombalbaye tried to put down these rebellions with the help of French troops and air force. This failed. In 1975 the dictator Tombalbaye was overthrown when the French switched their support to a group of military officers. Fighting continued as before, with repeated French intervention. Meanwhile the northerners were receiving some military support from Colonel Gaddafi's Libyan government and army. Interventions widened.

Chad became a battleground for diverse groups and interests, local and foreign. New rivals for power appeared. Divisions multiplied. In 1979 Nigeria led an attempt at mediation, but in 1980 civil war again shattered the fragile peace. As the scene of so many rival ambitions, whether foreign or local, Chad's whole future was in doubt.

There were lesser but still serious cases of intervention. External use of white-mercenary adventurers to overthrow African governments, in the interests of this or that foreign power, became quite frequent in the 1970s. Mostly, such attempts failed: as, for example, an attempt by white mercenaries to overthrow the government of Benin (former Dahomey) in 1977, and a similar attempt to overthrow the government of the Seychelles in 1981.

The fact or threat of military intervention by forces from outside Africa remained on the scene, and sometimes grew worse. Repeated military aggression by South Africa's armed forces against Angola and Mozambique began in 1975, and was renewed, especially against Angola, in 1978 and in following years. These South African attacks by air, land and sea were clearly aimed at undermining the newly-independent republics of those two countries, and replacing their governments by pro-South African puppets. In this they failed, but were very destructive of African life and property.

Countries in central and southern Africa also had to face great difficulties, in the economic field, caused by their support for the further liberation of southern Africa. Sanctions against the settlers' republic in Rhodesia (Zimbabwe), applied in 1966 and continued until 1980, placed a particularly heavy burden on Zambia, and, between 1975 and 1980, also on Mozambique. Zambia's economy suffered badly in those years, and there, too, setbacks in local farming and a widening poverty gap were hard to bear.

Searching for solutions

We can now stand back a little, and make another summary. Many of the troubles of Africa, after independence, followed on breakdown of parliamentary and administrative institutions set in place, at the time of independence, by departing colonial rulers. Those institutions failed to meet the problems left by past history, but, especially, by the legacy of colonial history.

Often enlarged by neo-colonial controls and interventions, such problems consisted of internal divisions, élitism, tribalism, and other forms of disunity. Patriotic leaders set themselves to solve those problems; selfish or corrupt leaders simply made them worse.

To these political difficulties on the road to stability, all of which were built into the situation on the day of independence, others of an economic and social nature were added. For what the new governments were obliged to take over, as Chapter 8 has shown, was not a prosperous colonial business, but, in many ways, a profound colonial crisis. There was poverty and hunger in wide rural areas. Towns and cities grew hugely in size as rural people flocked to them in search of food and jobs, and often could find neither. If a few persons managed to make money or get good jobs, the majority did not. Even before independence, the gap in living-standards between the few with money, houses, or good jobs, and the many who had none of those good things, was wide. It was also widely resented.

Yet the few with jobs and money were precisely that small minority who, as Chief Awolowo claimed in 1947, were 'destined to rule the country', because they had the necessary education and political knowledge. They duly took over power; but the gap in living-standards between them and the majority continued to widen. As it widened, so did popular discontent. And when that discontent exploded into strife or violence, the politicians proved helpless. Then the soldiers stepped in and took their place.

However painful, these breakdowns were often unavoidable. And they had one very positive side to them: they opened the way for new experiments in searching for stability. There were many experiments, as our few examples have indicated. Some of these experiments were firmly successful, and showed that Africans, left to themselves, could solve their problems and make progress. Other experiments were less successful, but were still useful in the lessons they taught and the experience they provided. Some experiments failed altogether. Nearly always, these failures occurred in countries subject to neo-colonial controls or repeated outside intervention, such as Chad or the Central African Republic.

This overview may be rounded off by looking at the record of the military rulers, and then at that of various kinds of political party.

The soldiers' record

Already by 1970, about half of Africa's then independent states were being governed by one or other kind of military rule. Why was this?

The reasons for military take-over may be divided, for the most part, into four:

1   Because parliamentary and administrative institutions had failed to overcome a destructive regionalism; or a threat of separatism; or a collapse of political power into intrigue and corruption.
2   Because popular discontents, largely economic in origin, had reached a point of explosion that undermined law and order.
3   Because, in weak or neo-colonial countries, foreign interests or governments wanted a change of government in their favour.
4   Because of personal ambition for power and privilege, with support from this or that élitist or tribalist grouping.

Such reasons were not, of course, peculiar to Africa. They had led to military rule at many points of European history. They had often produced military dictatorships in Latin America or Asia. But an examination of the African record brings out another point. There have been various kinds of military rule.

In the period examined here, there were patriotic military leaders who stepped into a power vacuum caused by the failures of civilian rule, and who then ensured the continued unity of their countries. They launched new experiments in national self-government, and were ready to hand back power to civilian rulers. Some of Nigeria's military rulers, such as Generals Murtala Muhamed and Oluṣẹgun Ọbasanjọ, were of this type. Their aim was to 'fill the gap' until new and better forms of civilian rule could be devised.

Other military governments were of different types. Some were imposed by men who acted for merely selfish or corrupt reasons. These men, like Amin in Uganda, had neither the personal wisdom nor the experience to bring unity and peace to their countries. Or, like Bokassa in the Central African Republic, they were military bullies who acted as the agents of foreign interests. Such men solved no problems. They only added to their peoples' woes.

In a record as complex as this, there were of course marginal cases, when useful military rule was mixed with useless military rule. Such cases have given rise to many sharp differences of opinion. Was it a good thing, for example, for the Ghanaian military to overthrow the one-party civilian rule of Nkrumah in 1966; and did that military government bring any improvement? Was it a bad thing, in another Ghanaian example, for Colonel Ignatius Acheampong to overthrow the multi-party civilian rule of Dr Kofi Busia in 1971; and did Acheampong then do better than Busia had done? How useful were the various military take-overs in Sierra Leone, or in Mali, or in Niger?

Broadly, the central political problem was to get rid of the dictatorial ways of colonial government, while, at the same time, finding new ways of democratic government. How to spread the use of power among all the people? How to ensure that votes at elections became a real use of power by masses of ordinary people? How to build ways of government by which people could begin to govern themselves, rather than being governed, as before, 'from the top down'? These became critical issues.

The record suggests that military government could be positive and useful wherever it prepared the way for new experiments in the search for democratic government. These positive examples are the ones that history will remember as steps toward unity and peace.

Several parties or one party?

Africans in past centuries found many ways of dealing with the abuse of power and privilege. They worked out a wide variety of checks and balances to control the behaviour of their chiefs or kings or other leading persons. They were accustomed to act against despots, to throw down tyrants, and to punish corruption.

But the modern world called for new ways. These were the ways of democratic election, representation, and discussion within modern states different from those of the past. They in turn called for political parties.

So long as there was colonial rule, such parties all had one central aim, and were organised to get it. They were parties or movements aiming at independence. Their situation was a simple one: on their side were the people to be organised to struggle for independence, while against them were the colonial government and its forces. But the situation changed after independence came. Then the sides became as many as the different and often conflicting groups of interest inside the new state.

The question then was: should each of these groups of interest have its own party, and try to reach its special aims by using that party in rivalry or combination with other such parties? Or would it be better to bring all these interests into a single party, and try to resolve their differences in that way?

Different answers were found in experiments after independence. Yet it remained clear, early in the 1980s, that the great debate was still open about which kind of system – the multi-party or the one-party – was better. There is no space here for a full discussion of the serious and difficult questions which underlie this debate: How best to exercise political power, and ensure that there are checks and balances on the misuse of power? How best to overcome élitism, tribalism, and other handicaps? But a brief survey of experiments can be made.

Various systems
We should note, to begin with, that multi-party systems were evolved in western Europe to fit a situation in which European peoples were increasingly divided into sharply conflicting classes. In that situation, it became generally true that middle-class (bourgeois) parties wanted a 'free enterprise' or capitalist system, while working-class parties hoped for a collective or socialist-type system. Essentially, the political battle was about *alternative policies*, even if, of course, it was also about persons and personal benefits.

The problem of evolving multi-party systems in newly-independent Africa was that class differences were much less deep and sharp than in Europe. This meant, in practice, that parties were seldom created to represent different class interests, and therefore different policies. Of course there were partial exceptions. The CPP in Ghana was thought to represent 'the masses', while the UGCC was thought to represent 'the chiefs'. Mostly, however, parties were created to represent different interests of a regional or similar kind, and to enable these rival groups to compete for power.

Secondly, most of the leaders and organisers of the parties and mass movements, during the 1960s, had to be persons of educational or other privilege. These persons, as Chief Awolowo had forecast in 1947, were 'the articulate minority destined to rule'. So it came about that the struggle between parties was not so much a struggle between alternative policies as a struggle between alternative persons; and elections were less about what to do with political power than about who should have the benefits of possessing that power.

Looking back over the first ten years of Nigeria's independence, Professor Billy Dudley wrote that politics in Nigeria was 'not about *alternative policies*, but about *the control over men and resources.*' That was the situation which had helped to produce the collapse of the first Nigerian federation (1960–66). The gap in living-standards between 'haves' and 'have-nots', for example, had grown ever wider, but there were no alternative policies which could have narrowed it. So the multi-party system, however democratic it was intended to be, had failed to work, and a new multi-party system had to be created in 1979–80.

Other countries devoted to free enterprise have done without a multi-party system. In the Ivory Coast, for example, the party which won independence in 1960, the PDCI, stayed in power under the uninterrupted leadership of President Houphouët-Boigny, though with many changes of persons. Was this the same as government by a privileged group? If so, how were the interests of the mass of ordinary people represented or protected? Would those interests have been better protected if the Ivory Coast had formed many parties? Here again are questions for discussion.

Checks and Balances

Strongly presidential systems are those in which the president has great power. They have been compatible with multi-party systems. On the other hand, Zambia has been an example of the combination of a strong presidential and one-party system. In Morocco, however, a presidential system run by the Moroccan king became a royal dictatorship in spite of the existence of parties.

Uganda, with a multi-party system until 1966 (see p. 179), offers another example. Once again, this was competition between groups and persons whose basic political ideas and policies were the same; and Uganda's multi-party system became, more and more, a destructive rivalry for the fruits of power. Not until 1969 did Milton Obote try, unsuccessfully, to introduce The Common Man's Charter as an alternative policy. Another example, which we discussed earlier (see p. 178), is illustrated by Somalia's multi-party system between 1960 and 1969. This in no way protected democracy. On the contrary, it declined into a corrupt fight for personal advantage.

One-party systems, on the other hand, could easily become 'no-party' systems, and degenerate into personal dictatorships, usually of a military nature. Censorship of the press, arrest of critics, falsifying of elections: all such abuses could be much easier when there was no elected opposition. This was what had happened in the last years of CPP rule in Ghana. Many Ghanaians then said that they were ruled by a single party which had become, in fact, a kind of dictatorship.

Yet one-party systems, like multi-party systems, could also develop checks and balances against the abuse or misuse of power. Kenya has offered a case of this. KANU, the major winner of Kenya's independence in 1963, remained in power; and within a year of independence Kenya had a one-party system. Critics suffered or were silenced. Yet checks and balances were also developed. KANU candidates for parliamentary election were encouraged to compete against each other at the polls. In Kenya's general election of 1979, no fewer than 740 all-KANU candidates competed for 160 seats. A number of former deputies, and several cabinet ministers, lost their seats. Later, such checks and balances were more severely tested.

Debate continues

Countries with a socialist-type leadership generally supported a one-party system. They argued that the important question was not the number of parties, but the degree to which ordinary people could really influence their governments. If ordinary people could not do this, they said, then many parties were even worse than one party. Why was that? President Nyerere of Tanzania summarised his answer in 1963. He said that there could be only one reason for the formation of many parties in a country like Tanzania. This reason was:

... the desire to imitate the political structure of a totally dissimilar society. What is more, the desire to imitate, where conditions are not suitable for imitation, can easily lead us into trouble. To try and import the idea of a parliamentary opposition into Africa may very likely lead to violence – because the opposition parties will tend to be regarded as traitors by the majority of our people; or, at best, it will lead to the trivial manoeuvrings of 'opposing' groups whose time is spent in the inflation of artificial differences in some semblance of reality 'for the sake of preserving democracy' . . .

He argued, further, that in Tanzania:

the only voices to be heard in 'opposition' are those of a few irresponsible individuals who exploit the very privileges of democracy – freedom of the press, freedom of association, freedom to criticise – in order to deflect the government from its re-sponsibilities to the people . . .

Clearly, then, the question of a party system is a complex one with many answers that deserve discussion. In any case, Africa's debate on this question continued. But it continued, during the 1980s, with a growing difference from earlier years. Much practical experience, and much new understanding, had been gained since independence.

Much more was understood about the possible advantages or disadvantages, benefits or risks, of different types of party and political system. Much more was realised about the small value or even the uselessness of a great deal of advice that came from outside Africa. Much more was known about national wealth, about natural resources, and how best to use these.

The revolution of 'people's power'
There were various experiments in renewal, within the strongly patriotic and therefore stubbornly independent countries, besides such examples, mentioned above, as Nigeria's new multi-party constitution of 1979. Algeria was moving ahead by a combination of

one-party rule, rapid development of education, and much industrial expansion. The big island of Madagascar (Malagasy Republic), at first under the lead of General Ramanantsoa and then of Commander Ratsiraka (elected president in 1975), had enlarged its independence from France and South Africa, and formed many *fokolona*. These *fokolona* indicated another trend in democratic experiment. As self-governing village communities, they aimed at a modern remodelling of ancient ways of self-government in the island, and at extending democratic controls.

A greater decentralisation of political power was meanwhile launched, on entirely new lines, in the countries of the former Portuguese empire: for example, in Angola, Mozambique and Cape Verde. There, one-party systems were closely linked to a country-wide organisation of 'people's power' or people's participation. In these countries, liberated from a very stiff Portuguese dictatorship, the driving idea of 'people's power' has been to draw as many people as possible into the actual tasks and responsibilities of local government, and then, step by step, upwards to national government. Communities in villages and towns in each country were led to form their own local assemblies, and elect their own local-government committees. These in turn elected regional assemblies, and the latter then elected a national assembly. The effort was to widen and strengthen the daily practice of democracy, and secure greater unity of work and understanding among all sections of the population.

In all parts of the continent, as the 1980s opened, there were examples of experiments in renewal that were beginning to yield results.

CHAPTER 19

Questions about development

The new nations of Africa had to come to independence in the midst of a deepening social crisis caused by colonialism. Their governments had to find the way to stability against new problems of rural poverty and of the rapid growth of cities, as well as against other legacies of internal division.

Some new nations were weak in unity and badly led; they made little progress. Others were strong in unity and well led; they were able to strengthen and enlarge their political independence. Winning more freedom of action, they could search for their own solutions to national problems. Increasingly, they were able to move ahead.

Yet the new governments had thoroughly to understand, and then try to throw off, another colonial legacy as well. This was in the field of economics: of working, earning, spending, managing the nation's wealth. And this economic legacy was heavier than the political and social legacy; it was harder to shift. Against this, too, a long struggle had to be launched, again needing many experiments.

The economic legacy

In economic affairs, the colonial legacy had two sides. On one side, the colonial systems had continually drained Africa of the wealth produced by African labour, land, and natural resources. As earlier chapters explained, that was largely what the colonial systems were for: they helped the colony-owning powers to become richer. But this draining of resources, this wealth-transfer, did not stop with independence. It continued.

On the other side of the economic legacy, all the newly-independent countries had to join a world, of trade and exchange, that was organised by much richer countries. In this world, formed by previous centuries, the advanced (that is, industrialised) countries possessed control of the markets in which world trade (exports and imports) was carried on. They could use their control so as to ensure that the wealth-transfer from poor to rich countries did not stop on the day of independence.

How did they do this? When independence came, the answer was unclear or unknown. For the colonial governments had never admitted to any such transfer of wealth; nor did they give the newly-independent governments any useful information on the subject. So new governments had to find out, by themselves, what was really going on. They had to discover how the economic legacy worked.

The power to make this discovery was among the principal gains of independence. It enabled African leaders to 'open the account-books' of the colonial legacy, look into the confidential files of government, learn the facts. Then the new governments, having analysed the economic legacy of wealth-transfer, could try to act against it.

Methods of wealth-transfer from Africa

This transfer of wealth to the industrialised countries was not easy to see: its 'machinery', for the most part, was in files and records that were out of sight.

With close inspection, it was found to work in several ways (see also Chapter 5, pp. 44–46). First, through the exchange of African raw materials for imports of manufactured goods. Secondly, through the fixing of export-import prices. Thirdly, through various forms of debt-interest paid on loans advanced by the industrialised countries. Let us look briefly at each of these. They formed an essential part of the background to post-independence economic progress and setbacks.

Africa's task, in the world of colonialism, had been to produce the raw materials needed by machines and factories in the advanced (that is, industrialised) countries. Consider, again, the case of cotton. If Europe had the machines and factories, it did not have the cotton: Europe had to get cotton from where cotton could be grown, for example Africa. So the British pushed the growing of cotton in Sudan and in Uganda, while the Portuguese, in another example, forced African farmers to grow it in Mozambique.

African farmers grew cotton and were paid for it; but that was where Africa's profit stopped. It was sold to foreign buyers, who took it to Europe and turned it into cloth, and then turned the cloth into shirts and other garments. These shirts and other garments were brought back to Africa for sale: usually, once again, by foreign merchants. So the value added to the raw cotton by manufacturing it into useful goods, as well as the profit made from selling these goods, went to foreign interests. Africans might produce the cotton. But Africans could have little or no share in the profits made from manufacturing and trading in that cotton.

A second way in which wealth was made from African labour, land, and natural resources, was in fixing prices. Mostly, the prices at which African products were sold for export were fixed by foreign companies backed by foreign governments. Only now and then were strong African peoples able to revolt against such prices: this happened, as we saw, in the Gold Coast 'cocoa hold-up' of 1937.

But the same foreign machinery of control also fixed the prices of goods imported into Africa. Again, nothing could lower import prices except mass action: this, too, we saw in the no less famous Gold Coast boycott of 1948. In colonies outside British West Africa there was practically nothing that Africans could do to make such protests heard. Fixed by oversea interests, the price-system meant that Africans had to sell cheap and buy dear.

A third method of wealth-transfer consisted in the interest-money that Africans had to pay on foreign loans. We will come back to this point later in this chapter.

This legacy was extremely difficult to throw off because, in many ways, it was built into the ways in which newly-idependent countries had to work and earn their living.

Export-crops or food?

By the 1960s, large rural populations were earning their living by growing cash crops – cocoa, groundnuts, coffee, cotton, and so on – and by selling these for export. This was a way of wealth-transfer overseas, as we saw above: it was part of the economic legacy of colonial rule. Yet the new government of Ghana, for example, could not simply say to the cocoa-farmers: 'Stop producing cocoa, start growing food.' For the cocoa farmers depended on cocoa for their livelihood. Besides this, the new Ghana government depended on cocoa exports for a large part of its revenue or income.

What that government had to do, and what it tried to do, was to cut down the size of wealth-transfer involved in exporting cocoa-beans, and to use the extra money for the national benefit. How far it actually succeeded in doing this remains a question for the detailed study of Ghana history. The big point for us here, is that the colonial economic legacy could not be thrown off from one year to the next: it could only be reduced, or removed, slowly. But real progress depended on doing this.

Another reason why it was desirable to cut down on cash crops grown for export was the need to produce more food. Wherever cash crop production became important in an African country, shortages of local food began to be felt. This was partly because the more land and labour that was taken for growing cash crops, the less land or

Fig. 10   The distribution of some important cash crops, in 1980

labour was there left for growing food. Local food shortages began to be acute, in some countries, as early as the Second World War. Even local famine broke out in the worst cases: as, for example, in northern Mozambique where the Portuguese forced farmers to grow cotton instead of food. Cotton, these farmers rightly said, became 'the mother of poverty'.

Increasing shortages of local food meant two things. There was less to eat than before, whether in villages or cities. Secondly, governments had to spend money on importing foreign food, often at high prices. So the result, by the 1960s, was that a continent whose population was still, largely, a farming population had become a continent which could no longer feed its own people. Here was another, and most serious, part of the economic legacy.

Go-ahead governments, after independence, began to act against this part of the legacy by trying to promote rural development and improve transport systems. It was hard to act quickly in such complex matters, calling as they did for better ways of production and higher productivity; but it was urgent to act quickly. Why was it urgent?

Population growth and movement

African populations began to grow in size, ever more rapidly, after the 1940s. Scientists are not yet sure why this happened, although one reason probably lay in the spread of preventive medicine – inoculations against disease, for example – during the late colonial period. By the 1960s, most African populations were growing at an average rate of about 2.5 per cent a year. This meant that most of the new nation-states would double the size of their populations in twenty or thirty years. If Nigeria had 100 million people in 1980, as seemed likely, Nigeria will have upwards of 200 million by 2000 or soon after. The same rapid rate of growth was general throughout the continent.

This huge increase in the number of Africans could present advantages for Africa. Most African countries still had much smaller populations than countries of comparable size in other continents. Angola, for example, is more than twice as big as France, and has great natural resources in minerals and crops. But Angola in 1975, when it became independent, had fewer than 7 million people while France had more than 45 million.

Yet doubling the number of Angolans could be good for them only on one condition; and here again was a general truth. This condition was that national skills, labour, teamwork, and planning could each year win more wealth, whether in food or other necessities, than the year before. For if the population went on growing, but the quantity of its productive wealth did not, then the population would get poorer. The average standard of living would fall, and would go on falling. A higher standard of living had to mean a better and bigger system of production, whether of food or other goods.

There was another reason why large economic changes were urgently desirable. If shortages of local food were caused by growing cash crops, they were also worsened by shortages of rural labour. We saw that the 1940s brought the beginning of a flight to the towns from villages where people had to suffer from forced labour and hunger. But once this flight began, it continued for other reasons as well. The towns grew even larger in size after independence came, because rural people, or at least rural workers, looked to the towns for a more comfortable life. In Ghana by the late 1970s, for example, there was not only a shortage of local food; there was also, in the food-growing areas, a shortage of local labour. Again it was the same in many countries.

But how were these new populations of the towns to make a living, and work in ways that would increase the national wealth? Here, too, the economic legacy called for a better system of production.

What, in turn, did this have to mean?

The meaning of development

All the new governments faced this difficult question, and tried to find good answers. Many efforts were made. The story of those efforts, in detail, belongs to each new nation's separate history. Here we can offer a general guide to what was attempted, and what was achieved.

Broadly, the problem of building a better system of production was to find out how to use national resources – in people and in things – so as to produce more wealth. What could be done, in practice, was governed by two factors. One was the quantity of natural resources, especially in soil fertility or minerals, which each country possessed. Some countries, such as Mauritania or Upper Volta, were generally poor in natural resources. The second factor was the amount of real independence which each country had won. There were rich countries, such as Zaïre, that remained under strong foreign control.

But all the new countries recognised their central economic task: how best to develop. It required more than the development of skills, methods, and organisation of work. It called as well for a big cultural change: from habits and attitudes of work that produced goods by hand, or by simple hand-worked tools, to habits and attitudes that produced goods by machines in factories. So development was not a simple process of ordering this or that change. It was a complex process in people's minds as well.

Seen in this light, the process of development had several major requirements. To begin with, the new governments had to win national control over national resources. This was difficult wherever foreign interests were deeply entrenched; and in the weaker countries it often proved too difficult. Next, they had to begin to build a new national infrastructure. That means providing the basic equipment for producing and exchanging more goods, such as more and better transport and communications, and much more electric power. Further, they had to make a vast improvement in the poor systems of education and public health left behind by the colonial governments.

Then, through the process of greater control *plus* more infrastructure, they had to decide on the plan or strategy by which they were going to help their peoples to move ahead. Should this be by the methods of free enterprise, or capitalism; or by the methods of collective enterprise, or socialism? Was the first priority to go to helping the rural areas or the towns? To farming or to industry?

Having settled such basic questions, the new governments had then to promote new methods of production, banking, trade, and other aspects of the economic system. Last but not least, each government had to decide how best to gather the national savings needed for infrastructure, industry, and public services; and how far it was going to rely on raising foreign loans for these purposes.

The strategy of private enterprise

We have touched on the matter of alternative policies: or, putting it in a different way, alternative strategies for economic development. In practice, of course, all the newly-independent countries had to rely on a combination of different strategies. Even countries most attached to the strategy of private enterprise, like Nigeria, kept some national ownership of production and trade. Even those most devoted to the strategy aiming at socialism, such as Angola, left farmers in private ownership of their farms. Yet the differences between the two strategies have been real and important.

Countries following the strategy of private enterprise can, in turn, be divided into two kinds. There were weak countries under strong foreign control or influence, such as Niger or the Central African Republic, which really had no choice: they had to do what they were told, and, above all, make sure of not offending foreign interests. In most of the countries of the former French empire, for example, France kept control of the national currency, by means of banking operations and the so-called 'colonial franc' tied to the French franc, as well as by keeping French troops on the spot (see p. 218).

But other countries, smaller in number though much bigger in economic weight, were able to choose private enterprise and build national economies. Notable among these was Nigeria after its first federation, which ended in 1966. Once the ravages of the civil war of 1967–69 were overcome, Nigeria moved rapidly to gain control of its national resources, and to ensure that foreign companies were made to serve local interests as well as foreign interests.

National planning was geared to the needs of private enterprise while, at the same time, providing for new kinds of infrastructure. Even before the 1980s, three Nigerian national plans produced a steady expansion of wealth and economic action. New factories and industries were built. Nigeria's large deposits of offshore oil were realised at a rate which soon made Nigeria one of the world's major oil producers; and there were corresponding benefits for the incomes of all the Nigerian states.

The whole economy became better balanced. Whereas agriculture in 1960, the year of independence, had contributed more than 60 per cent of Nigeria's 'gross domestic product' – broadly, its annual wealth – that proportion, by 1980, was down to less than 20 per cent. Yet it was also true that agriculture lagged far behind in improving output and productivity. As in other countries, low farming output remained the weakest point in national development, and continued to make necessary the import of expensive foreign food.

The Ivory Coast was another country of strong development of private enterprise, but its situation was different from that of Nigeria. On the one hand, the local position of foreign business interests was considerably stronger than in Nigeria. On the other hand, a big shortage of local farming labour could be made good only by a continual influx of migrant workers, chiefly from Upper Volta. These two factors in Ivory Coast capitalism indicated weaknesses which could become serious.

Kenya, again, was in a different position. Its national programme, declared at independence in 1963, was for a system aimed at socialism. Some currents of political opinion remained in favour of that. But others, more important, preferred private enterprise. Politicians went increasingly into private business. In practice, Kenya became a 'mixed economy' with private enterprise in a leading position. Social inequalities were sharply felt.

Other countries followed much the same type of mixed development, some with more private enterprise, others with less. Malawi remained strongly free enterprise in its policies and system. Zambia was a mixed economy with a large element of national ownership, as in its copper mines; but, at the same time, with an expanding private sector of Zambian businessmen and of politicians in private business. Uganda, in its brief moments of internal peace, combined support for co-operative production with a growing private-business sector.

Successes as well as setbacks were marked up by countries following the strategy of capitalism. But all of them had to face two central problems of private-enterprise development. One of these was the general failure to expand farming output and productivity. Even Kenya, in spite of some notable successes (see p. 204), failed on this front. Its farming output grew through the 1970s at a yearly rate of about 2.5 per cent. This was a very positive achievement. But Kenya's population grew still faster; and, to feed it, there had to be higher imports of expensive foreign food.

The second big problem in the private-enterprise systems was the poverty gap – the difference in living-standards between the minority of people who had good jobs and property, and the majority who had neither. Inequalities of this kind were not new. They had existed even in the distant past. But now they grew much bigger than before; the poverty gap became steadily wider. It was soon a major cause of discontent, and therefore of instability. But it was not, of course, limited to private-enterprise systems in Africa: its dangers and disadvantages occurred in such systems everywhere.

Strategies aiming at socialism

Countries which chose to experiment with strategies aiming at socialism also had their successes and their setbacks, again as elsewhere in the world. They, too, differed in their ideas and attitudes. In some of them, such as Cameroun or Senegal, official talk of socialism had no real meaning. In others, such as strongly independent Algeria, development took the form of industrial and business enterprise through powerful state-owned corporations, combined with experiments in farming enterprise through co-operative or other forms of collectively-owned production. In some ways very successfully, Algeria became a mixed economy in which private enterprise had no leading place.

Tanzania – but especially mainland ex-Tanganyika as distinct from the islands of Zanzibar and Pemba – developed another experiment in socialist-aimed strategy. Increasingly after 1967, Tanzania moved in the opposite direction from Kenya: that is, away from private enterprise, and towards state-controlled or collective enterprise. President Nyerere explained why. He said (in 1971) that Tanzanians, by 1967, were becoming discouraged after five years of independence.

He pointed out that there was 'an increase in the amount of inequality between citizens'. Apart from this widening poverty gap, there was waste of public money. There was growing dislike of the few who were getting rich. Tanzania, he concluded, was 'beginning to develop an economic and social élite whose prime concern is profit for themselves and their families, and not the needs of the majority for better basic living standards.'

After 1967 the ruling party of Tanzania, TANU, and its government began to seek other ways of development. Their aim now was to close this gap between the few and the many, bring the interests of people in villages into line with the interests of people in towns, and 'develop Tanzania without dividing it'. Important among its new experiments was the idea and policy of *ujamaa* (a Swahili word meaning 'neighbourliness' or 'community interest'). A big programme was launched to gather scattered hamlets and homesteads, in the countryside, into *ujamaa* settlements provided with schools, clinics, and the means of more efficient farming, such as better tools or tractors. Most foreign companies, at the same time, were taken into national ownership.

The *Ujamaa* experiment ran into serious difficulties in the late 1970s, largely of a political and administrative nature. But Tanzania now suffered badly, as did other non-oil-producing countries, from steep rises in the price of the oil they had to import for their national needs. World recession worsened this problem during the early 1980s. Many good plans and projects for development had to be delayed or even abandoned. All this became a general problem.

Other experiments, aiming at socialist systems, were made in the former Portuguese colonies: that is, in Angola, Mozambique, Guinea-Bissau, Cape Verde, and São Tomé. Powerful liberation movements in the first three of these former Portuguese colonies had destroyed the Portuguese colonial system. When independence came, they could make an entirely fresh start.

In the face of many handicaps, caused by the harsh legacy of Portugal's backward colonialism, they decided on socialist types of development. They took control of national resources, and extended the system of 'people's power' (see p. 188) into the economic field. Partly, this meant the extension of co-operative forms of production and trade. More important, it meant an effort to bring people in villages and towns directly into control of their work and enterprise.

The main task to be carried out, it was seen, was how to widen and deepen the effective participation of ordinary people in the government and public affairs of their countries.

In their various ways, these and other socialist-aimed experiments also had central problems. As with the capitalist or private-enterprise experiments, the greatest problem was to improve and raise the output and productivity of all types of farming. Another problem lay in the tendency for state-owned or national enterprise to become bureaucratic and inefficient.

We may note again, in concluding this brief review, that it was clear by 1980 that fresh efforts and experiments in development were necessary, whether in the private-enterprise systems or in those aiming at socialism. This was ever more urgent in the poorest countries, now hard hit by rising costs of oil and food imports, and of growing debts to foreign lenders.

Such points were emphasised in a report of April 1981 by Dr Adebayo Adedeji, executive secretary of the UN Economic Commission for Africa. 'With deteriorating economic prospects and a generally bleak outlook for growth', Adedeji warned, 'no continent has been worse hit than Africa. In the poorest or least developed countries people are as badly off as they were in 1970.' He added that: 'With drought in the Sahel countries and escalating new drought situations in East and Central Africa, many countries face imminent economic collapse.' Such hard-headed realism was another of the gains of independence.

National planning and infrastructure

In order to tackle problems of development effectively, the new nations had also to discover the real facts of their national situation. For example, what was the size of their populations? The colonial governments had merely guessed the answer. Now it was necessary to do better than guess. This called for detailed counting of people in national censuses. Or again, what natural resources in minerals and other wealth could the new governments command? The colonial governments had seldom known, or had kept their knowledge to themselves. Geological and other scientific surveys were necessary.

Armed with these kinds of vital information, the new governments could begin to make national plans. Centrally, such plans had to answer two big questions. How much money could the national economy command for its daily needs, and for its development? How should this money best be spent?

The first question concerned the amount of money for public purposes that could be found from taxation and foreign aid. The second required agreement on a list of priorities for spending that money: in the queue of things that each nation needed, which should come high on the list? Was it more useful to build a new port here, or a new river-dam there, or a new mine somewhere else?

Several priorities were generally agreed. One of them was to improve national infrastructure: that is, the basic equipment needed to expand the production of wealth, such as better roads, more railways, new deep-water ports, dams for the production of electric power. Here, much progress was made.

Colonial Africa had only a primitive infrastructure of modern equipment. There was, for example, a shortage of modern sea-ports. Ghana had only Sekondi for the export of minerals and cash-crops; Nigeria had only Lagos. There were few major sea-ports elsewhere along the western coast, or along the eastern coast except at Mombasa and Maputo. But independence soon improved this situation. New ports were built at Tema in Ghana, at Abidjan in Ivory Coast, and elsewhere in the west. There was also improvement of existing ports such as Dar es-Salaam in Tanzania.

Existing railways were improved, and some new ones built, notably from the coast of Tanzania to the capital and centre of Zambia. Great efforts were successful in producing electric power from major dams. One was at Akosombo on the Volta river of Ghana. Another was at Inga on the lower Congo river in Zaire; there, the steep fall of the river can produce, in theory, as much electric power as is used in all of Britain. A third was at Aswan in Egypt. A fourth was the great Kainji dam in Nigeria; even by 1975, before completion of the whole project, Kainji could provide Nigeria with twice as much electric power as the country had formerly possessed. Electric light for towns and even villages, as well as power for industry, began to become available as never before.

Other priorities were the provision of public-transport services, whether by buses in towns, or between towns, or by new ferries and modern vessels along the coast and between islands. Outlying areas began to be linked to the modern world for the first time in history.

The details of all this development of infrastructure is part of the history of each new nation. Here we have indicated some of the many forms it has taken in the years of independence. These improvements in infrastructure opened the way for the beginnings of industrialisation: that is, for the production of goods by machinery instead of by hand. Africa began to be less dependent on the outside world for everyday things that people need. African factories began to make

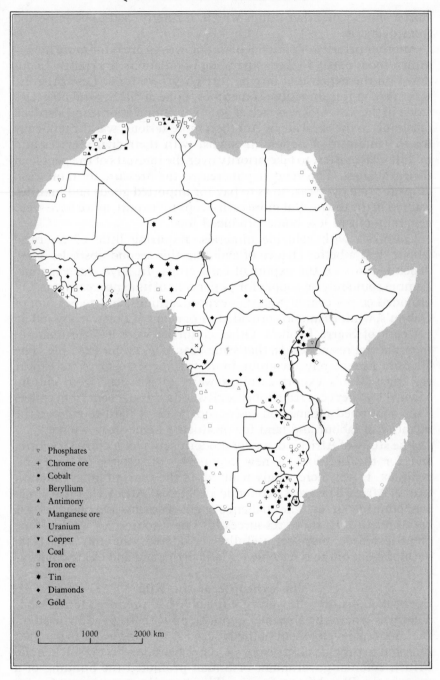

Phosphates
Chrome ore
Cobalt
Beryllium
Antimony
Manganese ore
Uranium
Copper
Coal
Iron ore
Tin
Diamonds
Gold

0   1000   2000 km

Fig. 11 Main areas of mineral exploitation in Africa, in 1980. (See p. 207 for oil.)

shirts, shoes, and other things which, formerly, had to be imported from overseas.

Another priority of national planning was to press for more home-grown food, partly to feed expanding populations, and partly to cut down on the expense of buying foreign-grown food. Less progress was made in this direction; sometimes, none at all. Several obstacles stood in the way. One was lack of good communications, and also lack of labour, in the rural areas. Another, more serious, was the tendency for the interests of people in towns, with their civil services and middle-class tastes, to take priority over the interests of the people of the rural areas. This tendency increased the pressure for more cash crops for sale overseas, so as to pay for imported goods and luxuries wanted in the towns. But more cash-crops for export, as we have seen, generally meant less home-produced food.

Countries with valuable minerals, requiring little or no rural labour, had a better chance of avoiding this second obstacle. They depended less on the export of cash-crops. In 1978, for example, Zambia could rely on copper for 93 per cent of its export earnings. Oil provided 90 per cent of Nigeria's export earnings, and 79 per cent of Gabon's, while diamonds provided 41 per cent of Botswana's, and 67 per cent of Sierra Leone's. Other countries were less fortunate in their natural resources. In that same year of 1978, for example, The Gambia had to rely on groundnuts for 76 per cent of its export earnings. Mali's export earnings were 47 per cent from cotton; Malawi's 56 per cent from tobacco; Rwanda's 72 per cent from coffee. This continued reliance on cash-crops made it hard to enlarge the quantity of labour and land for producing home-grown food.

The study of Africa's drive for modernisation of its infrastructure, and for the building of new economies of wealth, is large and complex. It was increasingly realised, in the years of independence, that if Africa had great economic problems, Africa also had great economic resources. The challenge to governments and planners was how best to turn those resources into new sources of wealth. One other example may be usefully considered: the infrastructural development of the river Nile for land-irrigation and electric power.

The example of the Nile

Far back in history, the waters of the Nile had produced fertile land. That was where the ancient Egyptians built their great civilisation. But modern development of the Nile, so as to bring water to parched soils and to provide electric power, dates back only to 1925, when the British colonial government of Sudan promoted the building of a dam on the Blue Nile at Sennar. This brought water to the Gezira region, and enabled the growing of long-staple cotton for factories in Britain.

The Gezira scheme was a major developmental success. By the late 1950s, the Gezira cotton-growing area of irrigated land was as big as 800,000 hectares, and supported 100,000 tenant-farmers. Then the great enterprise was taken over by the independent government of Sudan, and extended further. A second dam on the Blue Nile, at Roseires, was completed in 1966. This added another 40,000 hectares of irrigated land, now under full national control.

Meanwhile, the newly-independent government of Egypt, led by Gamal Abdel Nasser, decided to build a great Nile dam at Aswan, on the frontier of Egypt and the Sudan. Completed in 1968, this did much to improve the irrigation of land along the banks of the Egyptian Nile, as well as providing Egypt with electric power. Sudan also received benefits from the Aswan dam, thanks to an agreement between the two countries on the division of Nile waters between them. Lesser dams then added to these benefits.

At this point the Sudanese government turned its attention to the upper reaches of the Nile, where the great river flows northward from its source in Uganda. Here it is called the White Nile. Flowing northward through almost level country, the White Nile long ago created vast swamplands called the Sudd. Because of the flatness of the country, about half of all the water of the White Nile that flows into the swamps, near Mongalla, is lost by the time that the White Nile flows out of the swamps, near Malakal.

Cutting canals through the Sudd, so as to reduce this loss of water in the White Nile, had long been discussed; but nothing had been done. Then, in 1978, the Sudanese government began to cut the Jonglei Canal, a big one, so as to carry a large part of the White Nile northward with a smaller loss of its water. This great project would require years to complete, but then there would be more water for the parched lands to the north.

All such projects had to take account of many consequences. With the Jonglei Canal, for example, care would have to be taken to protect the grazing pastures of the cattle-raising peoples of the southern Sudan. If too much water was saved for the parched northern lands, these pastures would suffer.

Big dams created big lakes upstream: above Akosombo in Ghana, on the Zambezi river between Zambia and Zimbabwe, again on the Zambezi above Cabora Bassa in Mozambique, and elsewhere. These could provide new fishing industries. But they also meant that many people had to leave their homes. The creation of Lake Nasser above the Aswan dam, for example, meant that local farmers and their families had to be re-settled on irrigated land elsewhere. Dams also caused other problems, such as the silting-up of the lakes they made, the blocking of these lakes with weed, dangers from parasites, and the difficulties of fish-refrigeration and transport. But the long-term outlook, in spite of setbacks, was for more power and more irrigation: for new sources of wealth.

Rural development

National planning for more productive farming suffered, for a long time, both from the colonial legacy and from experiments that failed. Broadly, the reasons for failure were two-fold: first, too much reliance was placed on the advice of foreign experts who did not understand the real problems; secondly, there was a failure to consult African farmers on what best to do.

Severe famine in the West African grassland countries of the Sahel, during 1968–1974, showed an extreme case of failure. One of the countries to suffer worst was Niger. In 1974 its production of food-crops, chiefly millet and sorghum, was only about half of what had been produced in 1969–70. Between 1970 and 1974, on top of that, nearly 40 per cent of all the country's cattle were lost. Famine came, and people died.

Drought was the cause: but sufferings from drought were increased by failures of policy. The Niger government had encouraged farmers to use more land and labour for growing groundnuts. So there was less of both available for growing food. When drought struck, food reserves were small or non-existent. Meanwhile the same enlargement of groundnut production had pushed Niger's cattle-raising people to the northward. Their herds were packed into smaller pastures. These pastures were soon over-grazed. When drought came, the cattle died; and then the people.

By 1980, many governments were revising their plans for rural development. They were turning away from experiments and policies which had failed. In countries such as Sierra Leone, for example, the large-scale use of tractors was seriously questioned. Generally, it was seen that much more attention must be paid to the knowledge and skills of African farming communities. The big questions now became: How do farming communities think they can best be helped? What solutions do *they* recommend?

In this struggle for more food, big successes were scored with new varieties of seed. Kenya, for example, made a breakthrough with the use of hybrid-maize, capable of yielding a bigger harvest. Kenya's farmers were shown the advantage of hybrid-maize by pilot projects and farms. They rapidly adopted it. By 1975, as much as 30 per cent of all Kenya's maize-growing land was being planted with hybrid-maize seed. This 30 per cent was already yielding as much as 56 per cent of Kenya's maize harvest. An intelligent use of science was linked to close co-operation with farmers. The result was more food.

There were other such successes. One of a different kind was scored by the independent republic of Cape Verde. Very poor when independence came, its people are farmers who live on nine volcanic islands. Their biggest problem was the loss of rare but tumultuous rainfall, bouncing down steep hillsides into the sea. After centuries of colonial neglect, the independent government set out to change this.

Cape Verdeans were led to rebuild their country so as to conserve rainfall, and store water. They made a start in 1977, only two years after independence. By 1980 they had built 7,200 stone dykes and about 2,000 km of retaining walls so as to save rainfall. They had planted their bare hillsides with more than two million drought-resistant trees. They had begun to make a vast improvement in the natural condition of their rocky islands. More was achieved in four years of independence than in four centuries of colonial rule.

Foreign aid

In colonial times, as we have seen earlier, there was almost no foreign aid. There was only a little money, given mostly by the British and French governments, to help the colonial economies to export more wealth. After 1945, the same two powers put much more of their own taxpayers' money into enlarging the colonial economies. Sometimes this had very wasteful results, as we saw with the Tanganyika groundnut and The Gambia egg schemes (see p. 77). Little of it, in any case, was aid for African development. Most of it was aid for the enlargement of wealth-transfer from Africa to countries overseas. After 1950, money was also given by the American government for much the same purpose.

After independence came, the new governments nearly all had great need of foreign aid. Very few of them had been left with any reserves of capital (money to spend on development). Ghana was an exception, having reserves of capital built from selling cocoa. But most, like Zambia, had very small reserves because profits from mining minerals had been sent overseas. Tanzania, for another example, had almost no reserves. So foreign aid was necessary. It came, after independence, from many countries, with the USA high on the list. After about 1960, aid also came from the USSR and other communist countries.

The problem for the new governments was how to use this aid to the best advantage. Much of it, especially in new colonial countries, continued to enlarge the tranfer of wealth overseas. But more of it began to be used to help Africa's own development.

Yet this aid, even when well used, was found to have other disadvantages. Little of it was given. Most had to be paid for at high rates of interest. Indebtedness to foreign lenders soared alarmingly.

President Pereira of the Cape Verde Republic drew attention to this at a conference of 1981 to discuss aid to the world's least developed countries. Speaking on behalf of the twenty-one African member-states in that category, he pointed out that the size of their foreign debt in 1979 was four times' bigger than in 1970. Worse still, the 'service' on this debt (yearly payment of interest) had risen sharply in the same nine years, and was now, every year, as much as one-fifth of the total value of these countries' exports. So their national savings had to go to foreign lenders, not into their own development.

Foreign aid could present another disadvantage. The donor countries often wanted a political price as well as their interest money. In the nominally independent countries, this could mean that national policies and decisions were increasingly decided by foreign banks and governments. That is what happened in Zaire, for example, late in the 1970s when a severe economic crisis was relieved to some extent by foreign loans. But the foreign lenders, looking naturally to their own interests, more and more decided the economic policies of Zaire, and a neo-colonial situation was reinforced.

The amount of aid, in any case, began to shrink, especially after the industrialised donor countries moved into economic troubles of their own, late in the 1970s. Two conclusions began to be drawn. One was that foreign aid could still be useful, and even necessary, provided that it really went into new infrastructure and social improvement. The other was that it was dangerous to rely on foreign aid. Either this aid meant more wealth-transfer overseas, or else it failed to arrive.

In some countries, this led to policies of self-reliance in an effort to maximise local production, and to cut down on borrowing abroad. Mostly, the nominally independent countries found such policies too difficult. They slipped even more deeply into neo-colonial relationships with the industrialised countries. Sometimes, as in the countries of the Sahel, they entered a time of disaster.

But the strongly independent countries, large or small, began to make some progress towards self-reliance. Those with oil or other valuable minerals naturally found this easier. Nigeria was an example. In Nigeria's first national development plan, half of the total new investment came from foreign aid or foreign investment. In the second national plan, only a fifth came from foreign sources. In the third, almost all the money came from Nigeria's own resources.

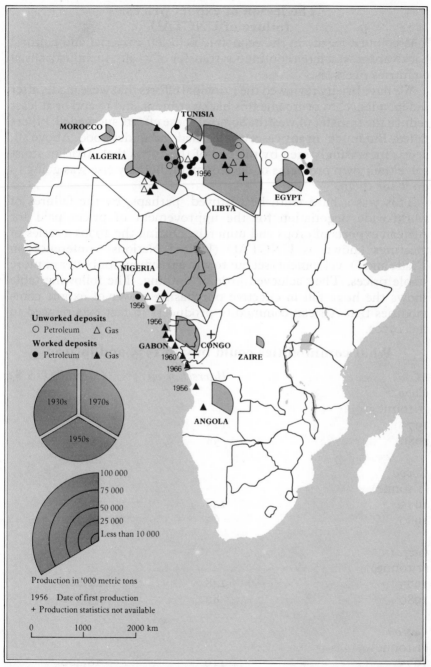

Fig. 12 Petroleum and gas production in Africa, up to 1980. Prospecting is currently being undertaken in many countries

The lesson of export prices:
failure of UNCTAD

The colonial legacy in the economic field left material and cultural backwardness; it left a continuous transfer of wealth to industrialised countries overseas.

We have briefly reviewed the principal efforts that were made, after independence, to overcome this backwardness, and to end or at least reduce the transfer of wealth. Some of these efforts succeeded; others failed. But much, in any case, was learned and understood. Above all, it was increasingly seen by the end of the 1970s that Africans must solve their own problems of development: nobody else was going to do it for them.

This was a hard truth best proved, perhaps, by the failures of world-wide negotiation for the improvement of prices paid for African exports of crops and minerals. During the 1970s a series of meetings known as UNCTAD (United Nations Conference on Trade and Development) set out to win agreement for better or more stable prices. They achieved little or nothing. The following table shows the huge fall in effective purchasing power of export commodities that African commodity producers in fact experienced in the 1970s.

What commodities could buy in 1975 and in 1980

	Barrels of oil	Capital (US $)
Copper (1 tonne)		
1975	115	17,800
1980	58	9,500
Cocoa (1 tonne)		
1975	148	23,400
1980	63	10,200
Coffee (1 tonne)		
1975	148	22,800
1980	82	13,300
Cotton (1 tonne)		
1975	119	18,400
1980	60	9,600

In the light of this failure, and the crisis in aid outlined above, African self-reliance became more than desirable; it became necessary. However difficult this might be, Africa must find its own way out of poverty; little real help, it now appeared, could be expected from the industrialised world. As thoughtful people saw this truth, they began to remember the old lessons of African unity.

Long before, during the early 1960s, Africa's prophet of modern unity, Kwame Nkrumah, had written a book called *Africa Must Unite*. He argued that steps towards an all-African unity were necessary to defend Africa's independence and build a better life. Only unity could give the strength to achieve those ends. His was a vision of continental unity, ahead of its time. Yet if continental unity was too difficult, why not now make a start with regional unity?

The question began to be asked again during the 1970s. So let us turn back to the history of Pan-Africanism. Here too, after many setbacks, new experiments seemed on the way.

CHAPTER 20
Questions about unity

Africans won success in building new and independent nations against handicaps of the colonial legacy, and against older divisions of the past. In spite of continued setbacks in the neo-colonial states, this success was growing wider by 1980. If the success remained far from complete, this was also because it could not be complete. The building of nations takes time; just as the struggle for independence, like the struggle for freedom, is one that can never end.

More years would have to pass before these nations could grow beyond internal disputes and rivalries. Dangers meanwhile threatened. The Nigerian historian G.O. Olusanya was speaking a general truth when he said, in a lecture of 1977, that in his own country there was still a lack of unity among Nigerians:

> Anyone who takes the trouble to monitor opinion, not only through the pages of newspapers but through contact with people, would realize that there are deep fissures within the body politic which do not provide confidence for the future.

But Professor Olusanya spoke also for the spirit of this new Africa of independent nations. He spoke for the confidence with which Africans could now face and solve their problems of unity.

We have looked at these problems of building unity *inside* new nations. We have studied efforts and experiments to overcome the legacies of division. We have seen that further efforts and experiments would be needed. But other problems of unity were coming into the foreground of discussion by 1980. These were the problems of building unity *between* new nations.

New questions were now being asked. Could the new nations defend themselves, and make progress, if they stayed in rivalry with one another, or even in conflict? Were the frontiers of the new nations, the old colonial frontiers, to act as barriers against solidarity and common action? Or were these frontiers to be down-graded, gradually, so as to become a liberating framework for regional and, later on, even for continental co-operation? If so, how could this be done? And in what ways, then, could new nations gain from joint planning, development, diplomacy?

To see why such questions came into the foreground, we need to turn again to the history of Pan-Africanism. In earlier times, during the colonial period, the ideas of Pan-African unity were far from the reality of daily life. Few persons knew about them; fewer supported them. The main task for the nationalists then, as people rightly saw it, was to free each country from its colonial system. The building of intra-African unity, of unity between Africa's nations, had to remain a task for the future, even the distant future.

But now, in the 1980s, this second task came closer. The ideas of unity between nations, of regional unity or even of still wider unity, began to seem useful. Let us see how the history of the last thirty years helped to make this happen.

A new vision and understanding

In Chapter 4 we left the Pan-African story far away in New York, at its fifth Congress of 1927 (see p. 29). A sixth Congress was held in Manchester, England, in 1945. With this Congress of 1945, attended by some of the future leaders of independent Africa, including Jomo Kenyatta and Kwame Nkrumah, Pan-Africanism came alive with a new strength of purpose.

A new vision of unity in independence began to develop in the years after that. A new understanding of the need for that unity began to spread. Here are two statements, among many, which define this vision and understanding as they now grew stronger.

The first is by President Julius Nyerere of Tanzania, in his book called *Africa's Freedom*. 'Only with unity,' he wrote, 'can we ensure that Africa really governs itself. Only with unity can we be sure that African resources will be used for the benefit of Africans.'

The second is by the Nigerian historian Adekunle Ajala in his book called *Pan-Africanism*. 'Africa has many untapped resources,' he wrote, 'and is majestically situated between East and West. With a population of 350 millions [but many more today] it exceeds those of the USA and the USSR. There is therefore nothing to prevent a united, stable, economically strong and highly-industrialised Africa from competing with them in world politics.'

The road to these new ideas about all-African unity and progress was long and difficult. It passed through several stages.

Early experiments

Africa's nationalists, before independence, had to put the building of national unity before any thoughts of building international unity. Yet Pan-Africanism was not forgotten. That was shown as early as the 1920s by the four-colony National Council of British West Africa (see pp. 30–31). Later, as independence came nearer during the 1950s, Pan-Africanist ideas took shape in other regional forms. None of them succeeded, largely because the struggle for national independence had to take, and keep, first place. But they deserve to be remembered.

In French Africa, for example, there were the efforts of the anti-colonial RDA, in its various territorial sections, to form two big independent federations, one for (ex-French) West Africa, and the other for (ex-French) Equatorial Africa (see Chapter 12). These efforts failed because France was against them, as were some leaders such as Félix Houphouët-Boigny of Ivory Coast and Hamani Diori of Niger.

But the 'federalists' went on with their campaign. Before independence, new national assemblies (parliaments) in Senegal, Soudan (now Mali), Dahomey (now Benin), and Volta each voted in favour of federal unity between them after independence. Dahomey and Volta pulled out of the plan under French pressure. That left Senegal and Soudan. In 1959 their assemblies voted to form a federal state called Mali. But this federation was prepared only 'at the top'. Too many differences still separated the two countries. The Mali federation fell apart in 1960.

When Ghana became independent in 1957, its leader Kwame Nkrumah at once threw his support behind a strong campaign for Pan-African progress. He declared then that Ghana's independence would be 'meaningless, unless it is linked up with the total liberation of Africa'; and this liberation, in Nkrumah's mind, was in turn linked to the ideas of Pan-African unity. In 1958, when Guinea became independent, its leader Sékou Touré shared Nkrumah's convictions. So the two new governments at once declared a Ghana-Guinea Union, soon joined by Mali (former Soudan). This union was only on paper. It could not be a real one, but was designed to point the way ahead.

The same linking of the ideas of freedom and unity – of *uhuru na umoja* in Swahili – were held by leading nationalists in the British East African colonies. A programme for *uhuru na umoja* was discussed, at a meeting in Mwanza (Tanzania) during September 1957, by 21 nationalist delegates. A second meeting, again at Mwanza during December 1958, decided to form the Pan-African Freedom Movement of East and Central Africa (PAFMECA).

At first, PAFMECA aimed only at common action for the national independence of these colonies. Later, the aim was broadened to one of East African federation between Kenya, Tanganyika (later Tanzania), and Uganda, together with any others that might want to join later. A third meeting, at Mbale in Uganda during October 1960, brought more nationalists from other countries. PAFMECA was widened to PAFMECSA (Pan-African Freedom Movement of East, Central and Southern Africa). Its aims were to work for independence, and for regional unity.

No progress was made on agreement for federation; and then, after independence, PAFMECSA was dissolved at the time of the formation of the Organisation of African Unity in 1963 (to be discussed later in this chapter). Efforts at East African federation were nonetheless continued. There was some progress towards regional planning and development within a new framework called the East African Community. But once again, as with the Mali Federation of 1959–60, the difficulties were too great; the plan for East African federation failed.

Other attempts at close regional co-operation were made before independence, or when independence came. One was a project for the federal unity of the Maghrib. Again the difficulties proved too great.

The All-African People's Conferences:
towards the OAU

These conferences began in 1958 under the leadership of Kwame Nkrumah and independent Ghana. They had two aims: to support the anti-colonial struggle in every part of the continent, and to strengthen the ideas of Pan-African unity.

The first conference organised by Nkrumah was a meeting at Accra, in 1958, between the eight states then independent: Egypt (United Arab Republic: UAR), Ethiopia, Ghana, Liberia, Libya, Morocco, Sudan, Tunisia. 'For the first time in the modern world,' wrote the Pan-Africanist historian V. Bakpetu Thompson in his book *Africa and Unity*, 'leaders of independent African states met to discuss common problems, with a view to working out common policies concerning political, economic, cultural and social matters'.

A second Accra conference followed in December 1958. This was a meeting not of governments but of nationalist parties. Delegates came from all parts of Africa, free or not, except from French Africa and Northern Nigeria. An All-African People's Organisation (AAPO) was formed with headquarters in Accra. It called for all-African liberation and steps towards an eventual Commonwealth of Free African States. Anti-colonial and anti-racist, AAPO was a channel through which the old ideas of Pan-African unity could develop in new forms and with new force.

Other AAPO conferences were held in Tunis in 1960, and at Cairo in 1961. An All-African Trade Union Organisation was launched.

213

Referring to this in 1963, Nkrumah argued that:

the development of a united African trade union movement will give our working classes a new African consciousness and the right to express themselves in the councils of world labour, unfettered by any foreign view.

These AAPO conferences, and other meetings of that time (including a second conference of independent states, then numbering twelve, at Addis Ababa in June 1960), were, in fact, useful steps towards a continent-wide organisation. Finally, this took shape at Addis Ababa in May 1963: 31 out of the 32 African states then independent (only Morocco failing to attend) agreed to form the Organisation of African Unity (OAU).

Non-alignment, Bandung, the United Nations

Several ideas powered the formation of the OAU. One of them was that Africa's independent nations must remain outside the 'big-power blocs' into which the rest of the world was mostly divided. Otherwise, Africa's nations would soon lose their new-found independence. This was the idea and policy of non-alignment. Africans, it said, must stand firm on their own ground. They must become free to make their own decisions.

Non-alignment as a world movement took shape first at a meeting in Bandung, Indonesia, during 1955, attended by representatives of 17 Asian governments and of 6 African governments (Egypt, Ethiopia, Liberia, Libya and the not-yet-independent governments of Ghana and Sudan). Later, most independent African governments joined the movement. Its aims were to defend newly-won independence; advance the interests of the poorer countries of the world; and assist in settling conflicts between them.

Another kind of co-operation helped towards the founding of the OAU. As African colonies won their independence, each new state became a member of the United Nations. Their delegates naturally worked together in the General Assembly of the UN, and in its various committees. Soon they formed an important grouping. This encouraged them to act together, and to pursue a common diplomacy.

But conflicts of opinion also divided the new governments. Different groupings took shape. One was the Casablanca Group, formed in January 1961 by the heads of state of Egypt, Ghana, Guinea, Mali and Morocco, together with representatives from Libya and the provisional independent government of Algeria (independent only in 1962). They wanted to urge common action to help patriotic nationalists in the Congo (Zaire) against breakaway secessions such as that of Tshombe in Katanga (Shaba). They wanted rapid progress towards an all-African organisation of unity.

A second grouping, known as the Monrovia Group, was formed in May 1961 at a meeting between the leaders of Liberia, Nigeria, and Togo. They were more conservative, and doubtful of rapid action for unity. They were joined by a third grouping, the Brazzaville Group. This consisted of representatives of former French colonies still under powerful French influence and indirect control. Generally, the Brazzaville Group was ready only to talk about all-African unity.

Though divided by differences of opinion, leadership, and personality, the two big groups, those of Casablanca and Monrovia, were both in favour of working for unity, while the third group, that of Brazzaville, was too weak to be able to stop them. So a compromise was possible. Out of this compromise there came the Organisation of African Unity (OAU), a major success of Africa's modern history.

Pan-Africanism and the OAU

The launching of the OAU in 1963 marked up a big African success for three reasons, each of them good for Africa's progress:

1 This launching proved that the new African states were going to begin their independent life, after the colonial period, with a determined effort to work together for common interests.
2 The OAU gave the new states their own means of settling disputes; of shaping joint policies; of combining in defence of African independence; of continuing the struggle for liberation.
3 Once launched, the OAU gave the old Pan-Africanist ideas a basis in reality. In doing this, it could point the way to overcoming the rivalries of nationalism and the divisions between nation-states.

The 31 heads of state who signed the Charter of Unity at Addis Ababa pledged that the OAU would:
(a) Work for unity and solidarity among Africa's nations.
(b) Plan and act together for a better life for Africa's peoples.
(c) Defend the sovereignty, independence, and territorial integrity of Africa's states.
(d) Get rid of all forms of colonialism in Africa.
(e) Work for common action with nations outside Africa, having due regard to the Charter of the United Nations and its Universal Declaration of Human Rights.

Other provisions of the OAU Charter affirmed the principles of:

1 Equality of all the member-states with each other.
2 Non-interference in the internal affairs of member states.
3 Respect for the existing frontiers of member states.
4 Peaceful settlement of all disputes between member states.

The Charter condemned all forms of political subversion and assassination. It pledged the member states to work for the liberation of African peoples still under colonial rule, and in South Africa. It declared the loyalty of member-states to the policy of non-alignment.

How was all this to be done? Meeting that question, the Charter provided the necessary political organisation. This consisted of an assembly of heads of state and government; a council of ministers appointed by the assembly; a general secretariat, based in Addis Ababa; and a commission to settle disputes. Money to run this organisation came from member states, each of which was asked to contribute on the same scale as its contribution to membership of the United Nations. A distinguished Guinean, Diallo Telli, became the first secretary-general.

The Charter was, in fact, a compromise between various opinions, chiefly those of the Casablanca and Monrovia Groups. Some leaders, notably Nkrumah, wanted to go much further, and begin to provide Africa with its own continent-wide parliament and government. Others, such as Abubakar Tafawa Balewa, thought that it was far too early for any such steps.

Generally, this compromise worked well. The Monrovia and Casablanca Groups were dissolved. The continent now possessed its own international forum; and this forum won the loyalty of all the states which became independent after 1963. Soon the OAU was making gains.

A start was made towards economic co-operation in the shape of an African Development Bank, formed in 1964 with the aim of channelling investment of African capital into a wide variety of enterprises. Other gains were in the settlement of frontier conflicts (see pp. 219–220). A special committee was formed to support the liberation movements in colonies not yet free, and to supply these movements with money and arms if wanted. A large majority of member states combined to oppose racist South Africa. This majority defeated a policy of 'dialogue' with South Africa, put forward by Ivory Coast, Malawi, and others, on the grounds that dialogue indicated acceptance and recognition of racist South Africa. The same majority insisted on a policy of boycotting South Africa as far as this might become possible.

Refugees were another of Africa's problems, after independence, in which the OAU could help with various forms of action and relief. In 1964 the OAU set up a special commission to work on refugee problems together with the UN High Commission for Refugees. In 1968 all member states signed a convention, or agreement, aimed at helping refugees, while, at the same time, preventing refugee problems from growing into inter-state conflicts. Such action proved very necessary. In 1976 the UN High Commission estimated that about one million Africans had fled from their own countries into neighbouring countries, some for political or social reasons, many others to escape from colonial or other wars.

Such gains and actions of the OAU were valuable. They lessened a number of troubles. They prevented others. But there were obvious limits on what could be done to build unity of policy and work. These limits could not be avoided. Like the world-wide UN, on which the OAU was partly modelled, the OAU was an assembly of heads of state or government. The OAU could only go as far as those national leaders wished or were able.

This being so, the OAU was unavoidably an organisation controlled 'from the top' of the new states, and not nourished 'from the base'. Further unification of Africa's peoples, through political parties and their elected delegates, was in no way possible yet. Until that could happen, the power of the OAU would have to stay within existing limits. As a sympathetic critic in the *Ghanaian Times* noted in 1963, the aims and means of the OAU Charter would be able to 'become a reality only if the masses of Africa are mobilised for action.'

OCAM, The Arab League

Meanwhile, even within these limits, the OAU proved useful.

Two large difficulties were usually overcome in the course of its conferences and resolutions. The first of these difficulties lay in the fact that the earlier division between 'moderates' and 'radicals' continued to exist. The other difficulty was that the all-African scope and nature of the OAU sometimes came into conflict with regional organisations. Such difficulties were unavoidable. They help to explain why the meetings of the OAU were at times reduced to little more than empty talk, or even to the echo of voices and interferences from outside Africa.

The first difficulty consisted, really, in a strong neo-colonial presence. This came from leaders, such as the Abbé Fulbert Youlou of Congo-Brazzaville – now the People's Republic of Congo – or President Philip Tsiranana of Madagascar, who both closely reflected the policies of France. Other leaders of influence, notably

President Houphouët-Boigny of Ivory Coast, were independent-minded; but they also believed that their countries should accept French leadership.

Others again, including some of the spokesmen of important former colonies of Britain, were much inclined to listen to the wishes of the USA or Britain, whenever any serious dispute arose. In those opening years of the OAU, for example, Nigeria scarcely possessed a foreign policy of its own. Over against these 'moderate' leaders were a number of 'radicals', notably Nkrumah of Ghana, Ahmed Ben Bella of Algeria (removed by Algerian military action in 1965), and Sékou Touré of Guinea. In between the moderates and radicals were many small states which lacked the power to take an effective independent line.

Some regional organisations or groupings also made it difficult for the OAU to work well. This trouble came chiefly from former French colonies which had formed the Brazzaville Group. They now formed a body of twelve states known as the Afro-Malagasy Union (in French, UAM), whose members were – Cameroun, Central African Republic, Chad, Congo-Brazzaville, Dahomey, Gabon, Ivory Coast, Madagascar, Mauritius, Niger, Senegal, Upper Volta.

All the UAM states had great dependence on France; generally, they were all neo-colonial states. They maintained a special relationship with France, even though this went against the OAU Charter. In 1965 they went further. Together with Congo-Kinshasa (Zaïre) and Togo, they formed a 'mini-OAU' of their own, the Afro-Malagasy and Mauritius Joint Organisation (in French: OCAM).

This dependence continued. In March 1981, for example, the Nigerian political scientist Yusufu Bala Usman pointed out that most of the then existing governments of Central Africa:

> were installed and are maintained by French military presence. The government of President Ahidjo of Cameroun was installed and is maintained by this presence. The government of President Bongo (of Gabon) was installed by French paratroopers who up to this day occupy the country. The government of President Mobutu has been maintained by a series of military interventions by NATO (the Western military alliance), spearheaded by France, since it was installed. .

And he went on to list other such cases.

So long as OCAM aimed at direct rivalry with the OAU, there was bound to be trouble. But gradually, after 1970, its main action was transferred to the economic field. It formed joint OCAM enterprises for postal travel, airlines, other matters. These had to be accepted by the OAU, given the reality of French presence, and, now, the arrival of the European Economic Community of which the OCAM states, as well as some of the non-OCAM states, became associate members.

The Arab League was another regional organisation with which the OAU had to come to terms. Founded in 1944 by Egypt, Iraq, Lebanon, Syria and Jordan, the League was later joined by African states which had an Arab-speaking or Muslim majority (Libya, Tunisia, Algeria, Morocco, Sudan, Somalia), as well as by other Arab states in the Middle East. Aimed at strengthening the security of these states, it rapidly became a forum for discussion between their governments, and a means of common action, especially against Israel and in defence of the Arabs of Palestine (see p. 63). Generally, the member-states of the OAU supported the aims of the Arab League. Any disputes between the two organisations were amicably settled.

Frontier conflicts

The new states now gathered in the OAU had to inherit some frontier disputes. Most of these were successfully settled by OAU diplomacy.

A small war broke out in October 1963 between Morocco and Algeria. It concerned a frontier area of Algeria that was claimed by Morocco. Acting as mediator, the OAU was able to bring about a cease-fire, and, in February 1964, an agreement for peace. Each side gained something, and agreed to co-operate in the economic development of mineral deposits at Tindouf in Algeria. But this failed to satisfy Morocco. OAU peace efforts had to continue. They were crowned with success by a new agreement of May 1970. Other disputes of this kind were settled; and the OAU proved a valuable instrument of peace.

Some large disputes could not be settled. One of these consisted in Moroccan (and, at first, Mauritanian) efforts to share out the ex-Spanish Sahara, and prevent the formation of a republic of the Western Sahara by its liberation movement, POLISARIO, which had Algerian and other African support. After a while Mauritania withdrew from this conflict, but fighting between POLISARIO and Morocco continued; and the OAU remained divided on the subject.

Another and bigger conflict concerned the frontiers of the Ethiopian empire, built by the Emperor Menelik at the time of the colonial partition. As mentioned in Chapter 10, the Somali people of the Ogaden province of the Ethiopian empire continued to press for their right of self-government or independence, and were strongly supported by the Republic of Somalia next-door. Fighting broke out in 1976 and led to an Ethiopian victory with the support of Soviet tanks and Cuban troops.

The former Italian colony of Eritrea, as we saw in Chapter 10, passed first under British military government, in 1941, and then, in 1952, became a federated state of the Ethiopian empire. In 1962, however, Ethiopia reduced Eritrea to a mere province or colony of the empire. To this the nationalists of Eritrea replied with guerilla warfare, and fighting continued into the 1980s. After 1974 a number of other minorities in Ethiopia, such as the Oromo, also began to revolt in order to win local powers of self-government.

New moves for regional co-operation

Generally, by 1980, it had become clear that the OAU could be useful and effective within its limits, but that little progress could be made outside those limits. What other road towards common action might now be open? Some important answers were already on the scene. These were echoed and reinforced during the 1980 meeting of African heads of state in Lagos, which emphasised a new interest in promoting economic co-operation between OAU member states.

Earlier efforts at economic co-operation between states, or between groups of states, had failed for several reasons, sometimes because they were tried too soon. But with the experience of more years of independence, and with a better understanding of Africa's real problems of development, it was now seen that co-operation was not only desirable, but was very necessary. Africa could face disaster unless much stronger systems of production and of productivity of goods, especially of food, were installed and made to work. We have examined the chief reasons for this.

Stronger systems of production and productivity called for new policies and plans inside independent states. But they just as surely called for co-operation between these states. New efforts and experiments began to be made. Here we can mention two of them.

In 1975, fifteen West African states signed the Treaty of Lagos. This formed the Economic Community of West African States (ECOWAS). The founding members were Benin, The Gambia, Ghana, Guinea, Guinea-Bissau, Ivory Coast, Liberia, Mali, Mauritania, Niger, Nigeria, Senegal, Sierra Leone, Togo, and Upper Volta; in 1977, the Republic of Cape Verde also joined. They pledged themselves to work together to promote more trade between them; to co-operate in various fields of enterprise; and to aim at self-reliance in regional development.

An important point about ECOWAS is that it linked strongly independent states which had come out of the British empire, and later out of the Portuguese empire, with much less independent states of the former French empire. This helped to reduce the strength of neo-colonial influence and financial control. Independence could gain. Another important point is that ECOWAS helped to build a common front of African self-defence in respect of the European Economic Community and of other outside groupings.

A further move of the same nature, as yet less advanced in form, began in 1980. Nine states of central and southern Africa (Angola, Botswana, Lesotho, Malawi, Mozambique, Swaziland, Tanzania, Zambia, Zimbabwe) decided to find ways of combining their development plans and policies. They aimed at preventing further expansion of racist South African influence. They looked for means of common action to improve their transport systems, food supplies, and industrial development. The urgency of these aims was strengthened in 1981, and after, by racist South Africa's military and other aggressions against Angola, Mozambique and Zimbabwe.

CONCLUSION
A time of unceasing change

This book has attempted to trace the decisive trends, ideas, developments and events that have shaped the history of Africa's peoples during the greater part of the twentieth century. It is a history that has carried the continent, and continues to carry it, through a process of unceasing change. That process has reached deeply into every aspect of African life, and with a revolutionary impact unknown in any previous time.

Africans had to regain their independence, and master the arts and technologies of modern life. They had to take their due place in the world, and cause their continent's weight and dignity to be recognised in every other continent. Making progress in all these ways, they had to face new problems, conflicts, and obstacles to further progress. Their struggles in this great contest for freedom and advance have formed the core and essence of the history in this book.

Twice in this century Africans were drawn into disastrous wars between the powers and super-powers of the industrialised world. A third such conflict, likely to be still more destructive than the other two, now seemed to threaten during the 1980s. Europeans and Americans argued that this danger arose from a clash of interests between 'West' and 'East': between the two super-powers and their respective allies and subordinates. But Africans affirmed, more and more, that the real clash in the world lay not between 'East' and 'West', but between the ex-colony-owning 'North', with all its wealth and power, and the ex-colonial 'South', with all its legacy of poverty and exploitation. This was the real world conflict: the 'South'-'North' conflict of interest and policy between 'developing' and 'developed' nations and economies in which Africans, like other ex-colonial peoples, must now defend themselves and their plans for progress.

TABLE 1

Key events and developments

Readers will have found a very large quantity of dates, referring to events and persons, in successive sections of the text. Besides these, an outline sketch of some of the important periods and dates in the making of modern Africa may be useful:

1884–5
Imperialist powers meet in Berlin to agree on the partition of Africa where, so far, they have only a few colonies. This is the so-called 'scramble for Africa' conference.

1885–1901
Many colonial invasions. By 1901, most of the colonial frontiers are fixed by agreement between the invading powers.

1901–14
Chief period of installing colonial power by military means. The invading powers put down continued resistance, and extend their control. Railways are built so as to export minerals and other wealth.

1914–18
First World War between the imperialist powers. Defeated, Germany loses its colonies to Britain, France and Belgium. These transferred colonies are called 'mandates' of the newly-formed League of Nations.

1919–29
Colonial governments continue to extend their control, act against further resistance, and develop civil services.

New mines are opened by large companies of one or another colonial power, notably for copper and gold.

Huge development of systems of migrant labour.

A few more railways are built, mostly again by forced labour.

Settlers continue to take land from Africans, notably in Algeria, Kenya, Northern Rhodesia (Zambia), Southern Rhodesia (Zimbabwe), Angola and South Africa.

Early attempts at national liberation, notably in Morocco and Somalia, fail against overwhelming colonial military strength.

Early forms of African nationalist protest, principally in West and North Africa, gain some ground.

Various other forms of popular resistance develop, notably by religious types of organisation.

1929–35

Africans face consequences of the Great Depression, a general collapse of the imperialist economies.

While the colonial powers introduce new forms of 'imperial protection' of their interests, African nationalism grows stronger. It begins to make demands for anti-colonial independence.

In some colonies, African workers begin to unite for better wages and less bad conditions of work.

1939–45

Second World War. Most colonial powers are weakened. USA becomes super-power. USSR, having defeated Nazi Germany's huge invasion of Russia and other Soviet lands, enters fully into world councils.

United Nations is founded at end of war as successor to League of Nations. League mandates are re-constituted as 'UN trusteeship territories'.

1945–52

Encouraged by the Atlantic Charter of 1941, which has promised that every people shall be free to choose its own government, Africa's nationalists strengthen their demands.

Parties formed by the 'educated few' begin to develop into mass movements of nationalism. Climax in 1951, when Ghana's Convention People's Party is able to win internal self-government for Gold Coast (Ghana), and when leading parties in southern Nigeria soon after achieve the same progress.

Most colonies are now in conditions of profound social crisis, deepened by forced labour in Second World War, and 'flight to the towns'.

1953–60

Nationalism continues to grow stronger.

Onwards from 1956, more and more colonies win their independence.

Widespread colonial warfare breaks out in settler colonies, notably Algeria and Kenya, which nonetheless become independent in 1962 and 1963.

In South Africa, meanwhile, 1948 has seen the coming to power of the extreme racist Afrikaner National Party, and the launching of full-scale *apartheid* (racist persecution and exploitation).

1961–80

Drive for independence continues, notably in East and Central Africa, with success.

1963

Organisation of African Unity (OAU) is founded.

1965–1980

White settlers in Rhodesia (Zimbabwe) rebel against Britain, declare their independence, and continue to build racist system. Zimbabwe African resistance replies with counter-violence. Africans win in 1980. Zimbabwe becomes independent.

Meanwhile, in Portuguese colonies, nationalists lead counter-violence which begins in Angola in 1961, in Guinea-Bissau in 1963, in Mozambique in 1964. They win these wars, make their countries independent by 1974–75, and, in so doing, cause the overturn of Portuguese dictatorship in Portugal itself.

Racist repression in South Africa grows worse; many kinds of African protest there are put down by violence.

Independent countries wrestle with the problems of the colonial legacy. Many military take-overs of civilian government. Economic problems become severe, but big oil discoveries are made in several countries.

Efforts to solve the problems of independence, and to overcome the colonial legacy, continue.

TABLE TWO
Independence dates

			Population (*1975* approx. estimate)
Already independent			
Ethiopia			24,470,000
Liberia			1,600,000
South Africa (only its racist regime being independent)			25,466,000

		Independence won from	Population (*1975* approx. estimate)
During the 1950s			
Egypt (UAR), process beginning in	1952	Britain	39,000,000
Ghana	1957	Britain	8,800,000
Guinea	1958	France	5,500,000
Libya	1951	Italy	2,257,000
Morocco	1956	France	16,700,000
Sudan	1956	Britain	14,500,000
Tunisia	1956	France	5,570,000
During the 1960s			
Algeria	1962	France	16,000,000
Botswana	1966	Britain	750,000
Burundi	1962	Belgium	3,750,000
Cameroun	1960	France	6,539,000
Central African Republic	1960	France	1,850,000
Chad	1960	France	4,100,000
Congo (People's Republic of)	1960	France	1,400,000
Benin	1960	France	3,150,000
Equatorial Guinea	1968	Spain	300,000
Gabon	1960	France	1,100,000
Gambia, The	1965	Britain	540,000

Ivory Coast	1960	France	6,673,000
Kenya	1963	Britain	13,399,000
Lesotho	1966	Britain	1,250,000
Madagascar	1960	France	8,500,000
Malawi	1964	Britain	5,400,000
Mali	1960	France	6,108,000
Mauritania	1960	France	1,400,000
Mauritius	1968	Britain	856,000
Niger	1960	France	4,900,000
Nigeria	1960	Britain	92,000,000
Rwanda	1962	Belgium	4,700,000
Senegal	1960	France	4,800,000
Sierra Leone	1961	Britain	3,100,000
Somalia	1960	Italy and Britain	3,340,000
Swaziland	1967	Britain	526,000
Tanzania (Tanganyika, 1961) (Zanzibar, 1963)	1961	Britain	15,155,000
Togo	1960	France	2,228,000
Uganda	1962	Britain	11,549,000
Upper Volta	1960	France	6,147,000
Zaïre	1960	Belgium	24,902,000
Zambia	1964	Britain	4,981,000

During the 1970s

Angola	1975	Portugal	6,761,000
Cape Verde	1975	Portugal	300,000
Comoros (without Mayotte)	1975	France	260,000
Djibouti	1977	France	210,000
Guinea-Bissau	1974	Portugal	750,000
Mozambique	1975	Portugal	9,200,000
São Tomé	1975	Portugal	75,000
Seychelles	1976	Britain	55,000
Western Sahara (disputed)	1976	Spain	75,000

During the 1980s

Zimbabwe	1980	Britain and white settler regime	6,290,000

Notes on further reading

Books about the history of modern Africa are very many. The student should ask for advice on the books that can help most in learning about this or that aspect of history. Meanwhile, the following lists, covering regional histories, general histories, specialised studies, and journals and occasional publications offer a short guide.

Regional histories

J.F.A. Ajayi and M. Crowder (eds.), *History of West Africa*, Vol. 2, Longman, 1974

G. Arnold, *Modern Kenya*, Longman, 1981

G. Arnold, *Modern Nigeria*, Longman, 1977

R. Davenport, *South Africa, A Modern History*, Macmillan, 1978

R. Denoon, *Southern Africa since 1800*, Longman, 1972

J. Iliffe, *A Modern History of Tanganyika*, Cambridge, 1979

E. Isichei, *A History of Nigeria*, Longman, 1982

S.R. Karugire, *A Political History of Uganda*, Heinemann (Nairobi), 1980

B. Munslow, *Mozambique: the revolution and its origins*, Longman, 1983

A. Roberts, *A History of Zambia*, Heinemann, 1976

P.J. Vatikiotis, *The Modern History of Egypt*, Weidenfeld and Nicolson, 1969

General histories

M. Crowder, *Cambridge History of Africa*, Vol. 8, Cambridge (forthcoming)

B. Davidson, *Africa in Modern History*, Penguin, 1978

Specialised studies

A. Ajala, *Pan-Africanism: Evolution, Progress and Prospects*, Andre Deutsch, 1974

S.K.B. Asante, *Pan-African Protest: West Africa and the Italo-Ethiopian Crisis, 1934–1941*, Longman, 1977

A.I. Asiwaju, *Western Yorubaland under European Rule 1889–1945*, Longman, 1976

E.A. Ayandele, *The Educated Elite in Nigerian Society*, Ibadan, 1974

E.A. Brett, *Colonialism and Underdevelopment in an African Working Class*, Heinemann, 1973

B. Davidson, *The People's Cause: A History of Guerillas in Africa*, Longman, 1981

B.J. Dudley, *Parties and Politics in Nigeria*, Macmillan, 1968

A.G. Hopkins, *An Economic History of West Africa*, Longman, 1973

C. Hoskyns, *The Congo Since Independence*, Oxford, 1965

R. Lemarchand, *Political Awakening in the Belgian Congo*, University of California Press, 1964

C. Leys, *Underdevelopment in Kenya*, Heinemann, 1975

C. van Onselen, *Chibaro: African Mine Labour in Southern Rhodesia 1900–33*, Pluto Press, 1976

A. Osuntokun, *Nigeria in the First World War*, Longman, 1979

R. Sandbrook and R. Cohen (eds.), *The Development of an African Working Class*, Longman, 1975

S. Stichter, *Migrant Labour in Kenya*, Longman, 1982

J. Suret-Canale, *French Colonialism in Tropical Africa 1900–1945*, Hurst, London, 1971

Journals and occasional publications

Journals which often contain articles on aspects of modern African history are –

African Affairs, The Journal of the Royal African Society, published quarterly

The Journal of African History (Cambridge University Press), published quarterly

The Journal of Modern African History (Cambridge University Press), published quarterly

The following issues of *Tarikh*, an occasional series of publications, published for the Historical Society of Nigeria by Longman, cover in greater detail some of the themes and issues raised in this book –

Tarikh 8 *France in Africa*
Tarikh 11 *Indirect Rule in British Africa*
Tarikh 12 *Independence Movements in Africa 1*
Tarikh 13 *Independence Movements in Africa 2*
Tarikh 19 *Protest against Colonial Rule in West Africa*
Tarikh 22 *White Society in Africa*
Tarikh 23 *Pan-Africanism*
Tarikh 24 *Portugal in Africa*
Tarikh 25 *Grass Roots Leadership in Colonial West Africa*
Tarikh 27 *Germany in Africa*

Index